W9-BZO-583

6/5/14 Ingram $25.00

ALSO BY THE AUTHOR

Understanding Tolstoy
Russian for Dummies

GIVE
WAR AND PEACE
A CHANCE

TOLSTOYAN WISDOM
FOR TROUBLED TIMES

Andrew D. Kaufman

Property of
Tyngsborough Public Library
25 Bryants Lane
Tyngsborough, MA 01879
(978) 649-7361

SIMON & SCHUSTER

New York   London   Toronto   Sydney   New Delhi

891.733
KAUFM
2014

Simon & Schuster
1230 Avenue of the Americas
New York, NY 10020

Copyright © 2014 by Andrew D. Kaufman

All rights reserved, including the right to reproduce this book or portions thereof in any form whatsoever. For information address Simon & Schuster Subsidiary Rights Department, 1230 Avenue of the Americas, New York, NY 10020.

First Simon & Schuster hardcover edition May 2014

SIMON & SCHUSTER and colophon are registered trademarks of Simon & Schuster, Inc.

For information about special discounts for bulk purchases, please contact Simon & Schuster Special Sales at 1-866-506-1949 or business@simonandschuster.com.

The Simon & Schuster Speakers Bureau can bring authors to your live event. For more information or to book an event contact the Simon & Schuster Speakers Bureau at 1-866-248-3049 or visit our website at www.simonspeakers.com.

Book design by Ellen R. Sasahara
Jacket design by Jason Heuer
Jacket photograph of book by Isabelle Selby
Jacket photograph of sky background © John Eastcott and Yva Momatiuk/National Geographic/Getty Images

Manufactured in the United States of America

1   3   5   7   9   10   8   6   4   2

Library of Congress Cataloging-in-Publication Data

Kaufman, Andrew D.

Give *War and Peace* a chance : Tolstoyan wisdom for troubled times / Andrew D. Kaufman.—First Simon & Schuster hardcover edition.
pages cm
1. Tolstoy, Leo, graf, 1828–1910—Appreciation. 2. Tolstoy, Leo, graf, 1828–1910—Influence. I. Title.
PG3410.K374 2014
891.73'3—dc232013024019

ISBN 978-1-4516-4470-8
ISBN 978-1-4516-4472-2 (ebook)

Excerpts of Tolstoy's *War and Peace*: From *War and Peace* by Leo Tolstoy, translated by Richard Pevear and Larissa Volokhonsky, translation copyright © 2007 by Richard Pevear and Larissa Volokhonsky. Used by permission of Alfred A. Knopf, an imprint of the Knopf Doubleday Publishing Group, a division of Random House LLC. All rights reserved.

The author is grateful to Natalya Alekseevna Kalinina, director of the L. N. Tolstoy State Museum in Moscow, for the photographs of Tolstoy and his family, the photograph of the page from the manuscript of *War and Peace*, as well as the photograph of the drawings from Tolstoy's diary.

FOR CORINNE AND IAN,
who inspire me every day
"to love life in all its countless,
inexhaustible manifestations"

To be able to affect others, an artist has to be an explorer, and his work of art has to be a quest. If he has discovered everything, knows everything, and is just preaching or entertaining, he makes no effect. Only if he keeps searching, then the viewer, or listener, or reader fuses with him in his search.

—Tolstoy's diary, December 1900

Contents

An Invitation to the Reader

Arriving at Amherst College in the fall of 1987, I was pretty certain I'd choose economics or political science as a major, and continue studying Russian language on the side, as I'd been doing since my junior year in high school. Gorbachev had come into power just a few years earlier and with business opportunities opening up in the then Soviet Union, my parents had wisely suggested that, even as a Michigan high school student, I start learning Russian at a local college. I had no idea at that time how such a seemingly insignificant decision made for pragmatic reasons, would lead straight to the most important spiritual journey of my life.

As a college sophomore I found myself in a Survey of Russian Literature class, in which within the first few weeks the professor had been ambitious enough for us all to assign what is arguably one of the world's most daunting novels, Tolstoy's masterpiece *War and Peace*. There I was, trudging around the rolling campus with that almost comically obese paperback, its pages splayed out, nicked and softened under the strain of that four-figure page count, the strain of so much use. Evenings I'd curl up with the novel on the ragged red love seat across from the stacks in the basement of Frost Library, or, when my roommates were out, under the covers of my creaky dorm-room bed. As I waded through the ocean of details, impressions, and barely pronounceable names, I found myself increasingly seduced by a world that, for all its foreignness, started to seem . . . strangely familiar.

One life-sized character in particular stepped forward as if to speak right to me: Pierre Bezukhov, the bumbling, bespectacled twenty-year-old who has just returned from a ten-year stay in Europe and is now trying to find his place in a rapidly changing Russia. As the proverbial small-town midwestern boy who'd just been thrown into what seemed to me a coldly competitive Northeast, I saw plenty of myself in this cloddish young soul, and in his passionate quest for a life that was meaningful, authentic, and complete. Pierre's long, tortuous journey toward truth captivated and inspired me. And so, if initially I'd been losing myself in Tolstoy, I soon enough began to find myself there.

Leo Tolstoy and I have been together for almost twenty-five years now. It has been one of my longest relationships, not to mention one of my most intense, as my wife Corinne recently observed, watching me with some concern as I lovingly caressed the tattered cover of that old college copy of *War and Peace*. We've had our ups and downs, Tolstoy and I, our disagreements, even a couple of separations. After graduate school I was so burnt-out by the academic life that I left the writer and Russian literature altogether to pursue what I saw then as a promising career as an actor. When I returned to the old count a few years later, I was surprised to find he had grown somehow even wiser in my absence, *War and Peace* as fresh and as important to me as when I'd first encountered it all those years earlier—all the more so, in fact. And, as with most long-term relationships that last, I rediscovered the reasons I fell in love in the first place.

It is Tolstoy's combination of skepticism and hope that I have always loved most about his work—that childlike curiosity about everyone and everything he sees, coupled with a wise awareness of who's who and what's what. I love his courage to believe in human goodness even when his rational mind offers a thousand reasons why he shouldn't, his total willingness to plunge right into the river of life, to play and splash and kick around in it, knowing full well that somewhere downstream a raging waterfall surely looms.

When Russian tenth graders today are assigned *War and Peace*, the boys often read only the "war" sections, and the girls, only those concerned with "peace." Yet by doing so, both are not just missing out, but, well, missing the *point*. It is perhaps worth pointing out that the word for "peace" in Russian is identical to the word for "world" or "cosmos"—*mir*, pronounced "meer." So, when Russians hear the title of the novel, they are hearing not just *War and Peace*, but also *War and the World*, which, in fact, captures an essential dimension of this novel missing in the English rendition. Whether you're ducking bullets on the battlefield or dodging your colleague's sally at a council of war; whether you're a commander preparing to oust the foreign enemy or a salon hostess trying to get rid of an annoying guest; whether you're a general navigating your troops through the Russian countryside or a teenage Russian boy preparing your father for the news that you've just lost forty-three thousand rubles, life, Tolstoy tells us, is a *battle*. It is also movement and change: "There is nothing stable in life," Tolstoy said when he was in his seventies. "It's the same as adapting to flowing water. Everything—personalities, family, society, everything changes, disappears and re-forms, like so many clouds. You hardly have time to get used to one social condition before it's already gone and become another."

Yet amid all that discord, out of all that conflict there emerges in *War and Peace* a strange, hopeful vision of the world as a place that does, in the end, make a kind of *sense*. And if this loose, baggy monster of a book refuses to tie things together into a nice, elegant literary package of the sort the American writer and critic Henry James was hoping for, neither does it leave us with the impression that, as some of Tolstoy's "enlightened" contemporaries believed, the world we inhabit is merely a vast interplay of physical, chemical, and biological stimuli. Life, Tolstoy shows, is both messy and meaningful, prosaic and poetic, sensuous and . . . sensible. And in order to communicate that vision, he needed to find a way of writing that was both more specific and more encompassing than that offered by the highly specialized, ideologically divisive worldviews of so many of his contemporaries.

"In clever art criticism," Tolstoy wrote to his friend, the philosopher Nikolai Strakhov, in 1876, "everything is the truth, but not the whole truth, and art is only art because it is whole." For that reason, he explained in another letter to Strakhov, "we need people who would show the senselessness of looking for ideas in a work of art, but who instead would continually guide readers in that endless labyrinth of linkages that makes up the stuff of art. . . .": people, in other words, who, rather than deconstructing a work of fiction to promote their own ideological or professional agendas, would attempt to reconstruct that work for the benefit of readers everywhere; people who, instead of dissecting a book as if it were some petri dish specimen, would strive to engage with it as fully as they might with any living, breathing organism.

I recently met the woman whose job is to preserve the manuscripts of Tolstoy's works at Moscow's Tolstoy Museum. When this smallish seventy-year-old with a weathered face and thin white hair talks about what it is like to touch the pages on which *War and Peace* was originally written, her soft, saintly eyes light up. She makes you want to be there in that room, feeling those pieces of parchment right alongside her. "They like it when you work with them," she says to me with a big smile, as if she were speaking about one of her own children or grandchildren. But, then, to her those pieces of parchment *are* alive. Indeed, the wisdom contained in her words ought to be plastered above the entrance to every high school or college literature classroom: *Literature is alive*; books *like* it when, rather than merely "studying" them, you engage with them deeply, personally, bringing your entire self to the reading experience, both you and the book expanding to dimensions you'd never have thought possible.

I have tried to be that kind of reader, the sort I think Tolstoy would have wanted for his work. Whether I've succeeded in that aim, I will never know. All I can say is that I have given *War and Peace* a chance, and hope you will, too.

*The Seeker: Tolstoy walking from Moscow to
Yasnaya Polyana in 1886 or 1888.*

Introduction

Times are tough, anxiety and fear are pervasive, and people are searching for answers to questions big and small. The country is at war, change is in the air, and the future remains uncertain. Welcome to Russia at the beginning of the nineteenth century. Welcome to the world of Leo Tolstoy's *War and Peace*.

Russia's greatest novelist has been dead just over one hundred years, yet the wisdom of his most famous novel is in many ways more relevant now than ever. Considered by most critics the greatest novel ever written, *War and Peace* is also one of the most feared. And at 1,500 pages, 361 chapters, or 566,000 words, it's no wonder why. Still, new editions keep appearing. For three years the novel has been one of the top fifty bestsellers in Amazon's world literature category, and its third-bestselling book about war. In addition to three new translations of *War and Peace* in 2006 and 2007, Oxford World's Classics reissued the celebrated Maude translation in 2010.

In July 2009 *Newsweek* placed *War and Peace* at the very top of its list of one hundred great novels, just ahead of Orwell's *1984*, which came in second, and Joyce's *Ulysses*, third. A 2007 edition of the *AARP Bulletin*, read by millions, included the novel in their list of the top four books everybody should read by the age of fifty. And a *New York*

Times survey from 2009 identified *War and Peace* as the world classic you're most likely to find people reading on their subway commute to work.

Oprah Winfrey's selection of Tolstoy's *Anna Karenina* for her 2004 summer book club certainly didn't hurt Tolstoy's popularity; nor did the 2012 release of the film adaptation of the novel starring Keira Knightley and Jude Law. A book filled with domestic troubles, broken marriages, steamy sex scenes, and one of the most heart-wrenching suicides in world literature—now, that's material tailor-made for Oprah and Hollywood. But *War and Peace*? What might all those *Newsweek* devotees, senior citizens, and harried commuters see in a book about the Napoleonic Wars of the early 1800s?

A mirror of our times.

The nineteenth century, you see, was a good deal less placid than many in our own war-torn, information-drenched, spiritually confused era might expect. And the setting for *War and Peace*—the Napoleonic Wars of 1805 to 1812—was a time of particularly deep social change, moral confusion, and hardship. Napoleon, or as many Russians called him, the "Antichrist," was a feared killing machine who had already conquered half of Europe. Even worse, from the point of view of the anciens régimes, he was a commoner who, having forced his way to power, was now spreading radical revolutionary ideas among the young.

It was no accident Tolstoy chose this troubled time as the setting for *War and Peace*. For the period in which he wrote the novel—the 1860s—was in many ways equally turbulent. His nation having been clobbered by the French and British in the Crimean War, Alexander II decided to redeem the loss by modernizing nearly every aspect of Russian society, and proceeded to introduce a series of sweeping social, economic, and political reforms, including the controversial Emancipation of the Serfs in 1861. This served only to sharpen the years-old rift between the liberals, who wanted speedier and more radical change, and the conservatives, who wanted to return to the familiarity of the old order. To add confusion to chaos, capitalism was being introduced into a society that for centuries had been fundamentally feudal and agrarian.

Alexander Herzen, one of the era's leading reformers, captured the crisis-ridden mood in his journal, fittingly called *The Bell*: "The storm is approaching, it is impossible to be mistaken about that. The Revolutionaries and Reactionaries are at one about that. All men's heads are going round; a weighty question of life and death lies heavy on men's heads." By the time Tolstoy sat down to write *War and Peace* in 1863, the "weighty questions" Herzen spoke about had overflowed the limits of intellectual journals and academic halls, flooding all corners of Russian society.

The social fabric was being stretched to the point of tearing, and Tolstoy felt it keenly. "We are starting over again from the beginning on new foundations," he wrote in his diary in 1861. As a socially conscious, guilt-ridden artist, he empathized with the peasants who had suffered for centuries under serfdom, and under the Tolstoy family, in particular. On the other hand, as a proud, landowning aristocrat, he had much to lose from the breakdown of a traditional social order in which generations of his family had thrived. His personal prestige was at stake, then, as was his financial security.

Wealthy landowning aristocrats like Tolstoy now had to make their way in the rough-and-tumble world of the free market. Many of them failed, and Tolstoy himself was no stranger to financial problems. For one thing, the thousand-acre estate at Yasnaya Polyana he had inherited wasn't producing the crop it once had. Fortunately, his shrewd wife had arranged advantageous publication terms for *War and Peace*, providing the Tolstoys with a temporary windfall. And so in 1869 he went on a land-buying trip, during which, in a hotel in the town of Arzamas, he suffered a severe panic attack. Tolstoy described the experience in a letter to his wife:

> The day before yesterday I spent the night at Arzamas and something extraordinary happened to me. It was 2 o'clock in the morning. I was terribly tired, I wanted to go to sleep and I felt per-

fectly well. But suddenly I was overcome by despair, fear and terror, the like of which I have never experienced before. I'll tell you the details of this feeling later: but I've never experienced such an agonizing feeling before and may God preserve anyone else from experiencing it.

Acute anxiety led him to the verge of suicide (no Xanax in those days). He even asked his wife to hide the knives, guns, and ropes in the house, for fear that he might kill himself. Fortunately, he did no such thing. What he *did* do was a lot of reading and thinking, which led him to the rather startling conclusion that the world-renowned author of *War and Peace* was an abject failure and had been living his life the wrong way all these years: "What, indeed, had I done in all my thirty years of conscious life? Not only had I failed to live my life for the sake of all, but I had not even lived it for myself. I had lived as a parasite, and once I asked myself why I had lived, the answer I received was: for nothing."

So Tolstoy decided to dedicate the rest of his life to writing moralistic essays and religious tracts encouraging people to live in accordance with the principles of the Gospels, which attracted him more and more. His famous contemporary, the novelist Ivan Turgenev, implored Tolstoy to stop moralizing and return to what he did best: being a great artist. But Tolstoy didn't take kindly to this advice from an erstwhile friend long since turned into a foe Tolstoy had once challenged to a duel.

To this day many scholars insist that there were "two Tolstoys"—the one before the crisis at Arzamas and the one after—as if a person's life, least of all that of a person as complex as Tolstoy, could be divided along such neat lines. This is, of course, nonsense. The fact is, Tolstoy's nervous breakdown in Arzamas was not the beginning of Tolstoy, Part Two, but rather the continuation of his quest, begun years earlier, in the difficult era of the 1860s, for stable meaning in a relentlessly chaotic world. And nowhere is that search more fully described than in the pages of *War and Peace*.

War and Peace is many things. It is a war novel, a family saga, a love story. But at its core it is a book about people trying to find their footing in a ruptured world. It is a novel about human beings attempting to create a meaningful life for themselves in a country being torn apart by war, social change, and spiritual confusion. Russian conversations about death, meaning, and spiritual enlightenment were all the rage in the 1860s, and Tolstoy's novel was perhaps the most ambitious contribution to those debates. Whether our own troubles at the opening of the twenty-first century may be leading to a spiritual awakening or simply a rude one is, well, less than clear. Either way, though, we find ourselves awakening to a rather strikingly new reality, and Tolstoy has important things to say to us at this moment.

Like us, Tolstoy's characters make mistakes, suffer, and hit dead ends. Every once in a while, though, under even the worst circumstances, they experience moments of transcendent bliss or sudden illumination: the comfortable familiarity of their smooth-running lives suddenly disrupted, their perceptions become . . . sharpened; their understanding of what it means to be alive, widened.

This may be of comfort to not a few of us today—the mother whose son was killed in Afghanistan; the father of four whose family savings were invested with Madoff; the young couple, laid off or simply laboring under crushing student loans, whose dreams of owning a home are impossible. Hard times would seem to be all around us. At a time when our country has experienced the greatest dissipation of wealth since the Great Depression, the specter of war far too familiar for far too long, and the future remaining for many uncertain, the existential angst of Tolstoy and his characters is entirely familiar.

Like most effective teachers, Tolstoy knew his subject well. The world was his classroom, experience his instructor, and trial and error—*lots* of the latter—his surest means of study. Henry James aptly called Tolstoy "a reflector as vast as a natural lake; a monster harnessed to his great subject—all of life!"

And what a life Tolstoy's *was*: a mess of paradoxes wrapped inside a web of contradictions. The bearded Russian sage who inspired both Mahatma Gandhi and Martin Luther King couldn't resist a blood-boiling bayonet fight, or a good duel with an old writer friend who had insulted him. This moralist who preached celibacy in and out of marriage had, in fact, a voracious sexual appetite and sired an illegitimate child by a local peasant girl. "I must have a woman," he wrote in his diary when he was twenty-five. "Sensuality doesn't give me a moment's peace." And again four years later: "Sensuality torments me; laziness again, boredom and sadness. Everything seems stupid. The ideal is unattainable; I've already ruined myself."

While serving in the army in his midtwenties, even as he pontificated to his friends about responsibility, Tolstoy lost his most prized possession, the house of his birth at Yasnaya Polyana, in a gambling bet. He may not have lost the land itself, but knowing that that noble structure would soon be physically dismantled, plank by plank, brick by brick, and carted away was a humiliation that cut deeply. "I'm so disgusted with myself that I'd like to forget about my existence," he wrote in his diary on the day of the devastating loss. Not two weeks later he wrote: "Played cards again and lost another 200 rubles. I can't promise to stop." His gambling sprees continued, as did his merry-making, his drinking binges, his womanizing, and his laziness.

He tried to curb his bad behavior by writing down daily rules of conduct, just as his hero Benjamin Franklin had done, and then grading himself the next day. But his grades, alas, remained low: "It's absurd that having started writing rules at fifteen, I should still be writing them at thirty, without having trusted in, or followed a single one, but still for some reason believing in them and wanting them."

The man who lent his voice to the Russian temperance movement drank himself into oblivion with the gypsies and smoked hashish with the Bashkirs. The fiercely patriotic writer who memorialized Russian history was more deeply influenced by French, British, and German thinkers and writers than by Russian ones. Even Tolstoy's unique brand of Russian Orthodoxy had more in common with the austerity and pragmatism of American Quakerism than with Orthodox Christianity. Yet even as he preached the joys of self-abnegation to family and friends, Tolstoy was enjoying elaborate meals on imported European china in the luxurious dining room of the main house at Yasnaya Polyana. He glorified domestic happiness, yet ran away from home at the age of eighty-two, and at the end, having for so many years railed against the trappings of fame, died nothing less than an international celebrity.

In his later years people flocked to Yasnaya Polyana from all over the world for advice on every subject imaginable. One John Levitt, an obscure American farmer, wrote to Tolstoy in 1909 to thank the Russian sage for showing him the meaning of life, following which he asked to borrow five hundred dollars. That letter, recently published by the Russian Academy of Sciences, has given Levitt fifteen minutes of posthumous fame among a tiny group of Slavic scholars, but it went unanswered by an irritated Tolstoy, who preferred to be solicited for wisdom, rather than money.

William Jennings Bryan, the Democratic Party presidential nominee and later U.S. secretary of state under Woodrow Wilson, was so taken by Tolstoy during his visit to Yasnaya Polyana that he asked Tsar Nicholas II, whom Bryan was to meet the next day, if they might reschedule. Indeed, in the last years of the nineteenth century it was often said that there were two tsars in Russia, Nicholas II and Leo Tolstoy, and that of the two, Tolstoy was by far the more respected.

After reading Tolstoy's lengthy essay "On Life" in 1889, Ernest Crosby, a thirty-three-year-old American diplomat who was working in Egypt at the time, decided that diplomacy wasn't his calling and instead dedicated the next twenty-seven years of his life to writing and lecturing about Tolstoy throughout the United States.

In his first letter to Tolstoy, Crosby thanked the writer for opening his eyes to the real meaning of life, telling his new spiritual mentor, "I am sure that I can never be as skeptical, as hopeless and as useless again, as I was before I read the book. I am sure it cannot be indifferent to you to learn that you are having a blessed influence on men of alien blood and in distant lands."

Less welcome was this radical personal transformation in the eyes of Crosby's powerful father, who, having helped his son secure a prestigious diplomatic post through family connections with future president Theodore Roosevelt, quite understandably envisioned a more traditional and lucrative career for his son. Yet even Crosby's father conceded defeat in the presence of the powerful muse who had come between him and his son. And if Ernest was going to become a Tolstoy fanatic, he should at least do so in style. To which end Mr. Crosby lent Ernest their New England summer estate as a retreat for his studies in Russian literature.

The internationally respected prophet who inspired Crosby with his message of universal love, however, had enormous difficulty either giving or receiving love within his own family. It was the stuff of newspaper tabloids, Tolstoy's tumultuous domestic life. Where today we are treated to the likes of *Jon & Kate Plus 8*, readers the world over followed the saga of *Leo & Sonya Plus 8*. (His wife Sonya had borne him thirteen children, just eight of whom survived toddlerhood.) This ongoing drama reached scandalous proportions as Tolstoy's life was ending. Had you cracked open the *New York Times* on October 31, 1910, this is the headline you would have encountered:

TOLSTOY IS FOUND;. WIFE TRIED SUICIDE

In Grief Over Husband's Departure to Turn Hermit, Sought Death by Drowning.

SAVED BY HER DAUGHTER

Aged Novelist, Who Had Asked Not to be Traced or Followed, Said to be on Friend's Estate.

The New York Times *headline about Tolstoy's flight from Yasnaya Polyana, published October 31, 1910.*

On the same day, the publication that has always prided itself on offering up All the News That's Fit to Print saw fit to use the occasion of Tolstoy's flight from Yasnaya Polyana and abandonment of his wife to engage in some celebrity psychologizing:

> That the novelist, who is over 80 years old, should desire to spend the evening of his days in solitude surprises no one acquainted with his career, but that he should deliberately desert the wife who had borne him thirteen children gives rise, even in the light of his well-known eccentricities of character, to the suggestion of failing mentality. This is accepted by many in explanation of the sudden leave-taking.

A writer for the *American Review of Reviews* put it even more bluntly: "No man is justified in inflicting martyrdom upon an unwilling wife and children whom he loves."

This conclusion to his life probably wasn't what Tolstoy had envisioned when, at thirty-one, he was creating the idyllic little story "Family Happiness" (1859), or when a few years later while working on *War and Peace*, he jotted down in his diary this thought about his early married life with Sonya: "There probably isn't more than one person in a million as happy as the two of us are together." Tolstoy wrote about the joys and tribulations of love as beautifully as any writer ever has. Yet he was sadly ill-equipped to master that complex emotion through the course of his own life. Often tender as a kitten, he could suddenly spring into the towering narcissism of a lion. Indeed, his life and conduct justified all too well his parents' decision to name their son Leo, or in Russian, "Lev," and that leonine ferocity, killingly attractive to his admirers across the globe, nearly destroyed his wife, who on multiple occasions during their stormy forty-eight-year marriage attempted suicide.

Why, then, should we listen to Tolstoy?

Because his own life of extremes and contradictions makes him not only a fascinating figure, but a surprisingly good teacher. If the Ameri-

Eighty-year-old Tolstoy resting at Yasnaya Polyana in 1908.

can philosopher and educator John Dewey was right that "failure is instructive," then Tolstoy's life is, well, an instructional gold mine. We can learn so much from this Russian writer who made one mistake after another, who went through the crucible of life and survived.

The writer who immersed himself deeply in the dross of life, and then described it as accurately as any other writer, Russian or otherwise, also had an unflinching faith in human possibility. At sixty-one, he advised a struggling friend: "No matter how old or how sick you are, how much or little you have done, your business in life not only isn't finished, but hasn't yet received its final, decisive meaning until your very last breath." This feisty, life-affirming spirit underlies not only Tolstoy's incredible life journey, but that of his characters, as well.

The world, Tolstoy tells us, is a mysterious place where things aren't always what they seem, today's tragedy often paving the way to tomorrow's triumph. Or, to quote Tolstoy himself: "Man is flowing. In him there are all possibilities: he was stupid, now he is clever; he was evil, now he is good, and the other way around. In this is the greatness of man."

Now, there *are* cases when we would be advised not to heed Tolstoy's advice, and certainly not to emulate his behavior. As a relatively levelheaded guy who grew up in a family of businesspeople, I, for example, have always found the wholesale rejection of capitalism of his later years troubling. I have been turned off as well by the way he treated his wife and children in trying to live in accordance with his rigid moral principles, insisting that everybody around him do the same. Tolstoy could be wildly unpragmatic, and the career advice he gave to his eldest son, Seryozha, upon graduation from the university—"Take a broom and sweep streets"—borders on what can only be called parental malpractice. As does his intention to give his and his family's property away to the peasants, and his renunciation of the copyright on all of his earlier works, including *War and Peace* and *Anna Karenina*.

A few years ago I had the dubious privilege of overhearing a debate regarding that decision taking place among members of the Tolstoy family who were in the audience during a talk I'd just given at the Tolstoy Museum and Estate at Yasnaya Polyana. Had he made the right decision? I asked the listeners. Ilya, the great-great-grandson, thought so on the grounds that his famous forebear hadn't wanted his eternal works of fiction turned into commercial commodities. The great-great-*great*-grandson (also named Ilya), on the other hand, disagreed: "Financial considerations are every bit as important as moral ones," he said, before adding half jokingly, "Just imagine how differently we'd be living today if he'd held on to the copyright." The truth is, not very, since in all likelihood the Soviet government, as part of their socialism-building efforts, would have requisitioned Tolstoy's remaining assets, in any case. Nevertheless, heated debates about Tolstoy's controversial positions continue among his descendants, in the hallowed halls of academia and the not-so-hallowed pages of Russian journalism, and even among members of the Russian Orthodox Church, which to this day refuses to officially withdraw the edict of excommunication placed on Tolstoy back in 1901, or to forgive the writer for his withering attacks on the Church.

The Church wasn't the only institution to suffer by Tolstoy's pen. Soviet literary critic Mikhail Bakhtin is not far from the mark when he summarizes Tolstoy's scathing indictment of modernity in his later years: "Every activity in this world, be it conservative or revolutionary, is equally false and evil and foreign to the true nature of man." Moreover, the man whom Vladimir Lenin would later dub "the mirror of the Russian Revolution," in a famous essay by that title, did indeed help to inspire a generation of revolutionaries who in 1917 successfully uprooted the imperial autocracy he had come to abhor. Tragically, of course, the Bolsheviks ushered in a society even more brutal and corrupt than the one they destroyed. Indeed, Tolstoy would have been horrified to see how some of his radical social ideas would be interpreted and implemented in the twentieth century. Still, he is hardly without blame for what happened in Russia in 1917. For when Tolstoy spoke, people listened. What, though, were they listening *to*? His moralistic ideas, I would argue, rather than his art. And therein lay the problem.

In the latter part of the nineteenth century, with a perfect storm of government oppression, revolutionary fervor, and rapid industrialization brewing, readers from all camps, all of them in search of solutions to contemporary problems, found in Tolstoy's polemical tracts either direct support of their own agendas or else a convenient ideological whipping boy. You think modern art has gone downhill? Well, then, *What Is Art?* (1898) is your pamphlet. Government the problem, you say, not the solution? *The Kingdom of God Is Within You* (1894) says it all. People consume far too much alcohol? Then run, don't walk (or stumble, as need be) to the bookstore and grab a copy of "Why Do Men Stupefy Themselves?," first published in 1890 as a preface to a book, *Drunkenness*, about the Russian temperance movement.

It's one thing to listen to Tolstoy's preaching, however, and quite another to immerse yourself in his artistic prose. An idea is something you can argue for or against, but a work of art, if it is great, transcends polemics altogether, offering a portrait of life in all its irreducible contradiction. No one understood this better than Tolstoy. How, after all, can you "agree" or "disagree" with *War and Peace*? You can't, for what Tolstoy gives us in that novel is not so much a set of *answers* to life's every challenge as an *attitude toward living*. Heeding his own advice in the quotation taken as the epigraph to this book, he invites us not to settle for the prescriptions of others (himself included), but to join him and his characters in their quest for deeper meaning, to keep asking the important questions and seeking out authentic experience on our own.

"The hero of my tale," Tolstoy wrote when he was just twenty-seven, "whom I love with all the power of my soul, whom I have tried to portray in all its beauty, who has been, is, and always will be beautiful— is Truth." Hardly a young author today with any literary pretentions would dare write such a sentence; it's not nearly ironic enough. But, then, Tolstoy wasn't trying to win a literary popularity contest with *War and Peace.* He was chasing the truth. And he wanted to help his readers do the same.

War and Peace is long. My own book is relatively brief, organized topically, with each chapter focusing on a timeless theme: Plans, Imagination, Rupture, Success, Idealism, Happiness, Love, Family, Courage, Death, Perseverance, and Truth. In the course of exploring these major concepts, I remind readers of something Tolstoy knew well: no word can capture the richness of the experience it seeks to describe. You think you know what happiness is? What success looks like? Or what courage is all about? Think again, Tolstoy says. No amount of words— not even 566,000 of them!—can absolutely record the messy grandeur of life. Yet in the necessarily imperfect empire of language, Tolstoy was tsar, coming about as close as *any* writer has to communicating through language that which is, well . . . incommunicable. Which is why, as you'll see, I quote so generously from the novel, sprinkling in quotations from Tolstoy's other works as well, in order to give readers as much exposure to the novelist's delicious prose as possible.

Give War and Peace *a Chance* combines biography, history, and philosophy with literary appreciation, while inviting readers to search alongside Tolstoy and his characters for answers to life's "accursed questions": Who am I? Why am I here? How should I live? Each chapter weaves in anecdotes from Tolstoy's life, as well as my own quarter-century journey with Tolstoy and the Tolstoy family in Russia and the United States. The book openly speaks of my own, sometimes tumultuous, spiritual journey, and seeks to enlighten and inspire readers with Tolstoy's wisdom much as I myself have been transformed by his art. The book's timely message is meant for both general readers searching for fresh approaches to today's challenges, as well as readers interested in learning more about one of the world's greatest writers and most captivating personalities.

Finding the man in the Great Man, and the living ideas in this Greatest of Great Books, *Give* War and Peace *a Chance* will, I hope, inspire a general audience to want to read—or *reread*—Tolstoy's works themselves. The ideal companion to *War and Peace*, this book should also be enjoyable to those who have never read a *word* of Tolstoy. Certainly it will help to make that masterpiece more approachable, relevant, and yes, even *fun*.

Even as he was working on *War and Peace*, Tolstoy explained his philosophy as an artist:

> The goal of the artist is not to solve a question irrefutably, but to force people to love life in all its countless, inexhaustible manifestations. If I were told I could write a novel in which I would set forth the seemingly correct attitudes towards all social questions, I would not devote even two hours of work to such a novel, but if I were told that what I write will be read in twenty years by the children of today and that they will weep and smile over it and will fall in love with life, I would devote all my life and all my strength to it.

The goal of my own book is to help that wonderful process along—to help readers weep and smile, and, with the benefit of Tolstoy's extraordinary vision, maybe even fall in love with life again.

1

PLANS

The mind's game of chess goes on independently of life, and life of it.

—Tolstoy's diary, March 1863

As a nineteen-year-old nobleman and proprietor of a vast estate, Tolstoy had big plans for his future. He listed them in his diary:

(1) To study the whole course of law necessary for my final examination at the university. (2) To study practical medicine, and some theoretical medicine. (3) To study languages: French, Russian, German, English, Italian and Latin. (4) To study agriculture, both theoretical and practical. (5) To study history, geography and *statistics*. (6) To study mathematics, the grammar school course. (7) To write a dissertation. (8) To attain an average degree of perfection in music and painting. (9) To write down rules. (10) To acquire some knowledge of the natural sciences. (11) To write essays on all the subjects I shall study.

And, in order to keep himself on track, he created an extensive list of rules that he'd intended to follow religiously. Here are just a few of the headings taken from his diary:

RULES FOR DEVELOPING THE PHYSICAL WILL

RULES FOR DEVELOPING THE EMOTIONAL WILL

RULES FOR DEVELOPING THE RATIONAL WILL

RULES FOR DEVELOPING THE MEMORY

RULES FOR DEVELOPING ACTIVITY

RULES FOR DEVELOPING THE INTELLECTUAL FACULTIES

RULES FOR DEVELOPING LOFTY FEELINGS AND
ELIMINATING BASE ONES, OR, TO PUT IT ANOTHER WAY,
RULES FOR DEVELOPING THE FEELING OF LOVE AND
ELIMINATING THE FEELING OF SELF-LOVE

RULES FOR DEVELOPING SOUND JUDGEMENT

A Man with a Plan: Tolstoy as a student in 1849.

Oh, and Tolstoy had one more rule: "The first rule which I prescribe is as follows: No. 1. *Carry out everything you have resolved.* . . . I haven't carried out this rule." Nor was he exaggerating. Within five years of writing down that list of intentions he had the following accomplishments to show for it:

- Briefly attended Kazan University, but withdrew without graduating

- Moved to Petersburg, planned to enroll in the university and enter the civil service, but having become distracted by cards, women, and booze, did neither

- Failed as a farmer, estate manager, and agricultural reformer

- Opened a school for peasant children on his estate with no success

- Gambled away tens of thousands of rubles (in today's money, around a half million dollars) at the card table

- Lost the house in which he was born in a game of cards

- Failed at every romantic relationship he attempted

- Visited a brothel with his brother, and wept from shame when it came time to settle the bill

- Was hospitalized on multiple occasions for venereal disease

- Exhibited increasing signs of severe hypochondria as well as pathological fear of death

- Lost his faith in God, regained it, and then lost it again

True, Tolstoy had been promoted to ensign for distinction in action in the Caucasus. And, interestingly, he'd enjoyed success in one pursuit he *hadn't* thought to include in his list of youthful ambitions: the writing of fiction. These were, however, among the very few bright spots on an otherwise dismal CV. Up to that point he'd failed at pretty much everything he tried, forcing him to come to a sobering conclusion: "It is easier to write ten volumes of philosophy than to put a single precept into practice." Not that this prevented him from trying. Future generations of readers, moreover, may be thankful that Tolstoy's life wasn't exactly turning out as he'd planned, for while he was amassing an impressive list of failures, he was also acquiring wisdom essential for the creation of *War and Peace*.

"The mind's game of chess goes on independently of life, and life of it," Tolstoy wrote in his diary in 1863. So it is with his characters' every intellectual conviction and rational intention. Whether in the ballroom or on the battlefield, as soon as they come into contact with real life, their ideas and plans disintegrate like so much meteor dust. The characters who come to recognize how little they know about what will happen, Tolstoy suggests, are actually the ones who know the most.

Toward the novel's beginning, the night before the battle of Auster-litz in 1805, a council of high-powered generals and military strate-gists prepare for the upcoming battle—analyzing troop movements, estimating the size of Napoleon's army, evaluating strategies. With all that planning you'd think victory was a sure thing, right? Actually, the Russians and their allies, the Austrians, will get trounced, and not in spite of all their good planning, but precisely *because* of it.

Hovering self-assuredly over a great map spread out before the council, the Austrian general Weyrother intones for an hour, in nause-ating detail (and in German), his written "disposition for the attack on the enemy's position behind Kobelnitz and Sokolnitz, 20 November, 1805" (261). Alas, unlike the map so beautifully illuminated by can-dlelight the evening before, the actual battlefield the next morning is shrouded in a fog that prevents the attacking army from seeing where in the hell they're going! As Tolstoy would write later in the novel about another battle, "[a]s in all dispositions, everything was beauti-fully thought out, and, as with all dispositions, not a single column arrived where it was supposed to at the appointed time" (994).

By the time the Russians do arrive at Kobelnitz and Sokolnitz, the place where they'd intended to begin the action, they are no longer the attackers, but the ones being attacked. It is a contingency Wey-rother's plan hasn't provided for. Nor did it include a provision for the vexation felt by the Russian troops toward their supposed allies, those "muddleheaded" Germans, or the ill-humor felt by the com-manders and superior officers, who are understandably frustrated that the action being undertaken bears no relation to what they'd proposed at the council of war. Dispirited to have arrived late, unable to see, and finding themselves now under assault, they are entirely unprepared to cheer up their troops.

Considering all of the crucial details that Weyrother's brilliant battle plan has left *out*, Commander in Chief Mikhail Kutuzov's decision to catch some shut-eye during the war council appears in retrospect a pretty good use of his time. "'There's nothing more important before a battle than a good night's sleep,'" Kutuzov murmurs to the chattering strategists at the military council, upon waking for a moment (264). For he knows what Tolstoy knows: nothing in battle ever goes according to plan—so just get some rest. That way when the unforeseen cannonballs are whizzing toward you in the morning, you may at least respond quickly and, with any luck, get out of their way.

History, Tolstoy reminds us, proved Kutuzov right. Though the Russians lost the battle of Austerlitz, they ultimately won the war against Napoleon in 1812, and no thanks to the bickering strategists, either. Kutuzov eventually defeats Napoleon not because he has a perfect plan, but because he manages to be present to what's happening in the moment. His nattering generals, motivated by self-interest and entirely removed from the realities on the ground, urge Kutuzov to attack the wounded French army after the battle of Borodino and hold on to Moscow. But "Kutuzov saw one thing: the defense of Moscow was *in no way physically possible*, in the full meaning of those words" (827).

And so, out of sheer necessity the Russian troops retreat, unintentionally luring the overconfident French army into the abandoned capital. That "conquest" is the beginning of the end of Napoleon's army, for while enjoying their wartime booty they are at the same time depleting the very resources needed for the long march out of Russia. How did Kutuzov, the nincompoop, as many of his compatriots called him, plan for *that*? He didn't, and that's just Tolstoy's point: "Kutuzov's merit consisted not in some strategic maneuver of genius, as they call it, but in that he alone understood the significance of what was happening" (990).

Kutuzov was in his sixties at the time, with a long military and diplomatic career behind him. But he had sufficient humility to throw all of his "knowledge" out the window when necessary, letting go of preconceived notions about how things are *supposed* to go on the field of battle, and embracing instead what is occurring right in front of him. Actors sometimes refer to this as "being in the moment." Buddhists call it "nonattachment to concepts." Tolstoy sees it simply as the key to living wisely and leading effectively in a radically uncertain universe.

To appreciate Tolstoy's interest in the topic of plans, it is helpful to know something about Russia in the heady days of the 1850s and 1860s. The hard sciences were becoming all the rage, and most educated Russians were convinced that you could solve the vast majority of problems facing their society through the rigorous application of the principles of science and reason. Leading that charge was the so-called radical intelligentsia, a motley crew of edgy intellectuals, journalists, and writers who studied French sociology, devoured Darwin, and traveled to Europe to worship at the feet of the German philosopher Karl Marx and the exiled Russian nihilist Mikhail Bakunin. The imprisoned revolutionary Nikolai Chernyshevsky's rather bad programmatic novel *What Is to Be Done?* (1863) was their bible, as it would be for nearly all future Russian revolutionaries, not least Lenin himself. The intelligentsia was ingesting, too, the writings of the French philosopher Charles Fourier, who envisioned a perfectly organized society that would feature seas made out of lemonade, androgynous plants that copulate, four lovers or husbands per every adult female, and approximately 37 million poets of the caliber of Homer and 37 million mathematicians with the genius of Newton.

Everybody in those days, it seemed, had a Plan—everybody, that is, except for Tolstoy, who by the early 1860s had hunkered down on his estate to write, hunt, have kids, raise pigs, tend bees, and picnic with his family in the sprawling fields of Yasnaya Polyana. It's not that he didn't care about what was happening around him; he cared very much, if his letters and diaries of the period are any indication, and for that very reason stayed out of the ideological screaming matches, which he believed were not only hurting everybody's ears but were in fact harmful to Russia itself.

Chastening personal experience had taught him that life's most important truths cannot be understood by means of scientific theory, that even the most brilliant social engineering project is bound to fail. That's because, while the *idea* of a perfect utopia is enticing, we imperfect humans are incapable of actually living in one. So, as Tolstoy understood, what begins as an intention to create heaven on earth almost inevitably leads to the exact opposite. Even a brief glance at twentieth-century Russian history, in which plans to build a social- ist paradise produced a totalitarian society far more brutal than the nineteenth-century autocracy it replaced, proves just how prescient Tolstoy was.

It's little wonder, then, that he rejected the fashionable insistence in the 1860s that the purpose of fiction writing was to promote the "cor- rect" social agenda. For starters, nobody at that time could agree on what that agenda *was*; and beyond that, the very notion of fiction as a vehicle for ideology was anathema to the man who said that the artist's goal is to represent "life in all its countless, inexhaustible manifesta- tions." Later in his life, of course, Tolstoy would not always practice what he preached, but at the time he wrote *War and Peace*, the author believed that fiction should do neither more nor less than tell the truth about things the way they are, rather than the way an author thinks they should be. And the way things are, Tolstoy reminds his readers throughout his greatest novel, is far more fluid and unpredictable than the dyed-in-the-wool proponent of one or another social agenda gen- erally cares to acknowledge.

Where was all this progressive thinking coming from in the first place? Tolstoy wondered. As early as the 1850s he searched for an answer to this question by delving into Russian history and became particularly fascinated by the so-called Decembrist Revolt of 1825, when a small band of Russian officers led thirty thousand men in a protest against the assumption of power by Tsar Nicholas I. Taking place just three years before Tolstoy's birth, the event loomed large in his imagination, as it did for many of his contemporaries. The poorly organized rebellion failed miserably, with some of the rebels executed, and the rest exiled to Siberia. Still, it was bitter confirmation of something most thinking Russians had long suspected: that their country was in dire need of social reform—reform, though, *not* a revolution as such, or some grand utopian project of the sort the more radical intelligentsia were advocating. For Count Tolstoy was loath to throw out what was precious in his country's past along with what was admittedly pernicious.

And so, with these ideas in mind, he set out to write a novel about a Decembrist returning to Russia in the 1850s after a quarter-century Siberian exile. It was to be a polemical work whose goal was to arouse sympathy for his hero's progressive aims while at the same time showing that he was a better breed of man than those shrill reformers he encountered upon his return to a changed Russia. The hero's name? Pyotr Labazov, the earliest incarnation of none other than Pyotr (aka Pierre) Bezukhov.

Where had all these good men gone? Tolstoy wondered. Come to think of it, where had they come from in the first place? They were forged, he concluded, in the crucible of the Napoleonic campaigns, and in that transformative year of 1812, in particular, a time of horror and shock during which the entire country—aristocrats, peasants, government, and all—came together in a spontaneous explosion of collective resistance against a foreign invader. In spite of all that hardship—or *because* of it?—Russians experienced a national unity they had never known before, and would not experience again until World War II, or, as the Russians call it, the Great Fatherland War. The crisis that tore the country apart, Tolstoy believed, also brought people closer together. Moreover, the future Decembrists were men who, traveling to the European capitals in the aftermath of the Napoleonic Wars, became acutely aware that Europeans not only enjoyed a higher living standard than Russians, but were less intimidated by their rulers, and freer to express their political opinions.

These insights came later, of course. All Tolstoy wanted to do initially was write a book focusing on Russia in the 1850s. But the more he worked, the more he realized that in order to understand his hero, it would be necessary to know how he lived at the time of the uprising in 1825. And to make sense of that event, it would be essential to understand the critical formative events of the year 1812. But wait: How could he tell the story of 1812 without first describing the years leading up to it, beginning in 1805? Fortunately for us, Tolstoy stopped with 1805, finding it, as a starting point, suitable for his purpose. Otherwise, *War and Peace* might have ended up 15,000 pages long rather than a mere 1,500.

One thing is clear, though: at no point did Tolstoy know what the final version would look like. He admitted as much when, at the end of 1864, he wrote in an unpublished draft of an introduction to his novel: "I cannot determine how much of my work will consist of what is now being published, because I do not know myself and cannot foresee what dimensions my work will assume." He wasn't kidding. The book came together over countless different stages of writing, during which the writer's interests and intentions continually changed, so much so that it seemed to some readers of the *Russian Herald*, where the novel was being published in installments, that later portions might have been written by someone else altogether.

Not only was the shape of Tolstoy's novel unclear to him; its very title eluded him. When he first conceived of the idea of a novel about a returning Decembrist back in 1856, he thought the book would be called, sensibly enough, *The Decembrists*. Having scrapped that idea soon thereafter, he then put the title *Three Eras* on his manuscript. By the time he actually started publishing the novel in the pages of the *Russian Herald* in 1865, he was calling it *1805*. The next installments, however, appeared in 1866 under a different title altogether: *War*. In April of that same year Tolstoy had another change of heart, confident that he'd finish the book the following year, and that it would be called, with apologies to Shakespeare, *All's Well That Ends Well*.

A lot can happen in a man's life over a year, particularly in one as dynamic as Tolstoy's. For instance, a well-known French philosopher by the name of Pierre-Joseph Proudhon, whom Tolstoy had met in Brussels several years earlier, in 1861, would suddenly die, unleashing a spate of articles about him in the Russian press. Surely Tolstoy was paying attention, for he was himself already deeply interested in Proudhon's highly publicized books about warfare, as well as social and economic issues. One of Proudhon's works in particular, which the Frenchman had completed just around the time Tolstoy met him in Brussels and appeared in Russian translation in 1864, kept flitting around Tolstoy's brain: it was called *La Guerre et le Paix,* or *War and Peace,* a title that Tolstoy, presumably rather liking it, now decided to borrow. This, of course, was the title he settled on through future stages of writing and publication, which took him another two years to complete.

Yet here is the interesting point: All those lost threads, failed plans, starts and stops, and shifts in direction—none of it amounted to time *wasted.* For almost everything, in some form or another, ended up in the book. The character of Pyotr, for instance, makes it through all of the drafts with just a slight name change, and the Decembrist theme, too, is still alive and well, for, as any Russian reader in the 1860s would have known, the heated political discussions taking place in the epilogue are harbingers of the future Decembrist uprising that would occur only a few years after the novel's ending. Even the planned title *1805* is not discarded, since the first quarter of the novel takes place in that pivotal year. The theme of *War* is omnipresent, as is the fundamental optimism about the world underlying the novel's previously plundered title, *All's Well That Ends Well.*

Had Tolstoy rigidly stuck to his original intention, the novel might easily have become just another long-winded addition to the ideological shouting matches of his time. But because he allowed the creative process to guide *him,* rather than the other way around, he ended up producing a masterpiece that manages to re-create life in all its unpredictable misery and splendor. The very existence of *War and Peace,* then, is testimony to the wisdom contained in the novel itself: Plans may very well not work, but plan*ning* is well worth doing anyway. Or, as General Eisenhower would put it nearly a century later: "In preparing for battle, I have always found that plans are useless, but planning is indispensable." So it is, Tolstoy continually reminds us, on the battlefield, in the creative process, in life itself.

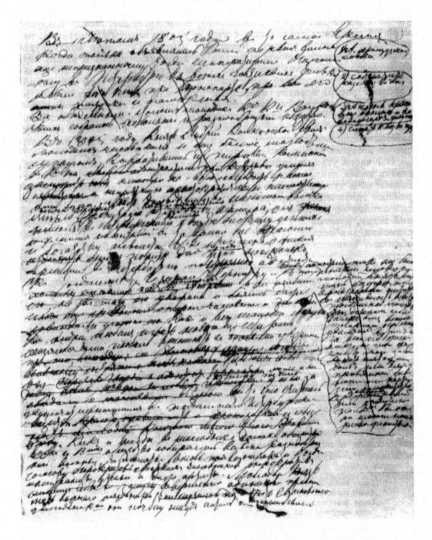

A page from the ninth draft of the opening of War and Peace:
Plans don't work, but they're worth making anyway.

2

IMAGINATION

What is *War and Peace*? It is not a novel, still less an epic poem, still less a historical chronicle. *War and Peace* is what the author wanted and was able to express, in the form in which it is expressed.

—"A Few Words Apropos of the Book *War and Peace*"

Reading *War and Peace* is a bit like sitting down to a Russian feast. If you can make it to the end (dessert usually being served around 3 AM, right after the fourth helping of salad Olivier, the third plate of steamed potatoes, and the seventh shot of vodka), you're likely to feel an uncanny sense of satisfaction. If, however, you leave before your stomach would seem at the breaking point, and your head spinning, then you will surely have missed something essential. You will not have had the *whole* experience. And the whole experience is what a Russian feast—and Tolstoy's fiction—is all *about*.

Henry James had a point when he famously called *War and Peace* a "loose baggy monster." For this beast of a book has hundreds of intersecting plotlines, and many hundreds of characters, who step forward for a moment only then to recede into the background, and then reemerge later, like the shifting whitecaps on a windswept ocean. And Tolstoy's writing is sometimes maddeningly clumsy. He often contradicts himself. He repeats exact words and phrases within a single paragraph, sometimes within a single sentence.

Adding insult to injury, halfway through the book he begins to plant in his already overflowing literary garden an odd species of philosophical disquisition about heroism, history, and free will. In the later sections of the novel, even as Tolstoy continues to add new characters and subplots to his dangerously burdened story line, these essays spread like weeds.

At the end of each writing day, Tolstoy's wife Sonya transcribed his notoriously bad handwriting into prose legible enough for the author himself to understand—a feat that often eluded him. Then, during the next sitting, he would often chuck out or completely revise the previous day's work, sending his overworked wife to her boudoir yet again until late in the night. And just as the *Russian Herald* was about to go to press with each new installment, the author would inevitably recall his work to make yet more additions and changes. This went on for six years, Sonya transcribing *War and Peace* alongside her husband no fewer than seven times. After all that, you might think Tolstoy ought to have had an inkling of how he wanted to bring his book to a conclusion. He didn't. And so he tacked on not one, but two epilogues, the second one being yet another one of his free-form philosophical treatises about history.

Hardly had the first installments of *1805* (the novel's original title) come off the press than critics over at the *Book Herald* started scratching their heads:

> [T]his *1805* presents us with something strange and ill-defined. The author himself apparently does not know how to define his work; its title says simply that it is some sort of attempt at a military-aristocratic chronicle of the past, interesting in some parts, and dry and boring in others. Reading the first two installments, it is impossible to give an account of the work's basic idea.

Another critic complained that "everything is mixed up into a general mass where one can see neither the reasons for nor the consequences of the events or the appearance of heroes or facts."

Someone else called the novel "a disordered heap of accumulated material," while still another diagnosed the writer's problem: "Evidently the author himself does not know what he is writing." And even Ivan Turgenev told a friend, "To my own deep disappointment I must confess that this novel seems to me to be positively bad, boring, and unsuccessful."

How did such a "badly composed book" come to be seen as the greatest novel ever written?

It's all a matter of how we view its strangeness. *War and Peace* is certainly no *Fathers and Sons* (1862), Turgenev's elegantly structured novel (which, as it happens, put Tolstoy to sleep when he read it one evening on Turgenev's drawing-room sofa). It lacks that latter's rigor, its poise, its deftness. But "bad writing" may in fact be very good, even great, writing *if* there is a reason for the quirks, the occasional careless flourish, the countless craggy edges. And Tolstoy had his reasons.

After six years of publication, however, installment after installment—some 1,500 pages in all—his readers still didn't get it. So in response to some of the early unfavorable reviews, the rather piqued author tried to explain himself:

> What is *War and Peace*? It is not a novel, still less an epic poem, still less a historical chronicle. *War and Peace* is what the author wanted and was able to express, in the form in which it is expressed. Such a declaration of the author's disregard of the conventional forms of artistic prose works might seem presumptuous, if it were premeditated and if it had no previous examples. The history of Russian literature since Pushkin's time not only provides many examples of such departure from European forms, but does not offer even one example to the contrary. From Gogol's *Dead Souls* to Dostoevsky's *Dead House*, there is not a single work of artistic prose in the modern period of Russian literature, rising slightly above mediocrity, which would fit perfectly into the form of the novel, the epic, or the story.

Overlooking Tolstoy's presumptuousness—vanity apparently coming to him as easily as anything else—we may notice that he was also making an important point, exhorting readers to stop trying to stuff his artistic creation into narrow paradigms about what a novel is *supposed* to be. Life, after all, doesn't often have a perfect beginning, middle, and end, nor clear heroes and villains, nor unifying plotlines. Why, then, should a book? Rather than shoving his world into nice, neat conceptual containers, Tolstoy invited readers to loosen up those containers to fit the very *largeness* of life.

War and Peace is long. But, then, so is the human journey. It is windy, but then so is life. And if its shape is inelegant, this is only because it mimics the shape of life. In short, this pockmarked, feisty, untutored monstrosity of a work reflects life in all its turmoil, all its roiling, overflowing possibility.

The fact is, the novel wasn't even supposed to be written. Having grown tired of the literary scene after the cool reception of "Family Happiness" (1859), *Polikushka* (1863), and *The Cossacks* (1863), Tolstoy had retreated to his estate to start a school for peasant children not unlike the one he'd unsuccessfully attempted to establish more than a decade earlier.

Tolstoy's Yasnaya Polyana home, in which War and Peace *was conceived and written.*

His real calling, he was by now convinced, was to teach. Beethoven, incidentally, is reported to have believed his true calling was the law, and sorry to have wasted so much time on music. But while it's hard to imagine the creator of the Fifth Symphony composing a brief legal memo, it *is* entirely possible to envision the author of *War and Peace* spicing up a pedantic point with a juicy story or two. For he *was* a good teacher—so good, in fact, that in 1862 the government raided his Yasnaya Polyana school for fear that Tolstoy was planting subversive ideas in young peasant minds. Nor was their fear entirely misplaced, for Tolstoy was indeed doing something revolutionary for a Russian educator in those days: encouraging children to think and create for themselves.

His pedagogical philosophy was simple: leave the children alone. On the sign above the schoolhouse entrance that greeted the pupils each day were the words "Free entrance and exit." Whatever this oddball teacher was doing to inspire his students, it seemed to be working; his pupils eagerly showed up every morning in their newly washed caftans, refusing to leave even at the end of the school day. And the feeling was mutual. His peasant pupils, Tolstoy insisted, were teaching him more about writing than those dusty old classics of German literature: "It seemed so strange to me that a half-literate peasant child would show the sort of conscious artistic power that even a Goethe, from the boundless heights of his development, could not attain," exclaimed the proud teacher after reading a story by Fedka, one of his favorite peasant students. "I would be very interested in knowing the opinion of other connoisseurs, but I consider it my duty to honestly express my own opinion. *I have never before encountered anything like these pages in Russian literature.*"

Gradually, the inspired teacher started toying around with the idea of returning to fiction writing himself, in between teaching, hunting, farming, beekeeping, gambling, occasional womanizing, and, in September 1862, getting married. With so much going on in his life, it's little wonder he had trouble settling on any single idea for his next book. He worked on "Strider," the story of an altruistic horse; a comic drama, *The Infected Family*; a strange little story called "The Dream," which nobody would publish; and a number of articles about his pedagogical experiments at the Yasnaya Polyana school. All the while, though, the idea of a historical novel was percolating. "I am now very drawn to writing a free work *de longue haleine* [on a grand scale]," he confessed in a letter to his future sister-in-law, Elizaveta Behrs, in October 1862, "a novel or the like."

"Or the like" is the key phrase here, because Tolstoy didn't know whether what he wanted to create was really a novel at all. All he knew is that this grand, free thing brewing in his imagination would have to be a work worthy of Fedka himself. A work, in other words, built by a bold and childlike mind unafraid to experiment with new forms, break some rules, and tell the truth about *everything* it observes.

Tolstoy in 1862 about to embark on War and Peace.

The secret of Tolstoy's technique, then, is perhaps best captured in the phrase "making strange," coined by a small but influential group of literary scholars living in the Soviet Union in the 1920s. Tolstoy's genius, the Formalists pointed out, lies in his uncanny ability to make our familiar, everyday world suddenly seem strange—and therefore fresh. Like Cézanne, who is said to have painted an apple in such a way that it seemed as though you were looking at one for the very first time, Tolstoy portrays life with an almost disconcerting truthfulness. Indeed, *War and Peace* thrusts readers raised on more polished literary fare out of their familiar paradigms and into a brave new fictional world, which, for all its strangeness, somehow starts to feel more "real" than reality itself.

Imagine your surprise as a Russian reader of the day, waking up on a crisp January morning in 1865, to encounter the first installment of this rather startling literary endeavor . . . Groping for your leather *tapochki*, or slippers, at the bedside, and lugging your well-fed body into a seated position, you would place the pince-nez on the bridge of your nose, and then, cracking open your copy of the *Russian Herald*, find yourself confronting the following:

—Eh bien, mon prince. Gênes et Lucques ne sont plus que des apanages, des помѣстья, de la famille Buonaparte. Non, je vous préviens que si vous ne me dites pas que nous avons la guerre, si vous vous permettez encore de pallier toutes les infamies, toutes les atrocités de cet Antichrist (ma parole, j'y crois)— je ne vous connais plus, vous n'êtes plus mon ami, vous n'êtes plus мой верный раб, comme vous dites. Ну, здравствуйте, здравствуйте. Je vois que je vous fais peur, садитесь и рассказывайте.

["Well, my prince, Genoa and Lucca are now no more than possessions, *estates*, of the Buonaparte family. No, I warn you, if you do not tell me we are at war, if you still allow yourself to palliate all the infamies, all the atrocities of that Antichrist (upon my word, I believe it)—I no longer know you, you are no longer my friend, you are no longer my faithful slave, as you say. Well, good evening, good evening. I see that I'm frightening you, sit down and tell me about it." (3)]

While the squiggly Cyrillic characters wouldn't have thrown a nineteenth-century Russian reader as they do most twenty-first-century English speakers, the sense of real disorientation would have been every bit as great: hardly have we cracked open this novel when we find ourselves suddenly under attack by an overly animated salon hostess lobbing veritable cannonballs of hot political gossip at unsuspecting guests. It is 1805. Russia has recently been drawn into the war against Napoleon, who has won decisive battles and is advancing eastward. The Russian army under Kutuzov's command has just left Petersburg to join the Austrian forces. Accosting the arriving Russian Prince Vassily Kuragin with the news of Napoleon's recent atrocities, this Anna Pavlovna Scherer threatens to end their friendship on the spot if, in light of recent developments, he fails to show sufficient Russian patriotism.

Oddly enough, Anna Pavlovna delivers her patriotic assault in the language of the French menace himself. A good 2.5 percent of this Russian national epic, in fact, happens to be in French—yet another feature of the novel that drove contemporary readers mad. Always on the lookout for a teachable moment, though, Tolstoy used this misunderstanding as an opportunity for a lesson in art appreciation: "The reproach that people speak and write in French in a Russian book is similar to the reproach made by a man who, looking at a painting, notices black spots in it (shadows) that are not found in reality."

Art isn't merely supposed to be a literal snapshot of reality. Rather, Tolstoy believed, it should also illuminate deeper, often hidden truths about life. The overabundance of French in the book made complete sense to him, for it highlighted "that French way of thinking" he believed had pervaded Russian high society ever since Peter the Great westernized Russia at the beginning of the eighteenth century. It simply took an actual invasion by France a century later, Tolstoy observed, to persuade Russians that they were not French, after all, and that this might be a *good* thing. It was those plucky Slavs, with their unorthodox military tactics and lice-filled greatcoats, after all, and not the rational Germans or the mild-mannered Brits, who succeeded in ending Napoleon's domination of Europe. What better way to celebrate than by re-creating this moment of awakened national self-consciousness in grand Russian style: throwing in everything, including the French-made kitchen sink?—hell, even making the vanquished Napoleon speak some Russian in the course of revolutionizing the European novel as people knew it!

And who might make a more fitting hero of such a book than Pierre Bezukhov, this odd amalgam of noble if uncertain Russian paternity and European upbringing, who has just returned to his homeland after spending ten years being educated in Paris? From the minute he steps foot in the door of Anna Pavlovna's home, this massive, portly, bespectacled young man with his cropped hair, his light-colored trousers, his jabot and brown tailcoat, is a social disaster waiting to happen. Everything about him—his size, his enthusiastic defense of Napoleon, his illegitimate birth—contributes to Anna Pavlovna's anxiety at the sight of his bumbling entrance, "like that expressed at the sight of something all too enormous and unsuited to the place" (9).

Nor is her fear unwarranted, for one of the first things Pierre does when he arrives is to lionize Napoleon to the Russian guests. After which he proceeds to walk away from a distinguished lady trying to have a conversation with him about her majesty's health. Oh, and just before leaving the party, he picks up a three-cornered hat with general's plumage, thinking it his own, and starts pulling out the feathers until finally the general is reduced to asking the younger man to give it back.

But even if he plays the game all wrong, Pierre is the one to whom all the really interesting stuff happens in the novel. How stimulating it would be to spend time inside the head of a young man who can dream at the beginning of the novel that he is Napoleon walloping the British and then later believe with total sincerity that he has been called upon to assassinate the so-called French Antichrist. And who wouldn't be a bit amused to observe this shy, bearlike Russian man sitting right next to an actual Russian bear, while driving around Moscow in a horse-drawn carriage with two friends? Who could fail to smile when Pierre fumblingly ties the bear to a policeman who tries to interfere with their amusement and tosses them both into the Moika River for a midnight swim?

There is something different about Pierre. His smile, which is "not like that of other people, blending into a non-smile," seemed to say, "'Opinions are opinions, but you see what a good and nice fellow I am.' And everyone, including Anna Pavlovna, involuntarily felt it" (22). Despite his oddness, or maybe because of it, few of Tolstoy's contemporaries who read the novel in installments guessed that Pierre would turn out to be one of the main heroes—not that Tolstoy gave them too much help, never furnishing his readers with the sort of potted biography other nineteenth-century novelists often did when introducing a major character. No, he simply tosses readers right smack into the midst of things, forcing them to decide for themselves who or what to focus on. "No hors d'oeuvres or anything," observes one book club reader. "We're into the main course right from the start."

But, then, part of the fun of the novel is that we get to know the characters in much the same way we meet people in real life. Most of us don't walk into a party, hang up our coats, proceed through the vestibule, and ask, "So, who's the one we're supposed to focus on here?" Rather, we're bombarded by hundreds of details and sensations while our minds work to organize all of these impressions into some recognizable pattern, resulting in judgments about who's who and what's what.

Unfortunately, because, like Anna Pavlovna, we are guided by limiting assumptions and personal biases, rather than by the truth of what actually happens to be in front of us, we are often, well, wrong. That fat, awkward "young man who did not know how to live" (10), as Anna reflexively characterizes Pierre, is, in fact, one of very few guests at her soiree who actually *does* know how to live. For in contrast to the self-assured folks in the room who believe that they have the world figured out, Pierre, precisely because he is clueless about how things are *supposed* to be, is less handicapped, less predisposed to error, than most. While he looks around everywhere at once "like a child in a toyshop" (10), the soiree guests spout prefabricated witticisms and perform on cue, rather like wound-up toys—and Tolstoy happens to be having some serious fun with . . . all of them.

The whole soiree, in fact, is described like a miniature battlefield of egos and interests that Anna Pavlovna appears to command with no less panache than General Bonaparte himself. But why stop at just one metaphor? Tolstoy also compares her hostessing skills to those of a good maître d'hôtel, serving up her guests like hunks of choice roast beef on a platter sprinkled with herbs. It all looks and smells quite nice on the outside, but living this way, Tolstoy suggests, is also slowly making spiritual minced meat out of them. *And* if culinary social commentary isn't your cup of tea, then how about this one:

> As the owner of a spinning mill, having put his workers in their places, strolls about the establishment, watching out for an idle spindle or the odd one squealing much too loudly, and hastens to go and slow it down or start it up at the proper speed—so Anna Pavlovna strolled about her drawing room, going up to a circle that had fallen silent or was too talkative, and with one word or rearrangement she set the conversation machine running evenly and properly again. (10)

"Tolstoy's *funny!*" exclaims an acquaintance of mine, as if in shock. "There's no less artificiality here than at a D.C. cocktail party," she adds. I'm not really in a position to evaluate, but I can say with some certainty that Tolstoy himself attended quite a few high-society parties when he was living in the Russian capital of Petersburg in his midtwenties and hated most of them. However dissatisfying these events may have been, they clearly supplied him with page upon page for later use. What *is* perhaps surprising is that one of the most opinionated men who ever lived, at least when it came to his art, managed to follow his own injunction to "relate, portray, but do not judge." Tolstoy may not like the cynical crowd of aristocratic courtiers very much, but he does understand them, and intends to help us do the same. They are simply people who, imagining they know how the world works, are doing what they believe they must in order to survive.

This well-oiled social machine may seem to be chugging along smoothly enough when we encounter it at the beginning of the novel, but a major rupture is about to take place in Russian society, laying a wrench right smack in the middle of that machine and the lives of the people, like Anna Pavlovna Scherer, ostensibly operating it. The characters who survive and thrive under such circumstances will be the ones most capable of embracing flux, of opening themselves to radically new ways of seeing and living. And guess what: that fat, klutzy kid earning the contempt of the entire drawing room will turn out to be one of them. As will Natasha Rostova, Pierre's female counterpart, and another one of those "broad Russian souls" with a big heart and a childlike openness to the world.

We meet this dark-eyed, vivacious thirteen-year-old as she comes screeching onto the scene at the very moment when the adults are trying to have polite conversation, her black ringlets all askew, thin shoulders popping out of her bodice. It's the name-day celebration of Natasha and her mother (the birthday of the saint they're both named for), and hundreds of guests file in and out of their well-known home on Povarskaya Street in Moscow to congratulate them. All of Moscow is buzzing with Alexander I's reported manifesto, declaring war and calling up Russian recruits. But who wants to talk about boring Bonaparte when there's Mimi, the doll, to play with. To Natasha, mind you, Mimi is quite real, and woe to the adult guest who merely feigns interest in Natasha's make-believe world by asking her, in condescending tones: "'Tell me, my dear, what is this Mimi to you? Your daughter, it must be?'"(39) Natasha ignores the question and gives the woman a serious look, as if to say that one doesn't *toy* with such matters.

Later, at dinner, with twenty guests seated around the large dining room table, Natasha interrupts the adult conversation because she absolutely needs to know, right now, what kind of ice cream is to be served for dessert. Let the grown-ups discuss, the politicians and pundits pontificate, the megalomaniacs menace, but by God, Natasha wants her pineapple ice cream! Annoying? Absolutely. Naïve? You bet. But to Tolstoy such mercurial and spontaneous behavior was far more attractive than, say, that of Natasha's prudish older sister, Vera, who prides herself on the fact that "'there can never be anything bad in my actions'" (47). Which, as far as Tolstoy is concerned, means there can't be much that is alive or authentic in them, either.

And, well, there *is* something about Natasha. When she dances in the folksy, free-spirited Russian style, people can't take their eyes off her: "Where, how, and when had this little countess, brought up by an émigré Frenchwoman, sucked this spirit in from the Russian air she breathed, where had she gotten these ways, which should have been long supplanted by the *pas de chale* [shawl dance]?" (512) Tolstoy proceeds to answer his own question: "from the Russian air she breathed"—from her immediate surroundings, that is, from Russian life itself. Had Natasha trained at the Bolshoi, she might have impressed the spectators with more technical precision, even as she bored them to tears. Instead, her dance elicits a different kind of tears from Anisya Fyodorovna, her uncle's servant, as she looks at "this slender, graceful countess brought up in silk and velvet, so foreign to her, who was able to understand everything that was in Anisya and in Anisya's father, and in her aunt, and in her mother, and in every Russian" (512).

What makes this teenage girl a delightful artist in this moment is that her creativity comes not from special technique or even talent, but from somewhere deep inside, from an instinctive responsiveness to the world, and an irresistible impulse for authentic self-expression. Her body finds its own form, discovers how to say what it needs to say, and says it well. "As soon as she stood there, smiling triumphantly, proudly, and with sly merriment, the fear which had first seized Nikolai [Natasha's brother] and all those present—that she would not do it right—went away, and they began to admire her" (512).

The fear Natasha initially evokes in Nikolai and the other onlookers is one all too familiar to artists of any stripe. As an aspiring seven-year-old actor, I was so scared to perform in front of my family that I'd hide under the dinner table and recite my lines while squinting and covering my ears for fear they might catch me making mistakes. But as Natasha demonstrates, sometimes allowing ourselves to do it wrong is the very key to getting it *right*. Tolstoy himself had to relearn this lesson while creating *War and Peace*. "I was afraid to write in a language different from that in which everybody writes," he admitted in a draft of an introduction to the novel written just after the first installments had appeared:

> I was afraid that my writing would fall into no existing genre, neither novel, nor long poem, nor history. I was afraid that the necessity to describe important personages of 1812 would force me to be guided by historical documents rather than by the truth. And while I was feeling all these fears time passed, and my work was not moving ahead. I began to cool towards it. Now, having tormented myself for a long time, I have decided to push aside all these fears and to write only that which I must tell, without worrying about what will come out of it all and without giving any name to my work.

Creating a rich work of art, Tolstoy says, much like living a rich life, is less a matter of target practice than, for instance, driving your carriage at night: rather than focus on the road directly in front of you, it is often better to soften your gaze, letting your wider, more intuitive peripheral vision guide you. Training your focus only on where you think you're *supposed* to go often makes it hard to get anywhere at all. A case in point: Napoleon's obsession with subduing Mother Russia. His monomaniacal pursuit of this one goal will lead him deep into a country that, with his "French way of thinking," he cannot comprehend—a country whose vast natural landscape, terrifyingly frigid winter, and fiercely proud inhabitants are enough to wipe out his seemingly invincible killing machine.

And so, in the famous scene when Natasha attends an opera for the first time, even as all the operagoers ooh and aah over a mawkishly acted love story starring the celebrated French ballet dancer Duport, Natasha sees only a stage consisting of flat boards, painted pieces of cardboard representing trees, a man in tight silk breeches singing something and opening his arms in front of a fat woman in a white silk dress sitting on a stool with a piece of green cardboard glued to the back of it. Phony performances may titillate the senses of some, but inevitably they fail to touch the soul in any meaningful way. Genuine art, Tolstoy insisted, should captivate the imagination by doing nothing more, and nothing less, than *telling the truth*.

The truth, of course, is riddled with sprained ankles and bruised hearts, as both Natasha and Pierre will discover over and over again in the course of the novel. So would it be better for these two dreamers to sober up? Not necessarily, says Tolstoy. Pain is the price we more often than not pay for being genuinely alive. The smug strategists who attend Anna Pavlovna's soiree may never know the emotional depths to which Pierre and Natasha descend. But neither will they experience these characters' exhilaration at a life fully lived.

In spite of, or perhaps because of, their frequent flights of fancy, these two masters in the art of living will eventually find their feet firmly planted in the soil of reality. By contrast, the socialites we meet at the soiree end up, by the book's conclusion, out of touch or out of sight, all their vitality, so carefully rationed, nevertheless drained. The Kuragins, whose family name rather significantly echoes the Russian word for dried apricots (*kuraga*), pride themselves on knowing how the world works. But when our social success depends on a carefully executed copycat existence, are we playing the game or is the game playing us? Better, says Tolstoy, to connect with our inner Natasha and wide-eyed Pierre. For it is these two "naïve" characters who end up happy, who end up alive. Like the child in "The Emperor's New Clothes," a story Tolstoy loved and quoted often, Pierre and Natasha may say and do all the wrong things; but it is they who see and experience life's deeper truth.

Among the many criticisms scholars and historians have leveled at *War and Peace* is that Tolstoy distorts historical fact in the novel for his own polemical purposes. A perfectly fair criticism, though perhaps beside the point. Tolstoy, after all, has done more to shape Russian readers' perception of their past than an ocean of factually "accurate" history books. Many Soviet soldiers given the 1812 sections of the novel to read in their barracks during World War II later claimed to have been stirred more by Tolstoy's descriptions of warfare than by the actual battlefield events unfolding before their eyes. And because of *War and Peace*, generations of Russians have regarded the war of 1812 and the famous battle of Borodino as a uniquely Russian *victory*. Tens of thousands of their countrymen were slaughtered at Borodino, but that battle happened to anticipate Napoleon's fateful retreat from Moscow. "It was not the sort of victory that is determined by captured pieces of cloth on sticks, known as standards, and by the amount of ground the troops stood and stand on," Tolstoy writes, "but a moral victory, the sort that convinces the adversary of the moral superiority of his enemy and of his own impotence that was gained by the Russians at Borodino" (820).

So, is Tolstoy's interpretation of history correct? Surely it doesn't really matter. The fact-versus-fiction debate is just too narrow to be applied to a book as sprawling and contradictory as *War and Peace*. In fact, it's just the kind of debate Tolstoy's Napoleon would have loved to engage in, because it's one you can win, if only you have at your disposal a big enough arsenal of information. But life, Tolstoy says, does not work so elegantly. Neither, he believed, should a novel. To truly understand the world and realize our individual potential within it, we need a fuller, more imaginative way of seeing, which is just what Tolstoy's behemoth of a book models for us. "A complete picture of human life. A complete picture of Russia of those days," wrote Nikolai Strakhov, one of the few critics in Tolstoy's time who actually *got* the novel. "A complete picture of the things in which men set their happiness and greatness, their sorrow and their shame. That is what *War and Peace* is." Or, as the member of a book club I attended recently put it: "*War and Peace* is life in HD!" And in HD, I would add, *everything* is visible.

More than a realist, then, Tolstoy is what Dostoevsky, referring to himself, might have called a "realist in the higher sense." That is, he doesn't so much hold up a mirror to the world as he illuminates it with a radiating lamp. Zooming in and out of our lives, moving back and forth between ballrooms and battlefields, marriages and massacres, private lives and public spectacles, Tolstoy invites us all to take a good, honest look at not only who we are, but who we might become. And in so doing, he offers a rather profound answer to the silly question Anna Pavlovna airily poses at her soiree: "'Is it possible to remain at ease in our time?'" (4). Maybe, Tolstoy suggests, we shouldn't be trying so hard to be. Maybe, by worrying less about remaining calm than simply staying *aware*, we may allow ourselves to truly live.

3

RUPTURE

"Once we're thrown off our habitual paths, we think all is lost; but it's only here that the new and the good begins."

—*War and Peace*, Volume 4, Part 4, Chapter 17

We've all had moments when our world suddenly snaps. It's as if we've just woken up from a troubled night's sleep—or perhaps even a good one—to find the earth shifted beneath our feet. Yesterday all at once seems ancient, the future unknowable, and the present . . . utterly strange. These moments of altered consciousness may be terrifying or blissful. They may engulf you all at once, or creep over you like a slowly unraveling nightmare, or a sublime dream. But they inevitably leave their mark for a lifetime. *War and Peace* is full of such moments.

Meet Nikolai Rostov, Natasha's older brother. This coddled young man from a happy family revels in the cocoonlike atmosphere of his home life. Yet at the same time he wants to cut the safe moorings and test his mettle out *there*, in the rough-and-tumble of the real world. Fortunately for him, a war with Napoleon is heating up, and if you were a young man looking for some adventure in those days, you couldn't do better than joining the fight against the archenemy of the

Western world. "'I'm convinced that the Russians must either die or conquer,'" blurts out the twenty-year-old future hussar (cavalryman) at Natasha's name-day celebration dinner (64).

But "the Russians," this hot-blooded young patriot will quickly discover upon joining the army, are hardly the monolithic group he imagines. How, for instance, is he to categorize that Russian comrade-in-arms, the soldier Telyanin, who steals money from right under Nikolai's nose in his very own barracks? Or make sense of the fact that, after exposing the thief in front of other soldiers, Nikolai is rewarded not with praise but a hearty chewing-out by the staff captain, who insists that *Nikolai* is the one to blame for attempting to besmirch the reputation of the regiment?

Oh, and the very next day, during the battle of Schöngrabern, just as Nikolai raises his sword to slash up the approaching Frenchmen, he is thrown off his horse onto the field. Lying on the ground surrounded by stubble all around him, he wonders:

> Where ours were, where the French were—he did not know. There was no one around.
>
> Having freed his leg, he got up. "Where, on which side now was that line which had so sharply separated the two armies?" (189)

Excellent question. Where *is* the seemingly clear line that divides "us" from "them"? Like Nikolai's earlier idealized conception of military valor, it is nowhere to be found. It's one thing to vociferate courageously in the comfort of your own home and quite another to be on an actual battlefield facing the real possibility of your own extinction:

> He looked at the approaching Frenchmen and, though a moment before he had been galloping only in order to meet these Frenchmen and cut them to pieces, their closeness now seemed so terrible to him that he could not believe his eyes. "Who are they? Why are they running? Can it be they're running to me? Can it be? And why? To kill me? *Me*, whom everybody loves so?" He remembered

his mother's love for him, his family's, his friends', and the enemy's intention to kill him seemed impossible. "But maybe even—to kill me!" (189)

What was he expecting? That they'd give him a high five, offer him some shots of vodka, carry him off to a tub and give him a nice warm bath like his nanny used to do? This gung ho hussar knows he's at war and in the middle of a live battlefield, and yet in his heart of hearts can't imagine that anybody would want to harm *him*, beloved son and master. As soon as the first of the charging Frenchmen is close enough for Nikolai to see his hooked nose and the expression on his face, he grabs his pistol in terror. But instead of firing it, Nikolai throws it at him and runs as fast as he can into the bushes.

The last we see of Nikolai in this early section of the book is when he is sitting around the campfire, writhing in pain, totally confused by what has just happened to him. Trying to make sense of the other wounded, moaning, bickering soldiers whose faces flicker like shifting shadows before him, Nikolai thinks, "'Who are they? Why are they here? What do they want? And when will it all end?'" (200) *They*, of course, are his comrades, each of whom hurts no more or less than Nikolai himself, and like him, seeks solace from the suffering. Still unable to recognize his connection to these strange men, however, Nikolai feels only his own pain. "'Nobody needs me!'" he thinks. "'There's nobody to help me or pity me. And once I was at home, strong, cheerful, loved'" (200).

But he's not in Moscow anymore. People in this new reality are neither all good nor all bad; things aren't always what they seem; and life doesn't necessarily happen the way we expect it to. In an irony as weird as those undulating shadows dancing about the fire, Nikolai will receive the soldier's St. George Cross for his supposed bravery in the battle he has just stumbled through. The disorientation of his first wartime experiences is an important first step on Nikolai's path to wisdom. But only a step, for, as so often is the case, inching his way closer to a firmer, more abiding sense of understanding, he must be struck by another blow or two.

A few months later, Nikolai comes home on leave and his family and relatives are jubilant at the return of their darling Nikolushka. The girls naturally swarm about Moscow's most eligible new bachelor, the handsome hussar lieutenant with a St. George freshly pinned upon his chest—and a very good dancer, to boot. Times are indeed good for Nikolai at home, where he sings, plays games, and shows off his dancing skills. "'Seize the moments of happiness, make them love you, fall in love yourself! That is the only real thing in this world—the rest is all nonsense. And that is the one thing we're taken up with here,' said the atmosphere" (331).

But if happiness is in the air, so is officer Dolokhov, the handsome, maleficent rake whom Nikolai has recently befriended. Dolokhov is now visiting the Rostovs in the hopes of courting Nikolai's cousin, Sonya—which creates something of a conundrum for Nikolai, since Sonya, whom he himself had once promised to marry, is still in love with him. And so when Sonya rebuffs her would-be suitor, Nikolai must both free himself from her advances and smooth things over with a now-vengeful Dolokhov.

Arriving at Dolokhov's farewell party held at Moscow's swanky English hotel, Nikolai is escorted into a private room and seated at a candlelit poker table with Dolokhov and twenty other men. The first thing Nikolai notices is his friend's cold, expectant gaze, as if he's been waiting for him. All too familiar to Nikolai is the mood behind this gaze, in which Dolokhov tries to curb his boredom with life "by some strange, most often, cruel act" (336). And so the settling of scores begins.

"'Why aren't you playing?'" taunts Dolokhov (337). So concerned with winning his charismatic friend's approval is Nikolai that he does not at first grasp that this is a game of cat-and-mouse, in which, naturally, he is to be the mouse—a mouse with a gambling addiction, as both he and Dolokhov know. Nikolai stakes five rubles and loses, repeats the bet, and loses again. He does this ten times in a row.

"'I let the others win, but you I beat,'" says Dolokhov. "'Or are you afraid of me?'" (337).

For hours the goading continues, the champagne keeps flowing, and eventually Nikolai leaves an eight-hundred-ruble bet on the table. Waiting with a sinking heart for the card that will determine his fate, he recalls the conversation he had only a week earlier with his father, who gave him two thousand rubles with the understanding that this was the last money he could afford to lend his son until spring. Nikolai fixes his eyes on Dolokhov's reddish, broad-boned hands, even as recollections of jokes with his younger brother Petya, warm talks with Sonya, duets with Natasha, and card games with his father flit across his mind. He cannot believe that "stupid chance, making the seven fall to the right rather than the left, could deprive him of all this newly understood, newly illuminated happiness" (338). But this is just what chance can and will do.

His head in a whirl, Nikolai tries to make sense of what's happening:

> "Can he really wish for my ruin? He used to be my friend. I loved him. . . . I've done nothing wrong. Did I kill anyone, insult or wish evil to anyone? Why, then, such a terrible misfortune? And when did it start? I was so happy, so free, so cheerful! And I didn't realize then how happy I was! When did it end, and when did this new, terrible condition begin? What marked the change?" (339)

When *did* Nikolai's misfortune start? When he sat down at the poker table? When he decided to go to the hotel? Started traipsing about with the shady Dolokhov in the first place? Or earlier yet, when he came home from the front? Tolstoy refuses to answer such impossible questions. For what if things sometimes happen just *because*? One minute you're this nice aristocratic boy from an excellent family with a St. George Cross pinned to your chest, and then you go and get drunk and gamble away a chunk of your dad's dwindling fortune to the stone-hearted bastard you thought was your friend. Where's the logic in that?

At first Nikolai thinks he'll just wiggle his way out of this one by adopting a self-assured tone and promising to repay his debt the very next day. But to actually come home alone to his sisters, his brother, and his parents, and ask for money to which he knows he has no right after giving his word of honor, that is another matter altogether. Sure enough, the full magnitude of the crisis hits him the minute he walks in the door. Enveloped by that joyous atmosphere filled with singing and laughing and card-playing, he feels none of it. He cannot understand why everyone else remains so happy when his own life is now in ruins. "'For them everything's the same,'" he observes. "'They don't know anything! What am I to do with myself?'" (341).

There is nothing he *can* do in that moment, Tolstoy hints, except let go of everything he thought he knew about himself, his family, and his world. Nikolai has again entered foreign territory. The giant glittering ballroom that was his life has just darkened, nasty Dolokhovs have crashed the dance floor, and he himself has turned out to be far less dashing than his lithe dancer's body or his medal of bravery might have suggested. In this moment Nikolai is right about just one thing: *they don't know anything*. Then again, neither does he; nor do any of us, really. And that honest admission, Tolstoy suggests, is an excellent place from which to start rebuilding his broken world.

"'A bullet in the head is all that's left for me,'" Nikolai thinks. But then he begrudgingly listens to his sister Natasha sing, something he has done any number of times before. Only this time he really . . . *hears*:

"What's happened with her? How she sings today!" he thought. And suddenly the whole world became concentrated for him on the expectation of the next note, the phrase, and everything in the world became divided into three beats: "*Oh mio crudele affetto* [Oh my cruel affliction] . . . One, two, three . . . *Oh mio crudele affetto* . . . Ah, our foolish life!" thought Nikolai. "All this misfortune, and money, and Dolokhov, and spite, and honor—it's all nonsense . . . and here is—the real thing . . ."

Oh, how the third had vibrated, and how touched was something that was best in Rostov's soul. And that something was
independent of anything in the world and higher than anything in
the world. What are gambling losses, and Dolokhovs and words
of honor!... It's all nonsense! One can kill, and steal, and still be
happy... (343)

Tolstoy isn't advocating stealing and killing, of course. What he is
showing is that in this moment of emotional crisis Nikolai taps into a
reality larger than himself. This swashbuckling young man who only a
day earlier was on top of the world, and more recently has come to feel
the weight of the world bearing down upon him, suddenly senses that
there is something in life that is bigger than his own ups and downs,
his narrow concepts of himself, or his familiar frameworks of understanding. Natasha's irrational joy infects him now, and just as mysteriously as his life had been transformed only hours earlier—undeniably
for the worse, it seemed to him—so is Nikolai suddenly transported
again, only this time to a state of momentary bliss.

Had he not lost forty-three thousand rubles, had his world not just
been turned on its head, would he have been able to hear the full
beauty of his sister's voice? Surely not. Tumultuous times, Tolstoy tells
us, can jar us into heightened awareness, expanding our sense of both
ourselves and life's possibility. Losing something valuable, that is, we
gain in return something invaluable: a radically widened perspective.

Tolstoy knew this to be so, because the scenes describing Nikolai's
wartime baptism by fire, not to mention his later, gut-wrenching gambling loss, were inspired by Tolstoy's own experiences as a young cadet.
At twenty-three he'd traveled with his brother Nikolai and joined the
army in the Caucasus with the aim of changing his libertine ways and
winning some glory on the battlefield. But war turned out to be far
less glamorous than he'd imagined; and his high hopes for personal

transformation, no match for the seductive gypsy girls and enticing poker tables he encountered. Open Tolstoy's diaries from his twenties and you'll find a morbidly entertaining portrait of a young man in a seemingly constant state of crisis.

"When shall I cease at last to lead a life without purpose or passion, or to feel a deep wound in my heart and know no means of healing it?" Tolstoy pined in his diary, while stationed in Simferopol. "God alone knows who inflicted this wound, but from birth I've been tormented by the bitter pledge of future nothingness, by wearisome grief and doubt."

Not that there weren't moments of contentment amid all the young Tolstoy's soul-searching angst—the period immediately leading up to the insane gambling spree that cost him the house he was born in being one of them. Tolstoy was twenty-six at the time, and things had actually been going rather well for him. He had twice been recommended for the St. George Cross for courage in battle, even though the notoriously absentminded young man couldn't get his official documents in order long enough to actually receive the honor. He was excited, too, about his concept for a military journal that had made it up the chain of command for consideration by the tsar himself.

Beyond these successes, Tolstoy was surrounded by acquaintances who enjoyed congregating in his rooms for long evenings of cards and vodka, punctuated by philosophical and literary discussions. The young count was even something of a jokester, "really the soul of the battery," wrote one of his fellow officers, known for making up and leading his comrades in nursery games: for instance, seeing how long you could balance on one leg atop a tent peg. Tolstoy enjoyed daytime hikes in the mountains, where he drank in the tableau of Turkish and British soldiers battling in the distance—sights that would inspire some of the grandest battle scenes in his later fiction. In the evening, when he wasn't drinking or gambling with fellow soldiers or chasing local beauties, he'd promenade about the charming little Tatar village of Eski-Orda and watch the southern sun setting on the snowcapped mountains.

An Officer and a Libertine: Tolstoy in 1856.

Then, after several months of living like this, in January 1855 he was transferred to a new battery station in the region of the Belbek River—a hellhole, as Tolstoy described it in his diary, consisting of shabby old huts, few interesting comrades or books, and worst of all, no women. The battery commander was "the dirtiest creature you could imagine," and Odakhovsky, the senior officer, "a nasty, mean little Pole" who embezzled battery funds and was a notorious cardsharp. "And I'm tied to, even dependent on these people!" lamented Tolstoy.

Nowhere was Tolstoy's dependency more evident than at the poker table. On the evening of January 28, 1855, just as he was settling down in his tiny hut, there was a knock at the door. It was Odakhovsky. "We're gonna start dealing in an hour," he told his young officer. They'd be playing shtoss again tonight. Tolstoy hesitated. He hadn't done anything all day. He'd meant to go for a walk, write some long-overdue letters. "Just for an hour," he said, though from long personal experience he knew perfectly well he didn't mean it.

The first hand had already been dealt when he arrived and joined the other officers at the table. He played cautiously at first, resolving to continue just long enough to win back his losses before quitting the table. A few hours later, he was only deeper in debt and unable to stop. The thick, pungent tobacco smoke, commingled with the scents of the chilled *chikhir** and hot pirozhki†, engulfed him in a toxic mixture of desire and frustration, much as only a few months earlier, a landlady's daughter had made him writhe under the influence of her jet-black hair, fiery eyes, and supple figure, ill-disguised by the thin, Oriental gown she was wearing. The self-induced torture continued for several hours more now, the champagne flowing, debts mounting. When dawn broke, the chips were in and the tallies counted. Tolstoy had lost a cool six thousand rubles—more or less what you needed in those days to buy a medium-sized country estate on a decent plot of land.

What killed Tolstoy even more than the serious financial loss was the fact that he had reneged on the word he had repeatedly given to his family, his fellow soldiers, and *himself*—that he'd put an end to his shameful gambling sprees. The cost of this broken promise was equal to that in significance: the loss of the actual house in which he'd been born. This house was one key symbol of stability in an otherwise mean-dering life, not to mention a central fixture on the estate bequeathed to him by his late parents, those scions of an older, agrarian Russia, descendants of one of the country's most important dynasties. Now, board by board, brick by brick, that mansion, with its three stories and forty-two rooms, would be dismantled, loaded onto horse-propelled telegas and hauled away to an estate some seventeen versts (around eleven miles) away. It would stand there empty until 1913, when local peasants tore it down for rubble brick and firewood. It was around the time of his 1855 loss that Tolstoy descended into yet another one of his depressive spirals.

Then, one evening in March, he took a walk on a gravel path near

---

* *chikhir*: strong Caucasian wine.

† pirozhki: stuffed pastries.

A stone today marking the site of the Yasnaya Polyana house lost at the card table. The inscription reads: "Here stood the house in which L. N. Tolstoy was born."

his barracks. For weeks he had been hiking, doing gymnastics, trying anything, in fact, to keep his agitated mind focused. But it all seemed mechanical, perfunctory—until this evening, when he sensed the stony mud path beneath his feet, smelled the first shoots of spring, glanced up, and for the first time in weeks actually *saw* that endless, inky vault above him, with its innumerable piercings of shimmering stars, every one of them suddenly alive to him. In an instant, weeks of emotional turmoil and self-flagellation seemed to melt away. Rather than falling down on his knees and extending his hands up to the heavens, however, Tolstoy would do even better: he'd bring heaven down to earth, for under the influence of that grand tableau combined with a conversation he had earlier that day with a fellow officer he was inspired with

a great idea, a stupendous idea, to the realization of which I am capable of devoting my life. This idea is the founding of a new religion appropriate to the stage of development of mankind—the religion of Christ, but purged of beliefs and mysticism, a practical religion, not promising future bliss but giving bliss on earth.

There he is, in the middle of a nondescript gravel pathway deep in some godforsaken village in the Crimea, and instead of cutting his own throat, as he knows he deserves, Tolstoy contemplates starting his own religion. Of course, founding a new faith takes a while, and in the meantime he continued gambling, sleeping with random Asiatic beauties, and waking up with hangovers at noon. The bouts of self-hatred, too, would continue: "It's amazing how loathsome I am, how altogether unhappy and repulsive to myself," he penned in his diary in June, only a few short months after his epiphany. But for a brief moment anyway, in the aftermath of one of his most devastating financial and personal losses to date, he was moved by a vision that would inspire his later art and thought—not least the pages of his most life-affirming masterpiece.

For if *War and Peace* can be said to espouse any religion, it is nothing more or less than the religion of life itself, encompassing all its joys, triumphs, and frustrations alike. The "bliss on earth" that Tolstoy was referring to in his diary does not suggest a belief in a world without pain so much as a deep fulfillment in life as it actually *is*. And who better to embody the tenets of this faith than the Rostovs, whose family name comes from the verb *rosti*, "to grow." Nikolai can lose a fortune, after all, without losing his mind, or his belief in the basic goodness of life. Sure, he has his moment of doubt and wants to put a gun to his head. But in that very instant, when he has been shaken to the core, he is lucky enough to hear Natasha sing, reminding him that sublime happiness and meaning are still available to him here and now, in the midst of his broken world.

Nikolai's story gained personal relevance for me a few years ago. Around the time the newspapers were announcing the so-called financial crisis, I received a call from my father telling me that a significant chunk of our family savings had evaporated in one of those Ponzi schemes then making the news. My situation that day was irrevocably altered. For weeks I kept asking myself: Why did this happen? With whom should I be angry? My father? The scoundrel himself? I thrashed about for answers, only to realize that I was asking the wrong questions. This "cruel joke," this "unfortunate event"—what should one even call it?—was not some riddle to unlock or another academic problem to solve. This was real life, and it couldn't be explained away by some neat rational framework.

Let the banks and businesspeople decide questions of financial oversight, gullibility, and greed, I suddenly felt. Let the courts debate questions of guilt and innocence. To me these issues were irrelevant. Something big had occurred—something I neither fully understood nor will ever forget—leaving not a few of my most basic assumptions seriously shaken. I was the guy, after all, who went to the best schools, grew up vacationing in Aspen, and who wrote pieces of his Stanford doctoral dissertation at his own private Yasnaya Polyana—my parents' Michigan home, replete with its woodsy lakeside paths, well-maintained tennis court, beds that made themselves . . . None of this seemed so exceptional to me, but in the back of my mind I understood there to be, you know, a safety net, should I ever need such a thing. Only after that net had been badly shredded did I realize how much I had relied on it for my psychological security.

Only now was I forced to realize that my father was as fallible as my future was unpredictable, and my entitled sense of security a precious gift that could be shattered . . . in an instant. Depression set in within hours of this discovery, and lasted, I'm not proud to say, for some weeks. Then one dreary afternoon, I was sitting in my rented Charlottesville, Virginia, home and closed the curtains, wallowing in self-pity when a funny thing happened.

I started filing through a collection of old CDs, and put on some random clarinet concertos by Carl Maria von Weber. It had been about twenty years since I'd last heard those pieces, around the time I quit playing the clarinet myself. Slouched there on the couch with my laptop, clicking back and forth between Outlook Express and the Palm Pilot desktop, I listened. I still don't know why, but as that clarinet sang over the orchestra, now with sad-sweet cadences, now with forceful, angry passion, something was kindled inside me. Memories of childhood assailed me, including images of my clarinet-playing. But it went beyond mere memory . . . I stood up, closed my eyes, and let those sounds wash over me, my body swaying to a beauty and mystery well beyond myself.

There I was, in the middle of my messy living room, in my unexceptional Charlottesville house, with the throw pillows strewn about and my poor, incontinent cat's shit stains amending the carpeting. And for a moment I was terribly happy. What are Ponzi schemes and stock markets and wash-out shysters in such a moment? Everything seemed irrelevant in comparison to that opening into eternity I glimpsed.

How many times I'd read and enjoyed that scene in which Nikolai listens to Natasha sing, but only now, in the aftermath of my own personal crisis, did I realize, for perhaps the first time, what that scene is *about*. Tolstoy is describing what you feel when your world has crashed, the ground beneath you has cracked open, and all you want to do is go to sleep—but then, out of nowhere, you hear or see something so beautiful, so strikingly real, that you suddenly awaken into a new consciousness, hoping the day never ends.

The moment didn't last, of course. For one thing, I had to start making hard decisions about what I was going to do. My once-omnipotent father now reduced to the status of mere mortal, it was up to me to take full charge of my life, to take a hard look at my priorities. I could finally be honest with myself about a lot of things, not least of which was the fact that I was growing tired of pumping out esoteric scholarly articles for obscure journals.

It wasn't merely the need to start making money from those hundreds of hours I had been spending at the keyboard; I realized that the ideas I'd been trafficking in among a narrow population of fellow academics are, in fact, vitally relevant to the times we now live in, and I wanted to share this with as many people as I could. With the perspective of even a few years, I can see now that the phone call from my dad was a crucial stage in my own journey, for it catapulted me into one of the most creative periods of my life. Indeed, I should probably *thank* the shyster who fleeced my family out of all that money, if only because that event created the circumstances that led to this book.

"You have learned something," observes one of George Bernard Shaw's characters in the play *Major Barbara*. "That always feels at first as if you had lost something." And although Tolstoy once told the wry British playwright in a condescending letter that "you are not sufficiently serious," he would have wholeheartedly agreed with Shaw's famous insight. We grow up, grow old, and if we're lucky, grow wise, but such wisdom always comes at a cost. Nikolai's own journey is an embodiment of this. As was Tolstoy's. As, I hope, is my own.

4

SUCCESS

There is no greatness where there is no goodness,
simplicity, and truth.

—*War and Peace*, Volume 4, Part 3, Chapter 18

On June 9, 1881, Tolstoy, fifty-two and frustrated with his life,
set out for the Optina-Pustyn Monastery, some seventy miles
from Yasnaya Polyana, disguised in a peasant's robe and bast sandals.
Carrying a wooden staff, he traveled by foot, and was accompanied
by luggage-toting bodyguards also in disguise: a schoolmaster and
a valet whose thick red sideburns and large round face must have
seemed fitting for his last name, Arbuzov, which, in Russian, is the
genitive plural of "watermelon." During their four-day trek through
the countryside, these three men, taken for holy fools in search of
alms, were offered lodging by their brothers and sisters in rural Russia.
But even the night spent sleeping on the floor of an old peasant's house
or the stopover in Krapivna were not enough to ease the bleeding of
Tolstoy's badly blistered feet, unused to those poorly fitting shoes
made of bark. As much as he wanted to experience Mother Russia in
all of her expansive, foot-shredding authenticity, Tolstoy's aristocratic
instinct took over when he gave in and bought himself a thick, fresh
pair of socks.

On the fourth day of their journey, the bedraggled, dust-covered trio finally arrived at their destination in time for dinner, but they were not allowed in the travelers' cafeteria. Instead, they were sent to the commoners' refectory, where they dined on borsht and kasha* and drank kvass† with the riffraff. Whether because his empty stomach wasn't accustomed to such heavy fare, or because of the stench of the insect-infected third-class dormitory where they had been sent to sleep, the writer threw up violently that evening. At this point the concerned Arbuzov, pressing a ruble into the hands of one of the monks, insisted that they be upgraded to superior accommodations. Upgraded they were, to a small room already occupied by a cobbler, whose snoring kept the exhausted travelers up for hours. "Wake that man up and ask him not to snore," Tolstoy whispered to his valet, who naturally did as he was told.

"So because of your old man I'm not allowed to sleep all night?" responded the startled cobbler. Fortunately for everybody concerned, the man turned his head to the wall and dozed off in silence for the rest of the night, and Tolstoy finally got some sleep.

The next morning, however, an even more serious problem arose. After gazing joyfully for hours at the monks working in the fields, Tolstoy returned to the monastery to learn that a rumor had spread that this rough-looking, shaggy-bearded wayfarer was no ordinary peasant, but Count Leo Tolstoy himself. As the monks started applauding and genuflecting before their famous guest in the monastery halls, Tolstoy knew his cover had been blown. "Hopeless," he grumbled, and told his valet to unpack his boots and good shirt, after which he proceeded to meet with monastery elder Father Ambrosy, a confessor and counselor known throughout Russia, in search of spiritual wisdom and career advice. We don't know what exactly transpired between the two men, but we may assume the Father's response was less than satisfying, for

---

* kasha: buckwheat oatmeal.

† kvass: Russian nonalcoholic beer made from fermenting rye or barley.

the very next day Tolstoy and his fellow travelers returned home by train—first class.

Okay, so let's get this straight: A middle-aged family man at the height of his intellectual and physical powers, the creator of *War and Peace* and *Anna Karenina*, a writer more famous than Dostoevsky and Turgenev, an all-around successful man with an annual income of 30,000 rubles ($85,000, or in today's money, around $2 million), decides to make a miserable, four-day trek through the Russian countryside in order to meet a famous monk and ask him the question *What should I do with my life?*

Success, apparently, is not what we may have thought it was. And think about it, Tolstoy *did*, from a very young age as a matter of fact. His diaries and letters are full of painfully honest confessions about his passionate longing for success, along with a fear that he might actually achieve it, but for all the wrong reasons. "[T]here are things which I love more than goodness—for example, fame," the twenty-five-year-old wrote in his diary. "I am so ambitious, and this feeling has been so little satisfied, that as, between fame and virtue, I fear I might often choose the former if I had to make a choice."

Nor were his fears entirely unfounded. In his *Confession*, written some three decades later, Tolstoy looks back on his journey to fame and fortune: "Lying, stealing, promiscuity of every kind, drunkenness, violence, murder—there was not a crime I did not commit," he wrote of his early years. Even his desire to become a writer was motivated by "vanity, self-interest, and pride." The literary and financial success that did start coming his way was less than satisfying: "'Very well, you will have 6,000 desyatinas [16,200 acres] in the Samara province, as well as 300 horses; what then?' . . . Fine, so you'll be more famous than Gogol, Pushkin, Shakespeare, Molière, more famous than all the writers in the world—so what?" His life, the internationally famous writer concludes, "was meaningless and evil."

Given all he'd achieved when he wrote this, we might be mildly amused by Tolstoy's public self-immolation, but the fact is, *he* wasn't laughing; he was deadly serious—indeed, he nearly killed himself. So what happened to bring him to this point?

Long before Rick Warren could make a lucrative business out of it, Tolstoy was talking about the "purpose-driven" life, and the unhappiness that may ensue from a life focused only on personal gratification, or achievement for achievement's sake. True, most of us will never be forced to justify the worthiness of a life that includes, say, an income of a few million dollars, the ownership of 16,200 acres of land, or the creation of two of the greatest novels ever written. Nonetheless we can surely relate to the challenge of defining what "success" really means to us, as well as the moral quandary that pursuing it and actually achieving it often puts us in.

"Success," Tolstoy tells us in *War and Peace*, is an image, an idea, a mirage. It's the elusive destination that you never quite reach, the pool of fresh water you glimpse in the desert. Once you've arrived, *poof*—it's gone. Perhaps it was never there in the first place.

Take Pahom, a well-to-do peasant who is perpetually dissatisfied with his lot in life. Every few years this hero of Tolstoy's 1886 story "How Much Land Does a Man Need?" uproots his family to go wherever he hears of a better landowning opportunity. One day he travels to the faraway land of the Bashkirs, where huge swaths of virgin soil can be bought for the amazingly low price of a thousand rubles. As much land as he can cover by foot in a single day will be his, provided he returns to the starting point by sunset. And so, off Pahom runs with his trusty spade, marking an irresistible little patch here, a to-die-for section over there. This land-buying spree goes on for hours until Pahom, suffering from exhaustion and noticing the sun dropping below the horizon, runs as fast as he can on his bruised feet while the Bashkirs cheer him on, and makes it to the finish line just in the nick of time. Whereupon he drops dead: "Six feet from his head to his heels was all he needed," the story tells us, by way of an ending.

A harsh message, perhaps, but universal enough—and inevitably timely enough—that it continues to resonate with readers of all ages and walks of life. "We see a nice guy driving a BMW or somethin' like that, and we'll want to get that BMW, not saying that exact BMW, but we'll wanna top 'im, so we'll try to get a better BMW," observed one resident at Beaumont Juvenile Correctional Center who had just read Tolstoy's story as part of my course, "Books Behind Bars: Life, Literature, and Leadership," in which University of Virginia students meet weekly with incarcerated youths to discuss classics of Russian literature. "It's funny how you can read, kin'a, you know what I'm saying, literature from years and years and years ago and still apply it to life today, ya know what I mean?"

I do. See, for many years I was obsessed with being "successful," without ever quite knowing what exactly I wanted to be successful *at*, or even what success *was*. No wonder I was perpetually frustrated. At the same time, even as my more competitive side kept pushing me to one conquest after another, there was a voice inside me urging me to seek some deeper sort of meaning. When I was a graduate student at Stanford, a professor at a monthly student-faculty meeting asked us if there were any issues we'd like to add to that day's agenda.

"Sure," I said with naïve enthusiasm. "Could we spend some time reflecting on our purpose in becoming Russian literature scholars?"

The room went silent, and people looked around nervously. Oops. I had obviously just made a big faux pas.

"The reason you're here is to *prove* yourself," glowered the professor who'd posed the original question. "The profession either accepts you or it doesn't," he added gruffly, as if personally insulted by my words.

The graduate students, myself included, dutifully nodded, of course. We were in no position to challenge this man's authority; what's more, we recognized in his response an all too familiar refrain we'd been hearing over and over since our college days: work hard, rack up the right credentials, jump through the right hoops, meet the right people, eventually publish in the right journals, and—voila!—academic success can be yours. But to what end? And at what cost? Were we all just emulous little Pahoms who'd come to graduate school in order to be turned into expert hoop-jumpers and skillful players in the game of academic advancement? And even if quite a few of us had, wouldn't it have been rather interesting to have an honest conversation with one another about why we thought that game was worth playing in the first place? But the silence that often accompanies such questions, in academia as well as other professional contexts, can be deafening—and deadening. More recently, for better or worse, with the much-discussed crisis in the humanities now a serious concern within academia, and the future of our country a frequent topic of conversation outside of it, there is a renewed interest in precisely the sorts of big, naïve questions I had been asking in graduate school—the same sort of questions Tolstoy poses in his art with such unabashed directness.

As a matter of fact, I recently learned that the members of the Young Presidents Organization (YPO), a group of corporate CEOs under the age of fifty, chose to read "How Much Land Does a Man Need?" as part of their annual educational enrichment program. My brother, a member of the organization, couldn't divulge details because of group confidentiality agreements, but he did say that Tolstoy's story got these high-powered young executives talking about things high-powered young executives don't often talk about in public. That these CEOs came to select a story whose message challenges much of what they have built their careers around is a testament not only to their intellectual courage, but to the urgency and relevance of Tolstoy's message.

War and Peace, although written decades before "How Much Land Does a Man Need?" and admittedly a far less moralistic work, invites readers to grapple with some of the same issues. According to the history books being read by most Russian schoolchildren in the nineteenth century, Napoleon was the greatest military genius the world had ever known. One had only to look at the sheer quantity of countries and peoples he'd conquered. Tolstoy's Napoleon, on the other hand, gloats as he's about to take the Russian capital, only to find Moscow almost completely empty. Then, having given him their capital, the Russians promptly set it on fire. Napoleon has thus achieved his long-cherished goal, and what was it worth? The death of nine-tenths of his overextended troops, for one thing, on the long winter march back out of Russia. To illustrate this point another way, consider this famous graphic by French civil engineer Charles Minard depicting Napoleon's march to Moscow and subsequent retreat. It first appeared in 1869, the year Tolstoy was finishing his novel:

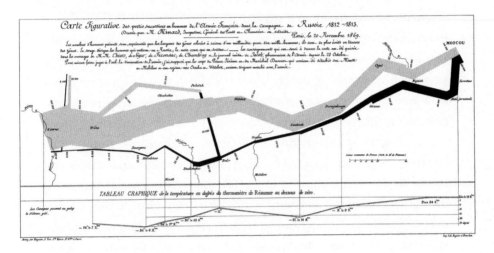

Napoleon's Invasion of Russia: the Costs of Success.

The gray shading represents the size of Napoleon's army when he first crossed the Nieman River into Russia in May 1812 with 422,000 troops. It then traces the steady dissipation of his army down to 100,000 troops by the time he reached Moscow (in upper right). The black line describes the continual thinning of his army down to 10,000 soldiers by the time he recrossed the Nieman. Minard's graphic shows visually in a single glance, then, what *War and Peace* illustrates narratively over hundreds of pages. The bottom line (literally) is that precisely when we think we're winning, we might actually be losing, or even planting the seeds of our own destruction.

Every generation is affected by its own version of the Napoleon Syndrome, and the characters in *War and Peace* are no exception. Early-nineteenth-century Russians feared and resented Napoleon, yet many of them also tried to emulate him. This self-made man who rose from humble beginnings to become the conqueror of all of Europe appeared to be everything they were not: omnipotent, pragmatic, ruthless, and, above all, French. If you were an ambitious young Russian male living in 1805, then, and wanted to make a name for yourself, you could do no better than beating Napoleon Bonaparte at his own game. That is exactly what Prince Andrei Bolkonsky sets out to do.

At twenty-seven, Prince Andrei has it all: good looks, plenty of brains, enviable breeding, and an attractive young wife who not only turns heads, but melts hearts. None of it, however, is enough for this nobleman whose perpetual boredom with life is readily apparent in his slow gait and weary gaze. And so off to the army he swaggers, abandoning his pregnant wife and, through his father's connections, landing a job as adjutant to Mikhail Illarionovich Kutuzov, commander in chief of the Russian forces. Smart, worldly young man that he is, Prince Andrei quickly makes himself useful to Kutuzov, advising him on military strategy, surveying battle plans, and disciplining unruly subordinates, who, understandably, aren't especially fond of their new supervisor. But Andrei doesn't care, for he is a man on a mission. Even after his participation in the battle of Schöngrabern, in which Russians successfully hold off the advancing French army, Prince Andrei himself fails to win the recognition he's sought. Yet, the disappointed prince refuses to waver in his single-minded pursuit. And a little over two weeks later, on the evening before the battle of Austerlitz, he is ruthlessly honest with himself about that fact:

> "I don't know what will happen ... I don't want to know and I can't know, but if I want this, want glory, want to be known by people, loved by them, it's not my fault that I want it, that it's the only thing I want, the only thing I live for. Yes, the only thing! I'll never tell it to anyone, but my God! What am I to do if I love nothing except glory, except people's love? Death, wounds, loss of family, nothing frightens me. And however near and dear many people are to me—my father, my sister, my wife—the dearest people to me—but, however terrible and unnatural it seems, I'd give them all now for a moment of glory, of triumph over people, for love from people I don't know and never will know." (264–65)

Whew! And I thought *I* was ambitious! What a load of inner demons this young glory seeker seems to be carrying around. Is he trying to prove himself to his imperious, emotionally distant father? To win the love he never received from his absent mother? Whatever the case, Prince Andrei is someone we have no problem recognizing from great literature, art, or even the evening news. From Achilles to Anna Nicole Smith, there are some people so obsessed by the allure of glory, they're prepared to sacrifice everything for it—including their own lives.

As the battle begins, Prince Andrei watches a curious skirmish between a French and a Russian soldier in which the two men seem to be engaged in some kind of weird dance around a cannon. Absorbed by this sight, the bemused spectator is suddenly clubbed on the head by a French soldier. What upsets him in this moment is not that this blow might lead to his capture or death, but that it prevents him from viewing the denouement of that interesting little fight. Who's winning? What's the score? Opening his eyes some time later after plunging to the dirt, he searches for the skirmishing soldiers:

> But he did not see anything. There was nothing over him now except the sky—the lofty sky, not clear, but still immeasurably lofty, with gray clouds slowly creeping across it. "How quiet, calm, and solemn, not at all like when I was running," thought Prince Andrei, "not like when we were running, shouting, and fighting; not at all like when the Frenchman and the artillerist, with angry and frightened faces, were pulling at the swab—it's quite different the way the clouds creep across this lofty, infinite sky. How is it I haven't seen this lofty sky before? And how happy I am that I've finally come to know it. (281)

How is it I haven't seen this lofty sky before?

Good question: How is it any of us fails to see the bigger picture, as we so often do, confusing the contentment we seek with the narrower visions of conquest we pursue?

Like Andrei, we frequently misunderstand the true nature of reality. Life, Tolstoy says, isn't a fast elevator shooting us up to the top floor, but a continuous river of individual moments flowing endlessly into one another. The battle of Austerlitz, which would go down in history as a terrible loss for Russia, is one of the great moments of Prince Andrei's life, but not for the reasons he might have thought. The majesty of battle would seem to be his for the taking (or at least the taking *in*), when wham!—life, in the form of a soldier's bayonet, hits him over the head and knocks him into a new consciousness. Through the haze of his blurred vision, he sees clearly for the first time the immensity of the universe, indifferent to his worldly plans and ambitions. And for a brief moment he *gets* it. Watching Napoleon collect his human trophies from the bloody battlefield some hours later, the usually silver-tongued nobleman is momentarily struck dumb as Bonaparte suddenly turns to address him:

[But] to him at that moment all the interests that occupied Napoleon seemed so insignificant, his hero himself seemed so petty to him, with his petty vanity and joy in victory, compared with that lofty, just, and kindly sky, which he had seen and understood, that he was unable to answer him. (292–93)

Such silent reverie is, of course, alien to the society to which Prince Andrei belongs. When they gather to give a hero's welcome to General Bagration for his brilliant victory at the battle of Schöngrabern, a few chapters later, the Moscow socialites are as chatty as ever. Alas, news of the Russian walloping at Austerlitz came in after the invitations had already been sent out. The Muscovites, of course, "felt that something was wrong, and that to discuss this bad news was difficult," but the party, they decided, must go on (306). And so they persist in their charade, basking in the illusory glow of triumph, much the way a recently broke businessman might show up to work in the same shiny Lexus and wearing those same golden cufflinks. And oh, the yarns those high-fiving Muscovites do spin about Austerlitz: "This one had saved a standard, that one had killed five Frenchmen, that one had loaded five cannons single-handed" (307). Of Prince Andrei, whom they assume to be dead, nothing is said.

Yet if you ask any ordinary Russian today what exactly happened at the battle of Austerlitz, most would be hard-pressed to remember much of anything about that military campaign, except for one little thing: that stirring moment in *War and Peace* when Tolstoy's hero has that powerful epiphany while gazing wounded up at the glorious sky. Such is the power of Tolstoy's art, not to mention the accuracy of his insight. Our greatest and most enduring personal triumphs, Tolstoy observes, are seldom the ones described in the headlines or the history books. They don't appear on the scoreboards or in our public celebrations. More often than not, they are those transformative moments we experience in the quiet inwardness of our souls when the cameras are turned off and nobody is watching. Except for God, that is—and Tolstoy.

Many of Tolstoy's contemporaries missed the point completely. In his essay "The Old Gentry," published in 1868, the influential literary critic and revolutionary activist Dmitry Pisarev perceived a real lesson about success in the character of Prince Boris Drubetskoi, son of an impoverished nobleman who, with the assistance of a relentless mother, claws his way to professional and social prominence. Pisarev considered Boris an exemplar of the then popular philosophy of "rational egoism," which posited that when strong, pragmatic individuals pursue their self-interest without constraints, society as a whole benefits. Boris, apparently, is a tough, clear-eyed realist who sees how the world actually works, in contrast to, say, his dreamy and impetuous childhood friend, Nikolai Rostov:

> The essential difference between these two young men is apparent from the moment they step out into the world. . . . Boris seeks for solid and tangible benefits. Rostov wants more than anything,

and come what may, bustle, glamour, strong sensations, effective scenes and bright pictures.

The problem is that, like most agenda-driven literary critics of his time, Pisarev was, well, a rather bad reader of Tolstoy. With his impulsiveness and idealism, Nikolai, of course, is the far more attractive character in Tolstoy's world. He believes in intangible, useless things like beauty and honor and sacrifice for a cause greater than himself. Whereas all Boris believes in, more often than not, is . . . Boris.

Oh, and this highly productive careerist, Tolstoy would have us notice, doesn't actually *produce* anything. He rises to a position of power not because of any distinctive qualities of imagination or courage or even productivity, but because of his "skill in dealing with those who give rewards for service—and he was often surprised at his quick success and at how others could fail to understand it. . . . He made friends and sought acquaintances only with people who were above him and therefore could be of use to him" (365). Such impressive skill does indeed demonstrate Boris's powers of observation—not to mention his blindness to life's deeper purpose. This young man, bemused by the apparent naïveté of his less pragmatic peers, is, contrary to Pisarev's reading, shown to be a rather odd specimen of humanity with a comically deformed worldview.

This becomes all the more apparent as we observe the parallel unfolding of the lives of these two friends. After his gambling fiasco, Nikolai is determined to pay back the debt to his parents in five years. All he wants to do, understandably, is return to the army, where "there were none of those unclear and undefined money relations with his father; there was no recollection of that terrible loss to Dolokhov! Here in the regiment everything was clear and simple" (395).

It would be nice, certainly, if that were in fact the case. But it would not be Tolstoy. Shortly after returning, Nikolai discovers that his regiment commander and friend, Major Vassily Denisov, is facing possible court-martial for having seized a transport of food to feed his hungry regiment, who had been denied provisions for two weeks. Determined to rectify this injustice, Nikolai first visits Denisov in the military hospital, where the older man is recovering from a slight injury while awaiting the decision regarding his case. There, amid the stench of dead flesh and the sight of pallid faces attached to mangled, bleeding bodies, Nikolai resolves to deliver a petition on his friend's behalf directly to the tsar himself in the Prussian town of Tilsit, where Alexander and Napoleon are about to sign a truce. What is this? wonders Nikolai. So many Russians wounded and dead, and suddenly Alexander I and the enemy, a self-styled emperor of negligible antecedents, are friends?

As it happens, Boris is also present at that significant event, although for entirely different reasons: "[F]or a man who valued his success in the service to be in Tilsit at the time of the emperor's meeting was a very important matter, and Boris, having gone to Tilsit, felt that from then on his position was completely assured" (408). Needless to say, the unflappable Boris is no more bothered by a wronged comrade than he is by a troubling truce; in fact, he uses this turn of events as a networking opportunity for himself, hosting one of Napoleon's adjutants in his quarters and even having several French officers over for a nice supper!

When Nikolai shows up at his friend's doorstep just as the table has been laid, Boris receives him coldly, clearly embarrassed by this mere hussar in civilian clothing who threatens to upset his otherwise smoothly running social affair. Immediately noticing the annoyance in Boris's face, Nikolai is at the same time "oddly struck in Boris's apartment by the sight of French officers in those same uniforms which he was used to looking at quite differently from the flank line" (408). The fiery young Russian patriot, you see, still wants to pump bullets into those enemy soldiers, whereas Boris would rather fill their tummies with wine and caviar, the better to advance his own career interests. When Nikolai requests Boris's assistance in getting the petition to the tsar, the latter, "crossing his legs, and stroking the slender fingers of his right hand with his left, listened to Rostov the way a general listens to the report of a subordinate, now looking away, now looking directly into Rostov's eyes with the same veiled gaze" (409).

In his final appearance in the novel, many hundreds of pages later, Boris can be seen speaking with a different childhood friend, Pierre Bezukhov, whom Boris has run into just before the battle of Borodino. Using this chat on the eve of what many fear will be a horrific affair as another career advancement opportunity, Boris waxes eloquent about Russian heroism just loudly enough so that Kutuzov, standing nearby, will notice him. Boris does, in fact, very briefly get Kutuzov's attention, and that's the last we ever see or hear of him. In all my years of teaching *War and Peace*, I've met few readers who are bothered by or even notice his sudden disappearance from the novel, ending up where such people often end up in life: forgotten. The ever-perspicacious Natasha, reminiscing with Sonya much earlier, senses Boris's fate from the beginning: "'I don't remember [Boris] the way I do Nikolai. I close my eyes, and I remember him, but Boris I don't'" (she closed her eyes), "'no—nothing'" (235).

Now, just to clarify: Boris is no evil monster. Indeed, this complex, full-blooded character is sufficiently charming not only to attract Pierre, but to make the (very) young Natasha fall in love with him. Moreover, Tolstoy reminds us, it is life circumstances that have made Boris into who he is: "'It's all right for [Nikolai] Rostov, whose father sends him ten thousand rubles at a time to talk about how he doesn't want to bow to anybody or be anybody's lackey,'" Boris muses at one point. "'[B]ut I, who have nothing except my own head, must make my career and not let chances slip, but avail myself of them'" (248). Okay, the guy's got a point: so much easier to be the proud, principled aristocrat when the cost of doing so isn't your financial security.

But, then, Nikolai is hardly blind to life's harsh realities. He knows that the world can be a frightening place—a place in which so-called friends let friends gamble drunk and then take their money, a place in which noble intentions are rewarded with a slap in the face, and ideals routinely besmirched, if not shattered. In such a world, Boris's self-focused, steely-eyed pragmatism might seem the wiser course. True, Boris will never know Nikolai's painful confusion as he watches everything he values come tumbling down at Tilsit, or Andrei's bewilderment as he looks up at the sky at Austerlitz and realizes that his dreams of glory have been nothing more than an illusion.

Nor will Boris experience the deeper satisfaction of a life courageously and authentically lived. For while the turbulence of historical change eventually sweeps him into the dustbin of irrelevancy, Nikolai and Prince Andrei continue to evolve, their road to self-discovery paved with the shards of one broken ideal after another. Trudging through that debris with an open mind and a searching heart will both strengthen and deepen them, just as Tolstoy believed that the hardship of those troubled years was good for Russia itself. "If the cause of our victory was not accidental, but lay in the essence of the character of the Russian people and army," he wrote in a draft of an introduction to the novel, "then that character must be expressed still more clearly in the period of failures and defeats."

One character intimately familiar with such failures and defeats is the tiny, stooping Captain Tushin, a poorly paid artillery captain who is no stranger to the injustices of nineteenth-century life. During battle this slight, unwashed man desperately tries to save his under-supplied, undefended battery from a merciless pounding by enemy fire. Adding insult to injury, he is later publicly chastised for defying orders to evacuate his position by General Bagration, the very man whose failure of leadership placed Tushin's battery in that predicament in the first place. Yet Tushin manages to find a deeper purpose in his bloody, thankless work, never descending to the level of bureaucratic sycophancy. On the contrary, it is in the thick of battle that he seems to come most alive.

Even as his battery is getting pummeled by the French, he can be seen barking out commands to his soldiers and running from cannon to cannon with the childlike enthusiasm of someone who loves what he does. In order to preserve his own sanity in this rather dire situation, he has created an imaginary world for himself: The enemy cannons in the distance are but little pipes from which an invisible smoker released occasional puffs of smoke, while his own firing guns are old friends needing a few words of encouragement. As for Captain

Tushin himself, he is a mighty man, flinging cannonballs at the French with both hands. In other words, he turns an unpleasant job he neither chose nor may leave into a daring game that offers fulfillment and even a little fun into the bargain. No wonder Prince Andrei, upon first meeting Tushin before the battle of Schöngrabern, senses "something special" in this otherwise ordinary, even slightly comical, little man.

Tolstoy is not asking us to pretend we don't live in the real world, with its many responsibilities, challenges, and financial necessities. Nor is he saying that we should quit our jobs, pack our bags, and head to a mountaintop in Siberia, or to a monastery, for that matter. Anybody with enough drive to produce ninety volumes' worth of novels, novellas, short stories, plays, essays, letters, and diaries, after all, is hardly an exemplar of monastic self-abnegation. Tolstoy loved work; he believed in the value of it. One of the most famous scenes in *Anna Karenina* is that joyous one in which Levin, exhausted and dripping with sweat, swings his scythe for hours through the thick hay, right alongside his peasants. What concerns Tolstoy is our *relationship* to our work. Does it enrich us as human beings, or just our bank accounts? Does it connect us more deeply with the world, or rather cause us to hunker down in little bunkers of self-involvement? And when we find ourselves confronted with a less-than-*ideal* work environment, do we merely trade our large spirits for the smaller comforts of job security, or, like Captain Tushin, find some way to infuse the mundane madness of the workplace with the spark of our own inspiration?

Moreover, should our efforts fail to pan out in the end, as is so often the case, does it follow that our lives have been a waste? The multimillionaire father of a college acquaintance of mine must have thought so, for when he lost his savings in the stock market crash of 1987, he blew his brains out. To which Tolstoy would say: If your raison d'être is so wrapped up in "making it" that failure leaves you with a gaping hole inside (perhaps all too literally), then maybe you *have* been engaged in the wrong kind of work; maybe you *have* been wasting your life.

At some point or another, we, like Tolstoy's characters, must face the truth that we are part of something greater than ourselves, prompting us to ask not "How do I get to the next rung on the ladder?" but "Is *this* the ladder I should be on in the first place? Is *this* the kind of life I want to lead?"

Good questions to ponder, for in such moments, Tolstoy says, we glimpse the kind of meaning to our existence that we almost always fail to see when caught up chasing the better job or the bigger house or the more beautiful plot of land. What that meaning *is*, each one of us must decide for him or herself. Sure, for some of us, at some times, it very well may involve donning a robe and a pair of bast sandals to trek seventy miles to the next monastery. But more often than not, if we look carefully enough, we will find what we are seeking right here, right now, on that bloody, beautiful battlefield known as everyday life.

Yasnaya Polyana today.

5

IDEALISM

"To seek, always to seek."

—Tolstoy's mumbled words to his daughter Alexandra
a few days before his death

Tolstoy's views about the limits of worldly success in *War and Peace*, far from offering him a pass on self-improvement, only reinforced his belief in the possibilities of human striving toward truth and goodness. I was newly struck by this dimension of his vision when, as a student at Moscow State University in 1990, my literature professor Aida Abuashvili-Lominadze invited me to spend a week with her and her husband at Peredelkino, the official summer retreat of the Union of Soviet Writers, just beyond greater Moscow. As I wandered among the grassy fields of this large property where writer Boris Pasternak once owned a summer home, the May air was thick with the scent of freshly blooming wildflowers. Three times daily we'd congregate in the cafeteria, where the clinking and clanging of silverware could be heard alongside the animated arguing, a common phenomenon in the heyday of Gorbachev's glasnost and perestroika.

One evening, the conversation turned to Russian literature, and Tolstoy's name was of course soon invoked. A recent article in a high-profile Moscow literary journal had argued that maybe it was time to remove Russia's most famous novelist from the required school reading lists. His time, the argument went, had come and gone. He was from a world far kinder and gentler, after all, than the one late-twentieth-century Russians inhabited, and thus had little relevance to the problems of Soviet Russia.

"He never lived through anything like Stalin's terror or fascist Germany," said one writer in his twenties at the dinner, eager to demonstrate his postmodernist credentials by agreeing with the author of the article.

No sooner had those words come flying out of his mouth than the clanging of silverware, the slurping of soup and compote, and the general chatter at our table of six ceased. I looked around in confusion. All eyes were on Sergei, Aida's husband, a smallish, well-built man in his sixties whose kind, intelligent face, with its bristling eyebrows and deep creases, contorted now into a look of both sadness and anger. Putting down his glass, he placed his thick, hairy forearms on the table.

"Young man," he said, slowly and quietly, peering directly into the eyes of the young writer. "When I was your age, I was serving a ten-year sentence in Stalin's Siberian work camps. I dug ditches. I was beaten. I pissed in my bunk at night because it was too frigid to go outside. I watched friends get murdered in cold blood. And you want to tell *me* about Stalin's terror!"

"I'm only saying, uh, that Tolstoy never, you know, went through . . ." the young writer stammered, his self-confidence rapidly fading, his face turning as red as the six untouched bowls of steaming borsht sitting on the table.

"Maybe I didn't serve long enough," Sergei continued, "because *I*, for one, still believe that [Tolstoy's] *Hadji-Murat* is the most devastatingly accurate story of man's inhumanity towards man ever written. And in *War and Peace*, the bestiality of battlefields drenched in blood . . . Or when Rostopchin [Moscow's governor in 1812] feeds a man to the crowd to be beaten to death . . . I saw these sorts of things with my own eyes." Pausing, he glanced around at us, then back at his young interlocutor, sternly concluding: "No, I can assure you, Tolstoy *understood*."

I later learned Sergei's story. His father, a high-ranking general in the Georgian army who had been suspected of treason, was ordered by Stalin to come to Moscow on urgent business. He knew perfectly well what that meant. This "enemy of the people," of which there were millions at the time, would be sent to the camps. And so he hanged himself. Unfortunately, under Stalin's rule, when one member of your family was an enemy of the people, so was the rest of the family. Years later, a seventeen-year-old Sergei, who didn't quite grasp this fact, unwisely penned and distributed among his classmates a poem with mocking references to the Soviet dictator. The school authorities found out about it, sent the poem to the regional authorities, and within weeks, Sergei was being escorted by security guards to Siberia. Still a teenager, he was about to begin a ten-year sentence of hard labor.

To this day, I remember that painful dinner conversation at Peredelkino, because it was my very first exposure to the concrete human realities of Stalin's Russia. I'd read books about twentieth-century Soviet history, of course, but there at that dinner, for perhaps the first time, I actually began to *understand*—and appreciate something else besides: Why Tolstoy still matters, and not just to Russians, either. To all of us.

Sure, the greatest Russian realist may not have lived through Stalin's terror or the Holocaust, or for that matter, the more recent threats of nuclear war or faith-based terrorism. He knew plenty, though, about the rank injustice, evil, and sheer brutishness that have ever dominated the world. He'd witnessed a public execution in Paris, for Christ's sake; had lived through the European revolutions of 1848, as well as the assassination of Tsar Alexander II, followed by the ultrarepressive regime of Alexander III. By the end of the century, Tolstoy was reading daily newspaper reports about workers' riots, bloody bombings by revolutionary terrorists, religious persecution, and pogroms. And what counts is this: having lived through *all* of that, he never lost his faith in the possibility of goodness, of human promise.

In his seventies, Tolstoy asked to be buried on the spot where, as a boy, he and his brother Nikolai had discovered a little green stick, a stick on which, they believed, was inscribed the secret to universal happiness. "And just as I believed then, that there is a little green stick, on which is written the secret that will destroy all evil in people, and give them great blessings," Tolstoy wrote in his *Recollections* (1902), "so now I believe that such a truth exists and that it will be revealed to people and will give them what it promises." Imagine *that*: someone who'd seen and done all Tolstoy had, still believing in "a secret that would destroy all evil in people." Was the man mad—or just some incorrigible Pollyanna?

Tolstoy's gravesite today, on the spot where he first discovered the little green stick that would "destroy all evil in people."

Some in Tolstoy's own time thought he was, well, a little bit of both. In one of the most famous of his later works of nonfiction, *The Kingdom of God Is Within You*, he responded directly to this criticism. "Blessedness," Tolstoy writes in that book, first published in Germany, in 1894, after being banned in Russia, "consists in progress towards perfection; to stand still in any condition whatever means the cessation of this blessedness." To tell somebody that striving toward such a high ideal is hopelessly naïve, Tolstoy writes, is just like telling a man who is struggling on a swift river and is directing his course against the current, that it is impossible to cross the river against the current, and that to cross it he must point in the direction of the point he wants to reach.

In reality, in order to reach the place to which he wants to go, he must row with all his strength toward a point much higher up.

True, the world may be filled with all sorts of obstacles to achieving our highest hopes, Tolstoy is saying. Yet if we cease striving toward those noble ideals, then not only will we fail ever to achieve them, but we will get carried so far downstream by the current of complacency that we will no longer even recognize the destination we wanted to reach in the first place. We'll end up, in other words, living without any ideals at all—in a state of either perennial despair or the kind of moral relativism that Tolstoy saw as one of the central spiritual illnesses of his times.

A quaint thought, even when he voiced it, but who in the "enlightened," modern world of the decades to follow could possibly have taken it seriously? A twenty-four-year-old barrister by the name of Mohandas Gandhi, for one. "[O]verwhelmed" by *The Kingdom of God Is Within You* when he first read it at the age of twenty-four, Gandhi was transformed by "the independent thinking, profound morality, and the truthfulness" of Tolstoy's vision. Gandhi dedicated his life to bringing the world a little closer to perfection himself, thanks in part to the inspiration of his Russian predecessor.

The word for "perfection" in Russian (*sovershenstvo*) is nearly identical to the word for "completion" (*sovershenie*). Of course, life is no more likely to be "complete" than it is to be perfect. A mere glance at today's newspaper will provide you with more than ample reason to doubt whether "perfection" even belongs in the human vocabulary at all. Tolstoy is here to remind us that it most assuredly does. Perfection, you see, is the goal we never quite reach, the thin, glowing horizon we may glimpse only in the distance. The closer we come to it, the farther away it would seem to get. Still, something compels us to move toward it, and by doing so, we bring a measure of sanity to the world, becoming better human beings ourselves in the process. There is a famous Jewish saying: "You are not required to complete the work, but neither are you free to desist from it." Tolstoy believed something rather similar. The world is badly flawed, he says, yet with every moment brimming with potential, it is up to *us* to try to perfect it.

No character in *War and Peace* embodies this insanely hopeful approach to living more than Pierre Bezukhov. Not that Pierre doesn't have plenty of reasons to be cynical about the world. After inheriting a great fortune, he marries the most beautiful woman in Russia: the empty-headed, fortune-hunting Hélène Kuragin, whose father, Vassily, a relative of Pierre's deceased father, skillfully orchestrates the union, while pocketing around forty thousand rubles' worth of the inheritance for himself. No sooner is the marriage consummated than it begins to unravel, thanks in part to that snake Dolokhov, whom Pierre challenges to a duel over suspicions that Dolokhov is having an affair with his wife. Hélène chastises Pierre for his groundless fears, while cruelly assuring him that there are few wives with idiotic husbands like him who *wouldn't* have taken lovers. At which point Pierre, in a paroxysm of rage, yanks from the table before him an enormous slab of marble and hurls it to the floor, leaving his wife appropriately shaken.

Following such an inauspicious introduction to the joys of adulthood and married life, you'd think Pierre might quietly hunker down in some funk-hole of self-pity, right? And indeed he does—this is Russian literature, after all. Far more interesting, though, is how quickly this soul-crushing depression is followed by an almost childlike readiness not just to forgive, but to *believe* again. First, though, the depression.

A few weeks after the argument with Hélène, Pierre gives her power of attorney over a large piece of his personal fortune, and then heads off to Petersburg, far away from the morass his life has become. Sitting in the Torzhok posting station as he awaits a horse transport, his mind turns and turns like a stripped screw, unable to catch on to anything solid or sensible. In this moment Pierre comes about as close as he ever will to thinking like one of those tortured nihilists for which nineteenth-century Russian literature is famous: Why, he asks himself, is he in this situation? What the hell should he do with his life? Why is anything the way it is? Of the peddler woman selling her wares at the Torzhok station, he thinks: "'And what does she need the money for? As if this money can add one hair's breadth to her peace of mind? Can anything in the world make her or me less subject to evil and death?'" (348).

When Pierre suspects the postmaster of trying to fleece him of even more rubles by delaying the arrival of horses, he concludes that the guy obviously needs the money, and Pierre can afford it, so, well, fleece away. After all, Pierre himself almost murdered Dolokhov, so who is *he*, really, to judge others? And while he's on the subject of senseless murders, what about those Frenchmen who chopped off King Louis XVI's head, or the fact that those who did so were themselves later executed for some reason. "'What is bad? What is good? What should one love, what hate? Why live, and what am I? What is life, what is death? What power rules over everything?'" (348). Things are not, shall we say, altogether well in Pierre's inner world.

Until, that is, a total stranger sits down on the bench next to him. This stranger, as it turns out, is the famous Freemason Osip Bazdeyev, whose glittering old eyes and calm paternal voice begin to soothe Pierre, even as he, at least at first, looks askance at the man's ideas. The more they talk, the more Pierre opens up about his despair, the depravity of his life, his wish to believe in God, and his inability to do so. Sensing Pierre's vulnerability, the old man explains to him that his current suffering comes from the fact that he is looking at things all wrong: the possibilities he imagines for his life are far too limited; there is another path toward truth and happiness, a path the fraternal organization of Freemasonry can help reveal to him. We watch as Pierre's mood shifts from despair to skepticism to a growing openness to Bazdeyev's message, and finally, to complete acceptance of it—all in a matter of just a few hours. No sooner has Bazdeyev shared with his soon-to-be young protégé this glorious vision of the possibility of perfection on earth than Pierre is seized with

> a rapture of renewal, picturing to himself his blissful, irreproach-
> able, and virtuous future, which seemed so easy to him. . . . In
> his soul there remained no trace of his former doubts. He firmly
> believed in the possibility of the brotherhood of people, united
> with the purpose of supporting each other on the path of virtue,
> and that was what he imagined Masonry to be. (353–54)

As the reader rather suspects, this is *not* exactly what Freemasonry is, and the transformation Pierre believes it will bring about in him is to prove more elusive than he thinks. What's more, Bazdeyev comes across as a bit of a spirituality peddler, not to mention a whack job. Still, he's not a complete sham; there *is* something genuinely kind and attractive about him, not least when compared with those high-society vultures Pierre's been moving among lately. Moreover, he gives Pierre something he badly needs in this moment: hope.

Inspired by the Freemason goal of reforming the human race, Pierre conceives a plan. Traveling to his estates in the province of Kiev, he summons the stewards (peasant managers) to let them know that he intends to set all of his peasants free. And while the details of their liberation are being worked out, he orders that peasants will not be overburdened by work, that women and children will not work at all, and that hospitals, almshouses, and schools should be built in every village. The stewards listen carefully, each interpreting the master's words in his own way. Some of them are fearful that Pierre is dissatis-fied with their work and perhaps displeased at the fact they have been concealing money from him, which, Tolstoy hints, they've been doing for quite some time. Others are amused by Pierre's lisp and the intrigu-ing new words he uses. Another group simply finds it pleasant to hear the master speak. Yet others, sharper of wit, politely nod their sweaty heads, all the while secretly calculating how best to manipulate Pierre to further their own aims.

When Pierre returns after a few months to see how the reforms are coming along, it is spring, and the southern sun warms the blossoming Russian countryside. His heart bursts with joy as his Viennese carriage progresses through his estates, each one, it seems to him, more picturesque than the last. "'How easy it is, how little effort it takes, to do so much good,'" he proudly thinks after being greeted at every stop with crowds of grateful peasants (380). But this royal tour is, of course, a sham carefully orchestrated by the stewards to impress and deceive their master.

What the stewards' glowing reports of a reduction in peasant labor don't explain, for one thing, is that the peasants, freed of their obligation to Pierre, are now being forced to work overtime for the stewards. Nor does Pierre understand that in one village, where a chapel is being built on his orders, or so he thinks, the only people who welcome him happen to be the wealthy peasants who had already started building that chapel long ago; nine-tenths of the peasants in that village are, in fact, destitute. Nor does he grasp that the priest who proudly exhibits the peasant children whom he has been instructing in reading, writing, and religion isn't quite as godly as his station in life and the thick cross hanging from his vestments might suggest; in exchange for the spiritual enlightenment he provides, he exacts exorbitant sums of money from the pupils' parents.

So, what are we to make of all this? Do we shake our heads at Pierre's naïveté? Get angry with him for being so blind? Admire his sincere intentions? Yes, yes, and yes, says Tolstoy. Indeed, there is something at once maddening and touching about this hopelessly good man who insists on doing "what he considered right" (381), even though he hasn't a clue, really, about how to carry out those well-meaning intentions . . . at least right now, that is. Pierre is only twenty-two, after all; we haven't quite reached the halfway point in the novel, and, well, a lot can happen in eight hundred pages. As Tolstoy reminds us over and over again, today's mistake may well become the "informed failure" that propels us toward some future triumph, just as what may seem like a conquest at one time may very well turn out to be a disaster later—or simply fizzle away into oblivion. We just don't know. Life has a funny (and often *not* so funny) way of reminding us of just how little control we human beings actually have over our destinies.

How, given such a fickle universe, are we supposed to live? Ah! . . . That is the million-ruble question all of Tolstoy's characters face—or avoid.

Were personal survival one's only concern, then any number of options would seem perfectly adequate, including, say, that of a post-master who takes advantage of a rich traveler, or a Petersburg beauty and her father who lure a recent heir into a financially lucrative mar-riage. Heck, even Dolokhov's pursuit of sadistic pleasure by cruelly messing with others' lives might constitute a fine choice—in a world, that is, in which questions of right and wrong aren't of concern. But human beings live on this earth, presumably, for a purpose; unlike animals, we have the ability to wrestle with big questions, make moral decisions, and perhaps become a little bit better tomorrow than we find ourselves today. Making full *use* of that capacity, Tolstoy says, is the key to leading a fulfilling life. Pierre does it in spades, which is why, despite the bad rap he sometimes gets from other characters, and not a few readers, he is such an attractive character in this novel.

One Russian acquaintance with whom I discussed this section of the book some years ago, for instance, was far less fond of Pierre than I am. In his fifties at the time, this shaggy-headed, plump scientist with a bristling beard and a fun-loving personality enjoyed giving folksy career advice to young people like me, who, not unlike Pierre, were struggling with a tendency toward idealism, uninformed by any pro-fessional focus. "Well, Pierre is obviously trying to sit in too many places with one butt," observed my mentor in his own colorful rendi-tion of a famous Russian proverb. "If you want to make a hole in the snow," he added, unable to resist a mixed metaphor, "you've got to piss in one *spot*."

I knew that, while ostensibly he was still talking about Pierre, he was referring to me, as well. And his message was perfectly clear: if you want to accomplish something, you've got to be focused, and strategic—

the very things that Pierre, chasing utopian dreams and continually switching from one thing to another, is most definitely *not*. But something I never quite understood from that conversation is why anyone would be so intent on making a hole in the snow in the first place. Urinating in multiple places, after all, you're bound to make a much more interesting pattern. Consummately bad planner that he is, Pierre ricochets pinball-like from one experience to the next, but he also happens to lead a rather fascinating life—a life that will lead him to the sort of abiding happiness that eludes many of the novel's more pragmatic characters. That's because Pierre is a genuine seeker, and as such, he can teach us something about living with deeper purpose in a world that, if it doesn't turn us into unthinking egoists, is just as likely to turn us into overthinking nihilists.

Pierre's inspired vision and infectious personality are strong enough, in fact, to lift Prince Andrei out of a slump of his own when Pierre visits his friend after a two-year hiatus. Arriving at Bogucharovo, one of the family estates recently acquired by Prince Andrei, the first thing Pierre notices is how everything bears the stamp of Bolkonskyesque efficiency and cleanliness. Yet there is something dead about the place, just as there is something less than vital about Prince Andrei himself.

Like Pierre, Andrei has been through a great deal since their last meeting. Two years before this he abandoned his pregnant wife Liza to join the army. Then, after the battle of Schöngrabern, in which almost nothing went according to plan, Andrei grew bitterly disappointed. Austerlitz, he hoped, would be a different story, and that it proved to be, but not in the way he'd expected: after being knocked on his back during that battle by a soldier's bayonet, he looks up at the lofty sky, only to realize that his longtime quest for personal glory has been an illusion.

Presumed dead after Austerlitz, Andrei is all but forgotten by his family and friends; then, on a stormy March night, he returns home to the amazement of everybody, including his wife Liza, who happens to be going into labor that very evening. What might have been a joyous homecoming, however, turns tragic, when Liza suddenly dies during childbirth. "'Ah, what have you done to me?'" says her lovely, pitiful, dead face to him as he enters the room where her body lies (327). Those words, and that face, will continue to haunt him for years to come.

And so it is with deep pangs of guilt and disillusionment that Andrei returns to the country, wishing to be left alone, to live out his days as quietly as he can.

Such is the state in which Pierre finds Prince Andrei when he visits. He is struck by the deadness of Andrei's expression—a gaze "expressive of a long concentration on some one thing" (382). What that one thing may be Tolstoy never tells us, but Andrei does indeed appear to be as focused and single-minded as he was during his former pursuit of glory, only far more depressed and guilt-ridden. Feeling awkward in Andrei's presence, Pierre restrains himself somewhat, in order not to appear naïve before his rather superior friend. Nevertheless, he tries to share with his old friend his current happiness:

> "I can't tell you how much I've lived through in this time. I wouldn't recognize myself."
>
> "Yes, we've changed very much, very much, since then," said Prince Andrei.
>
> "Well, and you?" asked Pierre. "What are your plans?"
>
> "Plans?" Prince Andrei repeated ironically. "My plans?" he repeated, as if astonished at the meaning of such a word. (382)

The more Prince Andrei talks, the more feverish he becomes, trying desperately to prove to Pierre that he's had it with life, and that anything he undertakes now is merely to survive and eke out a modicum of pleasure from the rest of his days. But Pierre, still flying high from Freemasonry, cannot stand hearing this. As the eloquent and embittered Andrei demolishes Pierre's noble arguments one right after the other, the latter fears for his friend's soul, and possibly his own. Pierre's plans to lighten the burden of the peasants' physical labor and build schools for them? Bad ideas, insists Andrei, for physical labor is as necessary to the peasants as mental labor is to the aristocrats; Pierre will merely be depriving the peasants of the animal happiness natural to them. As for the building of hospitals, that, says Andrei, is equally superfluous, for it would be simpler and easier for the peasants to just die. More will be born in any event; and, besides, medicine kills as many people as it cures (which, given the unsanitary state of rural hospitals in those days, would not have been far from the truth).

Shocked by his friend's callousness and yet feeling completely outgunned in the debate, Pierre suddenly sees a small opening through which to score a point: What about the fact that Prince Andrei is still serving alongside his father in the local militia, and that just a few weeks ago he dissuaded his father from hanging a civil servant for stealing boots from the militiamen? Surely that could be taken as proof that Prince Andrei is, in fact, concerned with building a more just society? Nope, insists Andrei; he joined the militia so as to have influence on his father and prevent him from doing something he might regret later on, which, given the nearly unlimited power the tsar has recently bestowed on the old prince, is a real possibility. All of which goes to show, Andrei insists, that his actions were motivated by self-interest. "'I pity my father—that is, again, myself'" (386).

"'Do you believe in a future life?'" Pierre then asks, changing tack, as he launches into his most impassioned monologue yet, ebulliently describing an invisible ladder that extends from earth to heaven and connects all living beings to a huge, harmonious whole.

"'Yes, that's Herder's teaching,'" responds Prince Andrei coolly, referring to a German philosopher popular in Russia at the time:

> "[B]ut that, dear heart, does not convince me; life and death are what convince me. What convinces me is to see a being dear to you, who is bound up with you, before whom you were guilty and hoped to vindicate yourself" (Prince Andrei's voice quavered and he turned away), "and suddenly this being suffers, agonizes, and ceases to be . . . Why?" (388–89)

On and on they argue. This hours-long debate starts in the little cottage on the lake where Andrei is currently living, and continues in a carriage ride to Bald Hills, and finally, on a ferry raft that transports them across a flooded river. To the astonishment of the lackeys, coachmen, and ferrymen, these two friends are still at it long after the horses have been hitched up on the other side of the river, the sun has already half disappeared, the evening frost has formed, and the stars have sprinkled the sky.

Even as Prince Andrei destroys Pierre's every argument, denying the existence of an absolute morality or of divine order, refusing to acknowledge the possibility of life after death, and insisting that he himself has no more plans, the fact is, he is still planning; he still *wants* to believe. For no matter how much the "facts" of his own situation might convince him otherwise, he finds confirmation of Pierre's glorious, future-oriented vision in each gentle wave that bumps up against the moored ferry raft on which they have been talking for hours in the stillness of this spring evening: "It seemed to Prince Andrei that this splash of waves made a refrain to Pierre's words, saying: 'It's true, believe it'" (389). And indeed, stepping off the ferry, Andrei looks up at the sky Pierre pointed to earlier, and

> for the first time since Austerlitz saw that high, eternal sky he had seen as he lay on the battlefield, and something long asleep, something that was best in him, suddenly awakened joyful and young in his soul. This feeling disappeared as soon as Prince Andrei re-entered the habitual conditions of life, but he knew that this feeling, which he did not know how to develop, lived in him. The meeting with Pierre marked an epoch for Prince Andrei, from which began what, while outwardly the same, was in his inner world a new life. (389)

Indeed, the seed Pierre has planted in time bears fruit, for in the next two years Prince Andrei will successfully bring about on his estate those very reforms against which he argued so passionately.

What I have always loved about these scenes on the ferry raft is how they encapsulate the optimism-grounded-in-reality that is at the heart of *War and Peace*. By no means does Tolstoy pull any punches with Pierre; as that little fiasco with his peasants demonstrates, he's still got a lot to learn about how the world works. But then, the far more worldly Prince Andrei has an equally important lesson to learn from Pierre: true wisdom is as much about *believing* as it is about . . . "knowing." By throwing himself into life completely and following that idealistic star of his, Pierre makes some foolish decisions along the way, sure, but he also manages to connect to the higher sort of truth that so often eludes his chronically skeptical friend. And it is ultimately through the power of his inspired state, rather than any particularly shrewd argument, that Pierre helps Prince Andrei do something he hasn't been able to for quite some time: rediscover what is best in him and in the world.

We may be forgiven for suspecting that Andrei's transformation won't last any longer than that profound illumination he experienced at Austerlitz. Just as Pierre, for his part, will eventually descend back into one of his familiar depressive states. But so what? Life is movement and change, with none of us ever knowing for certain what the future holds. The excitement of reading Tolstoy's novel, for me at least, lies in its masterly depiction of not only what life is, but also what it *can be*. Never could Pierre have foreseen that a chance encounter with a stranger at a train station would lead him out of his funk to one of the most important stages of his journey. Nor could Prince Andrei have guessed when he coldly greeted Pierre at his doorstep at Bogucharovo that many hours later he'd be looking back up at that high, eternal sky to sense possibilities for his life he hadn't felt in some two years.

I've read *War and Peace* maybe fifteen times, and I still root for these characters, knowing ahead of time full well what will happen to them. I want to believe that Pierre is right about the possibility of universal brotherhood on earth, even as I shudder to think he might not be. I find myself hoping Prince Andrei will carry that glorious vision of the lofty infinite sky with him into the everyday of his remaining years on earth, even though I know he won't . . .

Here they are, still asking the biggest, thorniest questions while others are predisposed to supply easy answers. To quote Dostoevsky's description of Levin in *Anna Karenina*, these two young searchers, Pierre and Andrei, are examples of "those Russian people who must have the truth."

And yet, no sooner than they think they've tracked down that mysterious *it*, reached a coveted goal, or achieved an ideal of perfection, life hits them over the head, suggesting otherwise: "Nope, not quite there yet." So they keep marching on, through every thicket of disillusionment or despair, persisting in their quest for perfection in a universe that inevitably has other plans.

6

HAPPINESS

He who is happy is right!

—Tolstoy's diary, March 1863

I f planning is ineffective, success an illusion, and perfection unattainable, is anybody ever happy in a Tolstoy novel? Yes, terribly so! When Tolstoy felt things, you see, he felt them *big*. And the same is true of his characters, who ache and search, certainly, yet also experience moments of unadulterated joy: Prince Andrei, knowing transcendent bliss as he gazes up at the lofty, infinite sky while lying prostrate on the battlefield; or Natasha, when she dances and sings, as if nobody were watching; or, as we shall see, Nikolai Rostov, experiencing ecstatic oneness with life during the hunt.

But what exactly are we talking about when we talk about "happiness"? A recent visit to the self-help section of my local bookstore suggests that even the experts can't agree. My head spinning with the superabundance of gurus and guides to personal transformation, I have no shortage of prescriptions about how to achieve this elusive thing we all supposedly want, but can't seem to define what *it* is. Pleasure? . . . Joy? . . . Peace? A Google search for the word *happiness* producing 322 million results doesn't help matters much, either.

So I return to Tolstoy, whose own search for a personal definition of happiness was no less tortuous (or torturous) than that of the rest of us. Still, he *may* help us think more clearly about what it is we are really searching for, not by reducing the notoriously elusive concept of happiness to a simple formula, but by revealing just how complex a phenomenon it really is, as well as offering possibilities for happiness we might never have considered.

"[T]he best way to true happiness in life," Tolstoy wrote in his diary in 1856, at the age of twenty-seven, "is to have no rules, but to throw out from yourself in all directions like a spider a prehensile web of love and catch in it everything that comes along—an old lady, a child, a woman or a policeman." The very next year would prove a difficult testing ground for his theory. He would live through the death of his older brother Dmitry, carry on a hopeless infatuation with the daughter of a neighboring landowner, and witness a public execution in Paris, which led him to conclude, "I will never serve *any* government anywhere." Even "[i]n Russia things are bad, bad, bad," he writes to his relative Alexandrine Tolstaya, whom he endearingly nicknames "Granny," less because of her age (she was only ten years his senior) than because of her groundedness, which contrasted so starkly with his own rather flailing tendencies.

If only Granny had seen, as Tolstoy recently had, how a lady in the street beat her girl with a stick, an official clubbed a sick old man, and a village elder abused a drunken peasant, then surely she would have understood how "life in Russia is continuous, unending toil and a struggle with one's feelings." And for a young man whose own moods could swing from Towering Inferno to Ice Station Zebra with impressive rapidity, the struggle was especially pronounced.

There was one constant in Tolstoy's life, however: a "shameful laziness," which, he admits to Granny a few months later, is the real reason for his failure to reply to her last letter. On the day he received it, you see, everything had been going beautifully: riding in the fields, "I experienced a feeling of joy that Lev Nikolayevich [Tolstoy] was alive and breathing, and a feeling of gratitude for someone for allowing Lev

Nikolayevich to breathe." But by the time he arrived home, all the pleasantness was rudely crowded out by nagging concerns about an upcoming land purchase and frustrations over having to arbitrate a local case of a peasant who'd beaten his wife. Not satisfied with a mere apology to Granny, however, Tolstoy generalizes his personal experience of that day into a theory of happiness accompanied by a series of illustrative diagrams. The head, shaped rather like an egg, contains two sets of drawers, the one on the left containing negative feelings and the one on the right containing positive emotions. The two sets of drawers are separated only by a corridor:

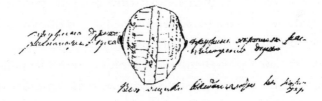

On an ideal day, the good-feeling drawers on the right are stuffed so full of positivity that they won't shut and even fill the corridors with their overflowing happiness. It works like a good mood catcher:

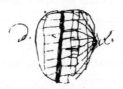

The normal state of affairs on a usual day, however, is that the drawers on both sides of the corridor slide in and out, filling the corridor now with good feelings, now with bad ones, leaving more or less space for emotional traffic to flow through the corridor between them:

What happened on that particular day, Tolstoy explains, is that the good mood catcher was in full force in the morning. As the day went along, however, the drawers on the left started opening and pouring their nastiness into the corridor to such a degree that the drawer on the right, containing Tolstoy's joy at receiving Granny's letter and intention to respond, was rudely slammed shut by the traffic jam of negativity in the corridor.

The first thing that becomes apparent from these annotated drawings is that Tolstoy could go to extraordinary lengths to explain his bad behavior. The second is that he was probably wise to have pursued a career as a writer, rather than a visual artist. And the third is that on any given day there must have been an awful lot of emotional drawers swinging open and closed inside this volatile young man. And so, he concludes his letter with an unsolicited mini-lecture: "It's only honest anxiety, struggles and toil, all based on love, that constitute what we call happiness." He goes on to chastise Granny for naïvely thinking, as he once did,

> that it's possible to create your own happy and honest little world, in which you can live in peace and quiet, without mistakes, repentance or confusion, in an unhurried and precise way. Ridiculous! *It's impossible*, Granny. . . . To live an honest life you have to strive hard, get involved, fight, make mistakes, begin something and give it up, begin again and give it up again, struggle endlessly, and suffer loss. As for tranquility—it's spiritual baseness. That's why the bad side of our soul desires tranquility, not being aware that its attainment entails the loss of everything in us that is beautiful, not of this world, but of the world beyond.

If happiness is what we seek, Tolstoy would seem to be suggesting, then we would do better, rather than attempting to mute the pain of living, to allow ourselves to feel it more deeply—in other words, rather than trying to lift ourselves out of flux, to immerse ourselves completely *in* it. Only by embracing everything down here do we get in touch, paradoxically, with what is transcendent, "not of this world, but *of the world beyond.*"

This is a far cry, to be sure, from his giddy "prehensile web of love," but it does bring us one step closer to understanding Tolstoy's view of happiness in *War and Peace*. For happiness in the novel, just as Tolstoy describes it in the letter, isn't so much a destination we reach by following a prescribed set of behaviors as it is a way of being in the world. It is what we experience when we come to know and embrace life as it truly is. This is what Pierre experiences later, as the French approach Moscow and catastrophe looms:

> He now experienced a pleasant sense of awareness that everything that constitutes people's happiness, the comforts of life, wealth, even life itself, is nonsense, which it is pleasant to throw away, in comparison with something . . . With what, Pierre could not account for to himself, nor did he try to clarify to himself for whom and for what he found it so particularly delightful to sacrifice everything. He was not concerned with what he wanted to sacrifice it for, but the sacrificing itself constituted a new, joyful feeling for him. (753)

Pierre's desire to sacrifice himself isn't about some abstract notion of being virtuous. Rather, it's the expression of his totally irrational wish to throw himself completely into the fray of the extraordinary events underway, without any concern for the outcome, or even whether doing so is good or bad, right or wrong. To be fully alive in Tolstoy's world, then, is to be connected deeply with that "something" Pierre senses that is bigger than all of our intellectual conceits and familiar frameworks of understanding—to embrace and love life in its totality: the good, the bad, the ugly, the beautiful.

Which is precisely what somebody like, say, the famous government reformer Mikhail Speransky, a secondary yet significant character in the novel, hasn't a clue how to do. According to the history books written later in the nineteenth century, this high-powered government bureaucrat held the fate of Russia in his hands. But in the world of *War and Peace* he is shown to be a dud, whose cold, grating laughter embodies the sterility of the man himself. It is Speransky's laughter, in fact, that first puts off Prince Andrei when he visits this man he has idolized at a dinner party with colleagues in Speransky's home. "There was nothing bad or inappropriate in what they said, everything was witty and might have been funny; yet that something which constitutes the salt of merriment was not only missing, but they did not even know it existed" (465). A man convinced that he controls the destiny of a nation, understandably, is not going to be able to feel the deep, irrational joy of living that is at the heart of *War and Peace*. A humbler, more emotionally attuned man like Pierre, however, can. As can the Rostovs, a family possessing a preternatural capacity for joy, as well as the ability to sense life's fundamental goodness, no matter the circumstances in which they find themselves.

Have we lost that capacity for finding deeper meaning and perhaps even some measure of joy in the midst of adversity? Have we exchanged an attitude of loving life on its own terms for an arrogant need to control the uncontrollable, on the one hand, or, on the other, a fearful disengagement from the world?

Neither of these approaches is the answer, Tolstoy would say, though both are as prevalent in our times as they were in his. Take the positive psychology movement in America today, a twentieth-century formulation of the conviction that we, as individuals, control our destiny. The original intention behind this movement was, according to Martin Seligman and Mihaly Csikszentmihalyi, two of its foremost practitioners, to help individuals, families, and communities thrive. An admirable intention, to be sure, but the more popularized versions of this movement often advocate a naïve can-doism that overlooks large swaths of human experience, failing to take seriously, Tolstoy would suggest, the possibility that there are, in fact, many situations in life in which we are at the mercy of forces entirely outside our control.

By trying to circumvent, or transcend those forces, to make them conform to our personal will, we only increase our frustration. What with hundreds of current titles of the All-You-Have-to-Do-Is-Set-Your-Mind-to-Whatever-It-Is-You-Want-and-You-Will-Get-It ilk, no wonder I come away from an afternoon in the self-help section of Barnes & Noble feeling, well, pretty lousy about my life. If everybody else is willing their way to happiness, I wonder, why can't *I*? What begins as a belief in endless possibility, then, put face-to-face with reality, can devolve very quickly into nihilistic despair.

So are we all supposed to walk around morose and feeling hopeless about things, then? Not at all. Gloomy fatalism, Tolstoy says, isn't the right response, either. *War and Peace*, after all, is a terribly life-affirming book that advocates not only realism, but a robust individualism, as well. Frankly, the nineteenth-century Russian philosopher Nikolai Kareev got it all wrong when he insisted that "the whole philosophy of history in *War and Peace* in actuality comes down to denying the role of individuality and the individual initiative in history: history for Tolstoy is mass movement, which takes place in a fatalistic way." Alas, Kareev's line of thinking still persists among certain Tolstoy scholars and Slavists; indeed, for years I was one of them.

Often depressed during graduate school, I consoled myself with the conviction that my suffering gave me special insight into the true (read: tragic) nature of life. It didn't help my mood that I was surrounded by academics, some of whom were high-minded about their chosen path of bookish self-abnegation, even as the rest of humanity persisted in their blissfully materialistic delusions. "*Nobody* who studies Russian literature is happy," a graduate school professor used to say, only half jokingly. Was my unhappiness attributable to my field, I often wondered, or had I, in fact, been drawn to it *because* I was unhappy? Moreover, as a Slavic scholar, was I doomed to a life of (noble) suffering?

But the more I immersed myself in Tolstoy's writing, the more I came to see the absurdity of these self-serving notions. Tolstoy himself detected precisely this sort of intellectual arrogance among many members of the intelligentsia in his own time, and responded to such thinking in a diary entry while working on *War and Peace*: "So-called self-sacrifice and virtue are only the satisfaction of one morbidly developed propensity. . . . He who is happy is right! The self-sacrificing person is more blind and cruel than the others." Human beings, in other words, are built for happiness. The only problem is that we sometimes try too hard to achieve it, or look for it in all the wrong places. Happiness rears its lovely head, more often than not, when we're not expecting it to.

This is a core lesson embodied by the Rostovs, one of the most blessed families in all of Russian literature. Yet for years I couldn't really relate to them. My thinking and writing about them tended to be abstract and full of generalizations about their earthiness, full-bloodedness, and other "-nesses," without ever quite understanding what exactly I was talking about or why. Nikolai rarely figured in any of my writing about *War and Peace* until my dissertation. Less fascinating than the questing Pierre or the tortured Prince Andrei, he had been relegated in my mind to the status of "lowbrow." Modeled on Tolstoy's own father, a high-spirited, hot-tempered aristocrat of the old school, Nikolai is, as the author describes him in a notebook, "very good at saying the obvious."

Indeed, his last name in an early draft of the novel, Prostoy, or Simple, captures something of his unconvoluted relationship to life that seemed so foreign to me, and that irked some of Tolstoy's more radical, "sophisticated" contemporaries to no end. "Since the world of thought is shut for Rostov, his development is finished when he is twenty years old," wrote radical literary critic Dmitry Pisarev, a brilliant, arrogant, and highly skilled assassin of fictional characters who failed to live up to his social and intellectual ideals. "All that remains for him is to grow more gross and stupid and then more senile and decrepit." Ouch. But if I never thought anything quite so scathing about Nikolai, I did share with Pisarev an elitism that made it a bit too easy for me to overlook one of Tolstoy's most important characters. This Mr. Simple appeared to me to be an ordinary bloke with ordinary values. What more was there to say?

Quite a bit, as it turns out. For not only is Nikolai at the center of some of the novel's most famous and memorable scenes, but there is also something . . . rather *extraordinary* about his ordinariness. Nikolai, I would now argue, has a gift for happiness that is uniquely his own, as well as being instructive for the rest of us. For one thing, he embodies the wisdom Tolstoy expressed in the sentence "He who is happy is right!"

It is 1809. Nikolai is still serving in the Pavlogradsky regiment, where he has become a squadron commander, beloved by his comrades, subordinates, and superiors. Ever since the signing of the truce between Tsar Alexander and Napoleon at Tilsit two years ago, things have been relatively calm on the European continent, if not on the Rostov home front. Nikolai, you see, has been receiving letters from his mother telling him that the family's financial affairs are in trouble, and that if he doesn't come home right away, the whole family will be ruined. Eldest of the Rostov sons, Nikolai knows that he has no choice but "to go from this clear, good world to somewhere where everything was nonsense and confusion" (489).

And so, a week later he shows up at Otradnoe, the Rostov estate, only to be thrust into a world that, for all its familiar charms, has fundamentally changed. Natasha, his brother Petya, and Sonya are growing up, for one thing, and his parents are arguing more often, mainly about money. Worst of all, he must get involved with "these stupid matters of estate management for which his mother had summoned him" (491). His inaugural executive decision is to visit the chief steward Mitenka. Demanding from this man "a full accounting," whatever that means, Nikolai proceeds to shower the bewildered peasant with a cascade of verbal abuse, then takes him by the scruff of the neck, kicks him in the rear, and sends him headfirst down a flight of steps.

"'I knew that I'd never understand anything here in this foolish world,'" Nikolai thinks to himself the next day after his father meekly remonstrates with him over his rather unorthodox management style (492). Admitting that he is not cut out for the finer aspects of estate management, Nikolai nevertheless proves that he has the makings of a true master in the old, autocratic Russian style. And as such, he develops a sudden, inexplicable passion for hunting with dogs, which has always been to Russian aristocratic culture what baseball is to the American way of life. Tolstoy doesn't tell us precisely how or why this happens, only that Nikolai pours himself into this new passion with as much vigor as he had in the course of his military duties. To go hunting or not is the only question that concerns him on that frosty September morning of his very first hunt. And like so many questions in the world of *War and Peace*, this one gets decided by forces lying outside the individual will.

As the hour arrives, the sky is overcast, the bare tree branches glistening with droplets of rain that hang in stillness, while the mist rising up from the warm black soil is like an endless curtain. Nikolai looks at the dogs, the sky, the earth, and Danilo, the wrinkled old peasant huntsman with whip in hand. Inhaling the intoxicating scent of dogs and fallen leaves, Nikolai glances into the dark, bulging eyes of his black-spotted bitch, Milka, who licks him on the nose and mustache, and the matter is resolved: a better day for hunting cannot be imagined. He "was already being seized by that irresistible hunting feeling in which a man forgets all his former intentions, like a lovesick man in the presence of his beloved" (494).

Within an hour about a hundred and thirty dogs and twenty mounted hunters with Nikolai at their head congregate without prompting at the porch. As in a regiment marching to battle, every dog and hunter knows his task, his place, and his purpose. Together they noiselessly spread out along the road and field leading to the Otradnoe woods. Vacillating between hope and despair, as if his life depended on the outcome of this chase, Nikolai crouches near the woods, awaiting his moment. And he prays. That's right. This earthy young man who pummels his peasants, who proudly bayonets Frenchmen on the battlefield, suddenly finds God: "'What would it cost You?' he said to God. 'Do it for me! I know You are great, and it's a sin to ask it of You, but, for God's sake, make it so that the old wolf comes my way and Karai, before my uncle's eyes, gets a death grip on his throat'"(499).

Such luck is not to be, he concludes. "'I am always unlucky, in cards, in war, in everything.'" But he

> again looked to the right and saw that something was running towards him across the empty field. "No, it can't be!" thought Nikolai, sighing deeply, as a man sighs at the accomplishment of something he has long awaited. What was accomplished was his greatest happiness—and so simply, without noise, without splendor, without portent. Nikolai could not believe his eyes, and this doubt continued for more than a second. The wolf ran on and jumped heavily over a hole that lay in his path. (500)

Does God exist, then? The skeptic in me says that it is a matter of random chance that the wolf appears precisely when Nikolai prays for it to. But even this more sober reading of the passage allows Nikolai the meaning of the moment, for in this moment he comes about as close to a religious experience as he ever will. Immersed utterly in the here and now, he touches the transcendent. Our greatest moments of joy are often like that. We struggle and search and all of a sudden, out of nowhere, the bliss emerges.

Tolstoy would have agreed, then, with one of his favorite American writers, Henry David Thoreau, who compared happiness to a butterfly that eludes you the more you chase it, only to come and sit softly on your shoulder as soon as you turn your attention to other things. There are quite a few moments of such butterfly-like softness in *War and Peace*—for instance, the wonderfully tender one when Natasha and her mother are curled up on the bed beneath the blanket, chatting on a crisp winter evening. But Tolstoy also points to another kind of happiness that isn't necessarily warm and cozy, but disorienting and intense, overtaking one without warning smack in the midst of life's chaos. That is what Nikolai experiences during the hunt.

Inevitably such "happiness" departs as mysteriously as it arrives. A second later another dog, unknown to Nikolai, flies down at the wolf, almost bowling him over, at which point the wolf suddenly gets up, snaps at his assailant, and the bloodied dog, its side ripped open, lets out a piercing squeal and buries its head in the ground. Thanks to this delay, Karai has time to head off the wolf, and pounces on him, while other dogs, not far behind, soon join in:

> That moment, when Nikolai saw the dogs swarming over the wolf in the ditch, saw under them the wolf's gray fur, his out-stretched hind leg, and his frightened and gasping head with its ears laid back (Karai had him by the throat)—the moment when Nikolai saw that was the happiest moment of his life. (501)

Wait: Wasn't the earlier instant when God sent the wolf his way Nikolai's "greatest happiness"? Yes it was, but so is this one. Tolstoy isn't being logical (there can only be one happiest moment in a person's life, right?), but he *is* being truthful in a deeper sense. With the animal-like thrill of the chase coursing through his body, Nikolai experiences things with a concentrated intensity unavailable at other times. If you've ever been to a sporting event and had your eyes glued to the ball moving down the court, across the field, or over the net in the final crucial moments, you know this feeling. Each basket made, each first down gained, each serve that goes unreturned—it can feel like the greatest happiness of your life, or most unbearable misery, depending on whose side you're on, over and over again, all within the span of minutes. To some viewers, it can seem almost like a religious experience. To the players, it often *is* a religious experience, as I myself know from one unforgettable squash match I played in college.

Darting about the court and literally diving for balls, as sweat pours into my eyes, my mouth, my ears, I hate my opponent every bit as much as he hates me. Not wanting to miss a single drop shot, I crowd behind the enemy so closely that his racket follows through right into my mouth. I fall to the ground, I later learn, though all I will remember is the high tinkling of a wineglass that for some reason has just shattered near me. As it turns out, that is the sound of my two front teeth landing on the wooden floor. I carefully pick them up, walk to the door at the back of the court, and hand them to my coach. He says something, but all I recall from that point on is the taste of the saltiness in my mouth—is it blood or sweat?—as well as the fleshy, toothless feeling and the piercing lemony sting as my tongue grazes the roof of my mouth where the two teeth used to be and now only the nerves dangle. I continue to play, as if nothing happened, winning that game over my shocked opponent, though losing the match to the better player.

Here's the thing: those forty-five minutes during which I was engaged in what seemed like a dance to the death on a sweat and blood-streaked squash floor were among the very happiest moments of my life—self-consciousness having dropped away as suddenly as my teeth. Everything worked together in perfect harmony. I was focused and flowing, and the world, weirdly right. This, I know, is what Nikolai feels on the hunt, sport having become nothing less than a connection to the divine, to life's most vital energies.

If you're having a bit of déjà vu, that's because . . . we've been here before—sort of anyway. The similarities between this scene and the earlier one in which Nikolai hears Natasha sing after his huge gambling loss are striking. In both scenes, there is a sense of at once disorientation, and heightened awareness. In both cases, Nikolai is in a state psychologists sometimes refer to as "flow," Buddhists as "samadhi," and athletes as "being in the zone." Totally immersed in what is happening in the moment, he loses his sense of both self and time, so acutely focused on the tiniest details of his surroundings that he has in fact merged with them.

"'No, it can't be!'" he thinks as the wolf comes his way, his prayer having been answered. Much as, when the notes start pouring out of Natasha, he thought, "'What on earth is this?' . . . And suddenly the whole world became concentrated for him on the expectation of the next note, the next phrase" (343). So, too, here—only he is focused entirely on the wolf's next move. And just as in the earlier scene, in which, "without noticing it, he himself was singing" alongside Natasha, so now Nikolai "did not hear his own shouts, did not feel that he was galloping, did not see the dogs or the space over which he was galloping; he saw only the wolf" (500).

In the earlier scene Nikolai experiences the world suddenly as infinitely larger than all of his previous frameworks of understanding. In such an expanded state, questions of right and wrong, good and bad play no part. "'One can kill, and steal, and still be happy!'" Nikolai thinks as he listens to Natasha sing (343). Something similar happens now: He heads back out to the fields with a distant relative and neighbor of the Rostovs, affectionately known as "uncle," and runs into Ilagin, a wealthy neighboring landowner who has just crossed over into the Rostovs' quarry. Greeting one another amiably, Ilagin apologizes for his accidental encroachment and suggests that the two parties join forces and hunt together on his property. As rules of politeness require, they compliment one another's dogs, and put up a façade of friendliness, with Ilagin going so far as to suggest that "'this counting skins, who brought in how many—it's all the same to me!'" (505).

Like hell it is. What matters most to these men is whose dog sinks his teeth into the hare's neck first. Violent? Sure. Ungentlemanly? Absolutely. And yet completely authentic, stripped of false modesty or social pretense. Cutting off the hare's leg and shaking it so that the blood runs down more quickly, uncle's victorious reaction of joy intermixed with anger and pride tells the larger truth about what this hunt is really all about:

> "There's a dog . . . outran them all, a thousand rubles or one—
> right you are!" he said, gasping and looking around angrily, as if
> scolding someone, as if they were all his enemies, as if they had all
> offended him, and he had only now finally managed to vindicate
> himself. "There's your thousand ruble dogs for you—right you
> are!" (507)

And right *he* is. For *he who is happy is right.* Uncle is in touch with a joy of living so visceral and truthful that it merges with disgust, pride, exhilaration, revenge, and a whole host of other feelings. Here is life at its rawest and most real, like something out of Homer's *Iliad*, a book that Tolstoy loved and read often, and to which he on one occasion proudly compared *War and Peace*. Natasha, sensing the intense energy of this moment, expresses its wild, epic thrill, not through words, but through

> a joyful and rapturous shriek, so shrill that it made their ears ring. With this shriek she expressed everything the other hunters had expressed with their simultaneous talk. And this shriek was so odd that she herself would have been embarrassed at such wild shrieking, and they all would have been surprised at it, if it had happened at any other time. (507)

But not in this instant they aren't. Later on, when life returns to its ordinary rhythms and patterns of behavior, the men will recover their "sham indifference." But in this moment the world is bigger and more heroic, as uncle becomes godlike in Nikolai's eyes, uncle's dog marches behind the horse carrying the bleeding rabbit "with the calm look of a conqueror" (507), and Nikolai is flattered beyond belief when, "after all that had happened, uncle still condescended to speak to him" (508).

For those who stand outside it, such full-blooded intensity may appear puzzling, if not repulsive. "Now, is that really the spirit of friendly competition?" asked an interviewer a few months later, bothered by the violent description of that squash match I'd included in a scholarship application. "Oh, I definitely believe in friendly rivalry," I responded. "I guess I was just trying to communicate my passion for the game," I added, with an aw-shucks smile. "Maybe I got a little carried away in my description." Satisfied, everybody on the interview committee nodded. But deep down I knew that I was fibbing, for like Nikolai, I'd experienced something big and special on the squash court that day—something that can't be captured by an ordinary phrase like "friendly rivalry." With age I have learned to temper my joie de vivre, to speak about such passionate moments in a more . . . socially appropriate way. But I often wonder with Tolstoy whether this routinely practiced sham doesn't rather mute our ability to identify the real thing when it happens, if not kill our very ability to experience it.

There is one important difference between Nikolai's experience of the hunt and his experience of hearing Natasha sing. The earlier scene occurs on the heels of a major rupture. Nikolai has just lost forty-three thousand rubles, along with his sense of honor, and he is ready to put a gun to his head. Whereas in the hunt scene no such rupture has taken place. Sure, he's had to deal with estate management issues, but beyond that, nothing major has happened. As often as it takes a crisis to catapult us into these states of intense experience, Tolstoy is show-ing, it is also possible to achieve them in the midst of everyday living and ordinary family life.

That Tolstoy chooses a hunt to communicate this message makes sense. Hunting, after all, had been a staple of Russian aristocratic life for generations. Whenever his writing wasn't going well, or he was out of sorts, Tolstoy himself would get his guns, pack his bags, call his huntsman, and head off for the woods for a day or more. He'd kill anything—fox, hares, wolves, even bears; in fact, once he was almost mauled to death by one of the last, a mishap he'd later recount in an adventure story for children.

The tradition lives on in the Tolstoy family. The writer's great-great-great-grandson Ilya still loves to hunt at Yasnaya Polyana. As he described to me his passion recently, I was acutely aware of myself as an American City Slicker, quite literally out of my element. What Ilya was trying to describe, and what Tolstoy depicts so effectively in *War and Peace*, is what it feels like to be in sync with life's most elemental forces. For generations of Russian peasants who lived in harsh land-scapes through subpolar winters that lasted almost five months out of the year, hunting was a direct confrontation with those forces. Hunt-ing in such an environment was a form of survival. But to later genera-tions of aristocrats, like the Rostovs or the Tolstoys, it would become a ritualistic reenactment of those good ol' bad ol' days on the Russian steppe, when man was put into direct contact with nature's simplest, most visceral truths.

Is it any wonder, then, that with centuries of hunting practice the Russians ousted the French in 1812? For the earthy wisdom and feeling for nature that are required of a good hunter were the very qualities Russians needed to lure and then destroy the French beast. And the novel's many analogies between hunting and warfare would seem to suggest that these connections were hardly lost on Tolstoy.

If you're not one for metaphors, you might also just enjoy these pages as some of the most thrilling Tolstoy ever wrote: you almost feel as if, rather than reading a work of fiction, you were experiencing, in Matthew Arnold's apt description of *Anna Karenina*, a "piece of life. . . . The author has not invented and combined it; he has seen it." And heard, touched, smelled it—*all* of it. In these pages there is brutality and bloodiness and beauty almost beyond words. There is unbearable rightness of being. This, Tolstoy is saying, is what it feels like to live in the *now*.

These scenes don't advance the plot, or tell us any more about Nikolai or Natasha than we already knew. They don't really seem to serve any purpose at all beyond themselves, and as such, would have been an easy target for those contemporary critics who blamed Tolstoy for breaking the rules of good novel-writing. But try to imagine *War and Peace* without them! You can't, for they *are War and Peace*. They contain its essential DNA. "The hunt is described so seriously, precisely because it is equally important," Tolstoy wrote in a draft of the novel's epilogue, anticipating readers' bewildered reaction to these scenes. In the 1860s, an era of grandiose thinkers with big plans for the human race, the hunt as Tolstoy describes it invites readers to come down from their castles in the sky and behold the gorgeousness of the here and now, in all of its raw splendor.

Russians have a saying: "In nature there is no bad weather." And in *War and Peace* Tolstoy says something similar: The bad times, like the good ones, are inseparable aspects of our human experience, and just as it takes both the sun and the rain to make a rainbow, so it takes both the joy and the pain to make a complete human being. Close yourself off to the flow of experience, live in fear of the unfamiliar, and you will enjoy a predictably comfortable numbness. Embrace life on its own mysterious terms, on the other hand, take the risk of living fully, and you will know your share of pain. But you will also feel the consummate joy of being alive.

7

LOVE

"Everything I understand, I understand only because I love."

—*War and Peace*, Volume 4, Part 1, Chapter 16

The phone rang one muggy August afternoon in Moscow a few years ago, and I recognized the deep, raspy actor's voice of my friend Vladlen. A charming man in his seventies with a gruff playfulness, and a name harking back to the fashion of the Soviet era (the name Vladlen blending *Vladimir* and *Lenin*), this guy has a positively Tolstoyan presence onstage, not to mention a proclivity toward the scatological in his humor. Like not a few former Soviet movie stars, Vladlen is, even at seventy-eight, arrestingly handsome, and, frankly, no stranger to marital troubles. He's also the kind of guy who likes to get straight to the point. "So who do you think was right, then," he asked right off, "Sonya or Tolstoy?"

I knew, of course, what he was referring to. In the vast ocean of Tolstoy lore with which nearly every Russian is familiar (and now, in the wake of *The Last Station*, a fair number of Americans, too) is the oft-recounted saga of the Tolstoy marriage, which was not always, shall we say, a reliable exemplar of domestic happiness. When Tolstoy and his wife were celebrating their twenty-fifth wedding anniversary with family and friends, the count responded to an old acquaintance who had just proposed a toast to their happy marriage by remarking, "It could have been better." These words wounded Sonya, naturally, and Tolstoy ought not to have spoken them. But sadly, they were true.

In the last twenty years of his life, Tolstoy tormented his wife with his priggish extremism, foolhardy decision making, impracticality, name-calling, and threats to leave her, which, in 1910, he finally made good on. Vladlen's analysis of their relationship? "She was a pain in his *zhopa*. That's why he left her."

Maybe, but while Tolstoy was railing in his later years against the evils of capitalism, the Church, and private property, the fact is that his wife made sure their own home at Yasnaya Polyana would not be dispossessed, and that her children had food, clothes, and a future. She set up a publishing business, for example, to bring in family income from Tolstoy's writings, a venture of which Tolstoy disapproved, believing it immoral for the family to profit from his labors. And so they fought ad nauseam about everything from copyright ownership to the education of their children.

One of the most hair-raising screaming matches took place about a week before Christmas in 1885. "I've come to say that I want to divorce you," Tolstoy said as he entered Sonya's publishing office, where she was at work. "I can't live like this. I'm leaving for Paris—or America."

"What happened?" Sonya gasped.

"Nothing. But you can only go on loading things onto a cart for so long. When the horse can't pull it anymore, the cart stops."

What exactly Sonya had been loading onto the cart was not entirely clear, but by the time her husband had progressed to the observation "Wherever you are the air is poisoned," she had heard quite enough. She went to her trunk and started packing, at which point Tolstoy broke down sobbing and pleaded for her to stay, while four of their children—Tanya, Ilya, Lyova, and Masha—looked on in horror.

"You know," Sonya wrote to her sister in a letter about that evening, "I drive myself insane by often asking: so, what's wrong, what have I done now?" Yet she would keep asking. Some twenty-five years later, on October 28, 1910, she woke up to discover a note her husband had left her in the middle of the night:

> My departure will distress you. I'm sorry about this, but do understand and believe that I couldn't do otherwise. My position in the house is becoming, or has become, unbearable. Apart from everything else, I can't live any longer in these conditions of luxury in which I have been living, and so I'm doing what old men of my age commonly do: leaving this worldly life in order to live the last days of my life in peace and solitude.
>
> Please understand this and don't come after me, even if you find out where I am. Your coming would only make your position and mine worse and wouldn't alter my decision. I thank you for your honorable 48 years of life with me.

Okay, let's face it: the genius who created *War and Peace*, the sage whose ideas have inspired hundreds of thousands, if not millions, the writer whom I have admired for nearly twenty-five years, was entirely capable of being . . . a complete *ass*. More to the point: this man who gave world literature some of its most beautiful scenes of human intimacy was surely one of the most love-challenged men who ever lived.

Opening Tolstoy's diaries from his twenties, we find a rather disconcerting portrait of the artist as a frustrated young man, yearning for love and yet acutely aware of his limited capacity either to give or to receive it. For several months he carried on a correspondence with Valerya Arsenyeva, the daughter of a local landowner, studying her as potential marriage material. "And really the main feeling I have for you is not love as yet," he confessed in one letter, "but a passionate longing to love you with all my heart," which marked the end of *that* relationship. Tolstoy eventually did find a mate, though on his wedding day six years later, in 1862, the thirty-two-year-old fiancé showed up at Sonya's home unannounced to give her one final chance to call the whole thing off—unless she was absolutely, positively, totally certain that she loved him. Frightened by his erratic behavior, Sonya seriously considered taking him up on the proffered out. And who could have blamed her? She was getting a good glimpse of a trait that in the years to come would cause her so much grief: not to put too fine a point on it, an extreme narcissism on Tolstoy's part manifesting itself in a need for total control over his emotional universe, even as he demanded reassurance that he was loving, and being loved, completely.

Bride Sofya [Sonya] *Andreyevna in 1862.*

And yet, I would argue that despite his own shortcomings in the arena of love—perhaps even *because* of them—Tolstoy has much to impart to us on the subject, whether we are falling in love, or out of it; are addicted to love, or sick of it; even if we've never loved at all and wonder what all the fuss is about. You'll need to ignore much of what he wrote after his spiritual crisis in 1869, however, for that sort of insight, and focus instead on *War and Peace*, a book written during a time when Tolstoy, still *in* love, offered his most reassuring, not to mention (for him) surprisingly realistic, views on the subject.

Not that the early years of Tolstoy's marriage were all bliss. The first few years were as excruciating as they were exhilarating; and it cannot have helped matters that Lev and Sonya were openly reading one another's diaries. "[O]ur happiness is terrifying," Tolstoy confessed in one entry, yet Sonya also received far more information about her libidinous husband's premarital liaisons—to say nothing of his ongoing sexual appetites—than this genteel eighteen-year-old newlywed was able to handle. Even Tolstoy's early fiction became cause for concern: "Every time he speaks of love or women I have such an awful feeling, such loathing, that I could burn the whole thing," wrote Sonya after reading a sensual description from one of Tolstoy's early works. "I want nothing to remind me of his past!" she continued, admitting that "[i]f I could kill him and create another new person exactly like him, I would do it with pleasure."

Reading this and other similarly chilling admissions in his young wife's diaries, Tolstoy began to wonder if he hadn't made a big mistake: "It's awful, terrible, and absurd," he penned in his diary in June 1863, within a year of his wedding, "to link one's happiness with material conditions—a wife, children, health, wealth. . . . The holy fool is right." Deep down, however, he knew what he had in Sonya, and being neither remotely holy nor completely foolish, decided to stay with the woman whom he had described as "impossibly pure and good and chaste," making sure to get her pregnant quickly and often. The lingering doubts remained, though, as did his bouts of narcissistic coldness, but rather than working through these issues in therapy, as one might today, Tolstoy did what any self-respecting nineteenth-century Russian novelist would have done: he gave them to his characters to deal with.

"'Never, never marry, my friend,'" the unhappily married, twenty-seven-year-old Prince Andrei advises Pierre early in the novel (28). "'[B]ind yourself to a woman—and, like a prisoner in irons, you lose all freedom'" (29). Pierre ignores his friend's advice, ultimately finding fulfillment in the imperfect bonds of marriage and family life, but then he learns to do something Andrei's never been able to: meet people where they *are*, rather than where he'd like them to be.

Prince Andrei is a good and noble man, but unlike Pierre, he cannot access his emotions for any extended length of time. Oh, they're there, all right: his external iciness and bitter sneer matched only by the volcano of desire inside him. Like his own father, he builds up protective walls between himself and others, even as he desperately wants to love and be loved by them. Lurching back and forth between grandiose ambition and depressive withdrawal from the pettiness of life, this man with impossibly high expectations is moved by the ideal of womanhood, yet woefully inept at loving an actual woman. Sadly, that is his approach to life in general.

Two years after that visit from Pierre at Bogucharovo, Andrei is still living in the country, successfully bringing about on his estate the very reforms that Pierre had tried and failed to accomplish on his. Yet the spirit with which he undertakes these activities is detached, perfunctory, whatever spiritual illumination he may have experienced with Pierre on that ferry raft long since passed. In the spring of 1809, the depressive prince embarks on a trip to his Ryazan estates to discuss business matters with the provincial marshal of the nobility, a certain Count Ilya Rostov. Cheerless and preoccupied with business considerations, Andrei pulls up to the Rostov country house in Otradnoe, which takes its name from the Russian word for "joyous." A crowd of girls suddenly runs across the path of his carriage. Yanked out of his dour self-absorption, he is struck by one of these girls—a dark-haired, "very slender, strangely slender" sixteen-year-old (420). What he feels, however, is not joy in her laughing face, in those lovely strands of loose hair happily flowing from beneath her white kerchief, but rather, sharp pain, his infatuation doused, even as it was ignited, by the infuriating realization that "this slender and pretty girl did not know and did not want to know of his existence and was content and happy with some separate—probably stupid—but cheerful and happy life of her own" (421).

"'And she again! As if on purpose!'" thinks Andrei later that evening as he overhears the dark-haired girl's voice speaking rapturously about the beautiful moonlit night from the balcony on the floor above him. "In his soul there suddenly arose such an unexpected tangle of youthful thoughts and hopes, contradictory to his whole life, that, feeling himself unable to comprehend his own state, he fell asleep at once" (422). This is a very good sign, in fact—the fact that Andrei can't figure out what in the world is going on inside him—for it suggests that his rational shell must be cracking, that he may be on the verge of an authentic emotional experience. And just *who* is this girl who has been put on this earth for the sole purpose of tormenting and confusing him? None other than Count Rostov's daughter Natasha, of course.

Over the coming weeks Andrei attempts to transform this elusive, unfinished diamond of a girl into the perfect gem almost in view within his own imagination. But, as is so often the case with this fellow, no sooner does the messiness of life rear its many-sided head than he runs for the hills, ignoring the wisdom of his own emotions and burying himself instead in a familiar cocoon of big ideas and beautiful ideals.

Right after meeting Natasha, in fact, he heads off to Petersburg, ostensibly on business, but in reality because he needs to find some outlet for the whirlwind of feelings she has unleashed inside him. Like an alcoholic reaching for the bottle whenever an uncomfortable emotion is just about to emerge, Andrei mistakenly conflates his sudden feelings for her with that old, familiar desire to be adored by the whole world: "'It's not enough that I know all that's in me,'" he proclaims to himself, under Natasha's rejuvenating influence. "'[E]veryone else must know it, too: . . . [E]veryone must know me'" (423). Rather than undertaking the more challenging and ultimately rewarding task of establishing genuine intimacy with another human being, then, he allows himself to be drawn right back into the intoxicating circles of political power.

Nevertheless, while in Petersburg he finds time to call on the Rostovs, who happen to be visiting as well, and he begins courting Natasha in earnest, much to the dismay of her mother, who rightly senses a false note in Prince Andrei's affection, an intrusion into their emotionally alive world, as dangerous as it is foreign. Nor is she off-base in this, for no sooner has he won Natasha's heart and her hand in marriage than her luster suddenly fades for him:

> Prince Andrei took her hand, looked into her eyes, and did not find the former love for her in his soul. Something suddenly turned over in his soul: the former poetic and mysterious delight of desire was not there, but there was pity for her woman's and child's weakness, there was fear before her devotion and trust, a heavy but at the same time joyful consciousness of duty that bound him to her forever. (479)

Suddenly those lifeless Bolkonskyesque abstractions of "duty" and "obligation" take over, killing the flower of authentic emotional connection that was just beginning to emerge. Having projected onto Natasha his own ideals and longings, Andrei can only be disappointed when the reality of her falls short of the image he has created. It need not have been like this, Tolstoy suggests: there is nothing more exciting than reality *if* we learn to view it properly—if, that is, rather than trying to impose onto the world our own limited ideas about things, we open ourselves to the wonderful messiness of life, of love. Unfortunately, that sort of perception makes itself available to us only under extreme circumstances, when something manages to puncture our familiar paradigms, forcing us to see beyond the limits of our ordinary assumptions. Absent such a revelation, one is all too prone to continue on one's unenlightened way—in Prince Andrei's case, chasing glory in all of its seductive guises: the grand conquest, the ideal woman, or, should neither of those quite pan out, the perfect revenge.

And, boy, do things *not* pan out the way Andrei hoped. In acqui-
escence to his father's demand that the marriage to Natasha be post-
poned for a year, he leaves for Europe, during which time a desperately
lonely Natasha falls for the charming rake Anatole Kuragin, and, in
her attempt to elope with him, breaks off her engagement to Prince
Andrei. The elopement doesn't come off, in the end, but only because
Marya Dmitrievna, the society matron and friend of the Rostovs,
intercepts correspondence between the two lovers and foils their plot.
It won't be long before Anatole is banished from Moscow, and Natasha, distraught over the realization of what she's done, falls seriously ill.
But all that is of little consolation to Prince Andrei, who is just returning from Europe when he gets the news about Natasha's infidelity. His
honor thus assaulted, and unable to forgive her, his all-consuming purpose becomes to return to the army, hunt down Anatole, and avenge
the wrong. And so, yet again, he misses the point: not only that such
grandiose gestures are inevitably ludicrous, but also that he, too, carries an equal share of the responsibility for what has happened. What
passionate teenage girl, after all, could possibly be expected to wait for
a fiancé while he figures himself out? Certainly not the kind capable
of turning the head of someone like Prince Andrei Bolkonsky in the
first place.

If Andrei frustrates me inordinately, it is at least in part because we
would seem to have more in common than just our first name: you
see, I too was in love with Natasha once, or so I thought. That slender
black-eyed Russian beauty, with her impulsive, fiery nature, jumped
right off the page and into my heart. Nor was I alone in my infatuation. "Akh, *Nataaassha*!" shouted an immense, pockmarked Moscow
taxi driver upon learning that his young passenger was a fellow admirer
of Tolstoy. "Now, *there's* a real Russian gal for you!" Teenage Russian
girls are quite quick to agree: most of them aspire to be like Natasha—
if, that is, they don't believe they already *are*. Little wonder that nearly

every Russian novelist after Tolstoy has tried to create his own version of this bewitching heroine. Only Boris Pasternak has come even close to succeeding, and, let's face it, *Doctor Zhivago*'s Lara Antipova just doesn't get under your skin quite the way Natasha does.

The maddening thing about Natasha, you see, is that as soon as you think you've got her pinned down, she pops up and defies all your expectations. That's what makes her so alluring, so real, and, well, so Tolstoyan. It takes a rare literary talent to capture that evanescent quality on the page, but leave it to an ordinary twenty-year-old Russian major from Amherst, fresh off the plane in Moscow, to convince himself that just about every attractive girl he meets is a reincarnation of Miss Rostova—even the fresh, blond-haired beauty I met while munching on a cabbage salad at the expensive Chinese restaurant on the fourth floor of the Intourist Hotel across from Red Square . . . All the clues were there, of course. This finely dressed, heavily perfumed postmodern lady of the night—Olga, I believe, was her name—was no graceful nineteenth-century countess brought up in silk and velvet. But it didn't matter. During the course of our short but enchanting conversation I *wanted* to believe that she was Natasha, and no amount of reasoning was going to convince me otherwise, thank you very much.

Such flights of fancy have occurred in my lifetime more frequently than I care to admit, almost always ending in disappointment. But they are at least instructive, helping me understand from direct experience a phenomenon Tolstoy illuminates over and again in *War and Peace*: that in affairs of the heart, we often find fantasy more satisfying than reality, a tendency that might well explain why prostitution and pornography remain about the most thriving industries, no matter what the economic situation, and why the worldwide divorce rate hovers at around 50 percent. If you really want to understand this curious facet of human nature—one with which Tolstoy had no shortage of personal experience—you might begin by contrasting the ways in which two of the novel's most important male heroes love (or fail to) one of the most lovable females in all of Russian literature.

Indeed, that is precisely what Tolstoy invites us to do in the way he structures this part of the book, for right around the time Andrei is falling in love with Natasha, or so he thinks, Pierre is again falling apart. "After the engagement of Prince Andrei and Natasha, Pierre, without any obvious reason, suddenly felt the impossibility of going on with his former life" (535). Of course, the reasons are perfectly obvious to us: the thrill of Freemasonry long since having worn off, once its internal politics and hypocrisies made themselves painfully apparent to Pierre, he is back to doubting and searching, drinking, and overeating. And now that his spiritual mentor, Bazdeyev, has died, Pierre has nobody to turn to for moral guidance. What's more, he is still sharing a house with his wife Hélène, whom he can't stand. At the obnoxious soirees she insists on throwing for the veritable who's who of Moscow society, Pierre is looked down upon by the guests milling in and out of his home as an affable if rather useless gentleman-in-waiting whose main virtues would seem to be his ready checkbook and his tendency not to get in anybody's way, like a nice piece of furniture standing unobtrusively off in a corner somewhere.

"'Had [Pierre] not wished with all his soul to establish a republic in Russia, then to become a Napoleon himself, a philosopher, a tactician, the defeater of Napoleon? Had he not seen the possibility and passionately wished to transform depraved mankind and bring his own self to the highest degree of perfection?" (536). Yes, he *did*, but none of it has come to pass, has it? And, as if that weren't troubling enough, how is he to deal with the realization that his feelings for his best friend's fiancée are perhaps growing stronger than they ought to? Increasingly uncomfortable in Natasha's presence, he makes a point of visiting the Rostovs as little as possible, and even leaves Moscow for a time under the pretext of having business in Tver. But his own best efforts at keeping a distance from the troublingly appealing Natasha are a poor match against fate, which finds a way of bringing the two together.

Upon his return to Moscow, Pierre receives an urgent note from Marya Dmitrievna asking that he come to the Rostovs on a very important matter. This, of course, is news of Natasha's attempted elopement, which has already become gossip at the English Club. Should Natasha's father find out, it is feared, he will be forced to challenge Anatole to a duel. Pierre has been called in to help patch things up, first by telling Anatole to get out of town, and next by trying to console the confused and still-defiant Natasha.

On his way to the Rostovs Pierre happens to run into Anatole in his sleigh, the latter dressed to the nines in the dashing accoutrements of a lady-killing military fop. "'Yes, indeed, there's a true wise man!'" thinks Pierre, who enviously eyes this suave man, the lower part of his ruddy face wrapped in a beaver collar, his white-plumed hat cocked, his pomaded curls of hair sprinkled with snow. "'He doesn't see anything beyond the present moment of pleasure, nothing troubles him—and therefore he's always cheerful, content, and calm. I'd give anything to be like him!'" (590).

Ah! How well I understand Pierre in this moment. What I wouldn't have given, say, at fifteen to be like Chris, that tanned tennis player from East Grand Rapids who had only to flash a smile from his well-chiseled mug for women to come sailing into his perfect world (or indeed, *with* him, on his father's yacht). Or, years later, to be like an old college acquaintance turned high-powered executive, nicknamed "the shark" for his seemingly limitless capacity to get whatever his voracious appetite might desire, whether in the boardroom or bedroom.

But wait, Tolstoy says: *Pierre* is, in fact, the wise one in this moment, whatever that word even means, precisely because he is acting out of a genuine concern for somebody *other* than himself. Certainly, it would have been easier for him to just stay at home on this winter night, curled up with a book and a bottle of wine, nursing his wounds over that failed marriage to Hélène and the general mess his life has once more become. Instead he has come in to clean up the emotional wreckage left by Anatole. Perhaps this is why, as much as Natasha would like to make Pierre the recipient of all her pent-up shame and anger, she finds herself taken aback, disarmed even, by the "meek, tender, heartfelt voice" of this fellow who has come to do right:

"Don't talk to me like that: I'm not worthy of it!" cried Natasha, and she was about to leave the room, but Pierre held her back by the hand. He knew he had something more to tell her. But when he said it, he was surprised at his words himself.

"Stop it, stop it, your whole life is ahead of you," he said.

"Ahead of me? No! For me all is lost," she said with shame and self-abasement.

"All is lost?" he repeated. "If I were not I, but the handsomest, brightest, and best man in the world, and I was free, I would go on my knees this minute and ask for your hand and your love." (599)

Later, Pierre will recall these incautious words with embarrassment, but in this moment, they are only truthful and thus completely appropriate. His reward for speaking what is in his heart, for acting out of instinctive kindness, rather than calculating self-regard, like Anatole, will be one of the grandest epiphanies of his life. For after he consoles Natasha, even as his cabman whisks him back through the wintry streets, Pierre looks up at the sky and sees the famous comet of 1812, which many Russians believed portended great danger. Not Pierre:

[F]or Pierre this bright star with its long, luminous tail did not arouse any frightening feeling. On the contrary, Pierre, his eyes wet with tears, gazed joyfully at this bright star, which, having flown with inexpressible speed through immeasurable space on its parabolic course, suddenly, like an arrow piercing the earth, seemed to have struck here its one chosen spot in the black sky and stopped, its tail raised energetically, its white light shining and playing among the countless other shimmering stars. It seemed to him that this star answered fully to what was in his softened and encouraged soul, now blossoming into new life. (600)

Come now. Shimmering stars? Immeasurable space? A flying comet that looks like a piercing arrow? What's next? A giant Cupid in the sky? Well, actually . . . why not? Had the Romans not already located him in the nighttime sky more than two thousand years before, Tolstoy surely would have. Because the things we notice, as he himself observed, are often less a reflection of our actual surroundings than of what is *inside* us.

Perhaps only Tolstoy, among modern writers, could pull off such an over-the-top moment of someone falling in love, delivered without so much as an ironic wink. He seems to feel no need to shy away from love in the grand key. And in this he is entirely at one with his character. Anyone as earthbound and self-focused as Anatole will never know the emotional heights glimpsed here by Pierre. Indeed, were a high-society socialite like the chatty Anna Pavlovna Scherer to see him right now, she would surely chuckle at the innocence of this "young man who did not know how to live" (10). Yet what a magical place the world may be for someone who, looking up at the evening sky, sees not darkness or danger but shimmering stars and shooting arrows.

True, Tolstoy says, love can make you stupid, but it also can make you wise in a way that little else *can*. For when you love, you see not just the truth about another person, but the *whole* truth all around us: the bad, the ugly, as well as the beautiful.

"Love us when we're black," goes a Russian proverb. "Anybody can love us white." Tolstoy is saying something similar through Pierre. It is easy to love Natasha when she is lighting up the world with her infectious singing, or dancing in her satin slippers and sparkling white ball dress. But what about those less glittering moments when she is petulant, annoying, and downright nasty? To his credit, it is precisely now, in Natasha's tear-stained eyes, that Pierre sees the radiance in the depths of her soul, and in so doing, glows a little more brightly himself.

As for the embittered Andrei, well, his hunt for Anatole having proved unsuccessful, he is soon enough back on the battlefield, and on the evening before the battle of Borodino, continues to muse about what might have been:

"I understood her," thought Prince Andrei. "I not only understood her, but it was that inner force, that sincerity, that inner openness, that soul of hers, which was as if bound by her body, it was that soul that I loved . . . loved so strongly, so happily . . ." And, suddenly he remembered how his love had ended. "*He* [Anatole] didn't need any of that. *He* saw none of it and understood none of it. He saw in her a pretty and fresh girl, with whom he did not deign to join his fate." (777)

But *had* Andrei really understood her? The memory of the whole affair stings him deeply, because he knows deep down that *he*, too, has behaved badly toward Natasha, that in heeding his father, rather than his own feelings, he did not join his fate to hers any more truly than the dreadful Anatole. Egoism is egoism, he would seem to grasp at least subconsciously, whether it is dressed in fashion or high-minded idealism.

And so, fed up with life after eight years of disappointment, he just sort of watches and waits as a grenade explodes in his face the very next day during battle. This wound, he senses, unlike the one he suffered at Austerlitz, may well be fatal. What he doesn't know yet is that this explosion will soon lead to one of the most important discoveries of his life: lying in the battlefield operating tent, writhing in pain, he observes another man who sobs like a boy as he stares aghast at his own amputated leg, still clad in its blood-caked boot. That man, it turns out, is none other than Anatole Kuragin, whom Andrei has expended so much energy in trying to chase down. Now, rather than pouncing on this opportunity to finish the blackguard off, the prince does something else entirely:

He now remembered the connection between him and this man, who was looking at him dully through the tears that filled his swollen eyes. Prince Andrei remembered everything, and a rapturous pity and love for this man filled his happy heart.

Prince Andrei could no longer restrain himself, and he wept tender, loving tears over people, over himself, over their and his own errors. (814)

What Andrei sees then is himself: a flawed fellow human being, neither good nor bad, but wounded and thus deserving of sympathy. "One can't help loving people," Tolstoy wrote a few years before embarking on *War and Peace*: "They are all—*we* are all—so pitiable." Indeed, the word "to love" (*liubit'*) and "to pity" (*zhalet'*) were often used synonymously in nineteenth-century Russia. Love, then, begins where the ego ends, where I see myself in you, and you in me, and we're both better, bigger human beings for it. That is the wisdom of Pierre when he consoles Natasha, and of Prince Andrei when he sees Anatole in the operating tent.

It is a sort of wisdom I saw as well in a Russian woman I once knew. During the Gorbachev reforms in the 1980s, when alcoholism was a major epidemic in Russia, I was often appalled by how women were reduced to caring for their dead-drunk husbands. "Why doesn't she just leave him?" I naïvely asked a Russian friend whose mother seemed always to be dragging her man home in her arms at night. "Because she loves him," responded my friend plainly. "It would kill her to abandon him." Having been raised in a therapy-drenched culture in which anything even remotely smacking of codependency set off internal alarm bells, I instinctively dismissed their relationship as unhealthy, even pathetic. But then one evening I watched my friend's mother, her fifty-year-old form slightly stooped, as she supported that man in her stocky, weathered arms, her dirty, calloused fingers digging into his torn shirt, while he exhaled his stinking breath in her face and blinked his shame-filled eyes up at her. It was one of the most striking things I had ever seen, as tender as it was dreadful, and I simply looked and listened, bearing witness to the kind of compassionate love that Tolstoy believed lies within every human being.

In a passage that has made more than a few readers weep, a badly wounded Andrei lies in a room at the back of a cottage in the town of Mytyshchi, some thirteen miles outside Moscow; he has come there with a caravan of evacuated civilians and injured troops. As fate would have it, the Rostovs happen to have been leaving Moscow at the very moment that Andrei and other wounded troops were brought to the capital and are now traveling in the same caravan, spending the night in the very same cottage. Natasha, who has not seen Andrei for several months, soon learns of his presence. Later, when everybody has fallen asleep and the red glow of burning Moscow fires can be seen and felt in the distance, she tiptoes catlike to his room, her heart thumping so heavily that she thinks the cottage walls must be moving.

A delirious Andrei concentrates on the red circle of light around his bedside candle, or the rustling of the cockroaches over the floor, or the rhythmic buzzing of a fly hovering just above his face, now descending to touch his burning skin, now rising alongside a strange, airy imaginary edifice of needles, which seem to whisper the weird sounds "Piti-piti-piti." Might he subconsciously be hearing in the fly's humming the French word for "pity"? Quite possibly, for in this moment of profound openness, Prince Andrei sees, hears, and feels as never before. And it is through this haze of widened awareness that he glimpses a pale sphinx standing in the doorway, then moving slowly toward him, kneeling, and at last gazing up at him with fearful, shining eyes. This sphinx is of course Natasha, who moves closer to Andrei on her knees, takes his hand, and begins to kiss it. Andrei sees her now with sudden clarity and depth:

> "Forgive me!" she said in a whisper, raising her head and glancing at him. "Forgive me!"
>
> "I love you," said Prince Andrei.
>
> "Forgive . . ."
>
> "Forgive what?" asked Prince Andrei.
>
> "Forgive me for what I di . . . did," Natasha said in a barely audi-

ble, faltering whisper, and she began to kiss his hand more quickly, barely touching it with her lips.

"I love you more, better, than before," said Prince Andrei, raising her face with his hand so that he could see her eyes.

Those eyes filled with happy tears looked at him timidly, with compassion and joyful love. Natasha's thin and pale face with its swollen lips was more than unattractive, it was frightful. But Prince Andrei did not see that face, he saw radiant eyes, which were beautiful. (922)

What he sees, in other words, is what Pierre saw on that wintry night a year earlier: the real Natasha, radiant in her full-blooded humanity. And in so doing, he taps into a form of understanding greater than either the cool rationalism of his deflated periods, or the apparent high-mindedness of his glory-seeking ones. He embraces, that is, the perceptive powers of love: the only form of knowledge, Tolstoy believed, that allows us to see people, places, and things as they truly *are*, without preconception, without judgment, in all their mysterious beauty, all their interconnectedness. Whether this new-found wisdom will stick, or disintegrate as quickly as so many of his other epiphanies have, remains to be seen. Natasha, at any rate, doesn't concern herself with what may or may not be, but simply stays present with what *is*, and from that day on, through the rest of the Rostovs' journey, remains at Andrei's side.

Given her reconciliation with Andrei, the thought crosses everyone's mind: Might their engagement be renewed, should he recover? But nobody speaks about this, least of all Andrei or Natasha, for there are bigger concerns hovering in the air. With Napoleon now in Moscow, "the unresolved question of life and death hanging not only over [Andrei] Bolkonsky but over Russia shut out all other conjectures" (923).

Forty years after Tolstoy wrote that moving scene, he himself would lie in a tiny, dimly lit room in the red stationmaster's cottage at the Astapovo train station. Sonya, having learned of her husband's where-

The Tolstoys' forty-eighth wedding anniversary in September 1910, two months before Tolstoy's flight from home and death in a train station.

abouts, had come against his wishes, and, kept at bay by Tolstoy's disciples, was not allowed to see him until he'd nearly lost consciousness. Entering the room cautiously, she crouched by her withered husband's bedside, and, listening to his heavy breathing, whispered, "Forgive me, forgive me." Only he did not hear her. He died a few hours later.

For all they'd been through—not least during those all-too-dramatic last few weeks—the Tolstoys stayed married nearly fifty years, an impressive accomplishment in *any* age, and especially at a time when the average life expectancy hovered at around forty. Ten years after the writer's death, Tolstoy's oldest daughter, Tatyana, asked her mother whether she still thought of papa. "Oh, constantly," the old countess responded, "constantly. . . . [I]t tortures me so that I lived badly with him. But, Tatyana, I say to you before my death—I never, never, loved anybody but him." Her love surviving all of the pain of their marriage, Sonya was, in the end, an exemplar of the very sort of emotional courage and compassion that Tolstoy celebrates in *War and Peace*.

8

Family

The family is flesh. To give up the family—this is the
second temptation—is to kill oneself.

—Tolstoy's diary, May 1881

Vladimir Ilyich Tolstoy has not forgotten his roots. The writer's
great-great-grandson, director of the Leo Tolstoy Museum and
Estate at Yasnaya Polyana, is known for his success in keeping the whole
family together. Once every couple of years a hundred and fifty or so
of the more than 350 Tolstoy descendants from twenty-five countries
descend upon Yasnaya Polyana at Vladimir's initiative for some sort
of reunion, be it a wedding, a birthday, a funeral . . . I happened to
be there on the day of one such event, the fiftieth birthday party of
a great-great-granddaughter who lives in France. I'd learned about it
just a day earlier when I ran into Vladimir's nephew, Ilya Ilyich, a
friend of mine, on the first floor of the Hotel Dvoryanskaya Usad'ba,
or "Nobleman's Estate," where I was just then attending a conference.
This was a family-only celebration, naturally, so I wasn't invited. Still,
this was not something I was about to miss, even if I had to enjoy it
from afar.

I was standing under a great linden tree with enormous, thickly foliated branches when the rain started to come down lightly, the droplets ever so slightly breaking through the canopy above me. It was a breezy, balmy June night, and I loved being there, listening to the sound of the gentle rain against the giant leaves, feeling the wetness in my hair, on my shirt sleeve. The joyous melodies from the Russian folk quartet hired for the occasion drifted over me from fifty yards away, where the party was in full swing under a great tent that had been set up on the lawn near the hotel.

"To a wonderful woman, whom we love and admire, and who is very much needed in our lives," proclaimed a stylishly dressed middle-aged man in French, raising a shot of vodka. As the music struck up again, I noticed several young boys dressed in khakis and white button-downs playing a game in the yard. Not far from that, two twin girls with adorable, identical bright red cloth flowers sewn on the back of their lilac dresses skipped across the lawn, hand in hand, their girlish giggles punctuated every so often by a delighted scream. A few slightly older girls were jumping rope, while a pack of teenage boys strutted their stuff out on the dance floor.

Standing beneath the dripping tree and inhaling the general atmosphere with delight, I thought to myself how the author of *War and Peace* would have loved to be there that night. I recalled the many joyous name-days at the Tolstoys' I'd read about, the family birthday parties, the picnics in the fields, the troika* races and the mummer† celebrations during which the great author often played a bear. I remembered the stories about Grandpa Lev tossing his grandson into the air with one arm and then catching him on the way down, and called to mind the famous photograph of the writer holding up his fingers to show his grandchildren Ilya and Sonechka just how big that cucumber in the fairy tale really is.

---

* troika: Russian sleigh drawn by a team of three horses.

† mummer: merrymaker in a costume during festive occasions.

*Grandpa Lev telling grandchildren Ilya and Sonechka
the story of the cucumber.*

For the hour or so in which I stood there in the darkening woods dreaming of a world that once was, I felt that mixture of sad-sweet longing Russians call *toska*: a yearning for a long-departed world that continues to stir one's imagination with all the force of reality . . .

Tolstoy's contemporaries, well, they weren't buying it. "The family, that warm and cozy element . . . which once gave the novel its content, has vanished from sight," wrote the satirist Mikhail Saltykov-Shchedrin in the early 1870s. "The novel of contemporary man finds its resolution in the street, on the public way, anywhere but in the home." Saltykov-Shchedrin was referring here to stories like Nikolai Gogol's "The Overcoat" (1842) and novels like Dostoevsky's *Crime and Punishment* (1866)—fiction that depicted the poverty, crime, and prostitution sweeping through Russian urban centers in the second half of the nineteenth century. But, of course, this very sort of development was what impelled Tolstoy to put that warm and cozy element back *into* the literature of his day, through depictions of the Rostovs' troika races and Christmas games, as well as the dinner parties and name-day celebrations at their well-frequented home on Moscow's Povarskaya Street.

"[I]t really is all gentry-landowner literature," Dostoevsky remarked of Tolstoy's novels, by which he meant the sort of literature created by privileged aristocrats ensconced in their private kingdoms, envisioning an idyllic, orderly Russia that no longer existed. Yet with all due respect to nineteenth-century Russia's *second*-greatest novelist, most readers I know would not be opposed to spending a few weeks in the world described in *War and Peace*, just as they wouldn't care to live out two hours in that of *Crime and Punishment*. Dostoevsky's "accidental families" of drunkards, prostitutes, and copy clerks all tossed together in run-down tenement houses, while real enough and certainly worthy of compassion, are simply not going to inspire us with a model to live by. *War and Peace*, on the other hand, *can*. It does so not by sugarcoating the harsh realities of modern life, as Dostoevsky suggested, but rather by showing us what is possible in *spite* of those realities.

Now, even Tolstoy would agree that there is such a thing as a toxic family, in which relationships are so torn as to be unmendable. And to veterans of such family hell, well, what Tolstoy suggests in *War and Peace* might appear a bit far-fetched. Then again, we've all seen examples of people coming from horrific backgrounds who charge into the future with redoubled commitment to creating families of their own, determined not to repeat the pattern of their own upbringings. Where the courage for such an outlook comes from is one of the greater mysteries of the human heart. Yet it reminds us of something Tolstoy knew from personal experience: that even those family relationships that appear fundamentally broken might be in fact more reparable than we suppose.

What the writer says of Moscow after the war, after all, is true of the whole world of the novel: "everything has been destroyed, except for something indestructible, immaterial" (1108). That "something" is the life force, which, continually renewing itself, can heal even the most seriously ruptured of family bonds. Or, as the poet Robert Frost would put it much later: "Home is the place where, when you have to go there, they have to take you in."

The Tolstoys in 1887. Standing from left: Marya, Andrei, Tatyana.
Sitting from left: Sergei, Lev, Tolstoy with his daughter Sasha,
Sonya, Ilya, Mikhail.

Tolstoy saw the family as society's primary social unit. When families break down, he observed, societies break down, and life itself falls apart. The very breakdown in family structures that Tolstoy wrote about so passionately in *Anna Karenina* was already taking place ten years earlier, in the 1860s, as he was working on *War and Peace*. Even then, the shift from agrarian to industrial economy, with the latter's emphasis on individualism, competition, and consumerist gratification, was having its effect. Not only were peasants abandoning their communes in the countryside in favor of the economic opportunities in the cities, but Tolstoy observed a shift in attitude even among those in his own aristocratic circles, and watched with disappointment as his friends and relatives began getting divorced.

What's more, the so-called woman question was heating up: nineteenth-century Russia's equivalent of what today we would call feminism. The most progressive thinkers at the time (most of them young, unmarried, or both) encouraged women to pursue more important work beyond the chauvinistic confines of married life. One of the most famous examples of this argument was found in the radical Nikolai Chernyshevsky's novel, *What Is to Be Done?*, written over four months from December 1862 through March 1863, during the author's imprisonment in Petersburg's Peter and Paul Fortress. That book, which would inspire the Russian "free love" movement in the 1860s, not to mention future revolutionaries, tells the tale of Vera Pavlova, a poor girl living with her brother and a mother who wants to marry her off to the owner of the tenement house in which they live. Vera is saved from this loveless marriage as well as her poverty by a young medical student who marries her and helps her to set up a successful sewing business.

Tolstoy remained uninspired by Chernyshevsky and his model of the self-determined "new woman," not least because he believed that, while running a sewing business with a doctor in training might well improve the quality of both one's wardrobe and medical care, it hardly guaranteed one's chances for long-term happiness. In the end, Tolstoy responded to the female emancipation movement with a character of his own, named Anna Karenina—a character who he felt offered a rather more realistic account of a "modern" woman's prospects. Here was a passionate lady who managed to escape a loveless marriage and find her own freedom, only in the end to stick her head on the tracks before an oncoming train.

In *War and Peace*, too, Tolstoy offers something of a response to the progressive thinkers of his day, this time through the story lines of Natasha Rostova and Princess Marya. Freedom, alas, isn't all it's cracked up to be, as the nineteen-year-old Natasha realizes while suffering from a severe case of "option-itis," unable to choose between the juicily romantic Anatole and the jaded but morally superior Prince Andrei. Thankfully, she avoids throwing herself in front of any fast-moving ironclad vehicles, although after her failed elopement attempt, she does try to overdose on arsenic pills. That fiasco, however, serves as a watershed moment in her evolution from a rather narcissistic adolescent into the sort of mature young woman who learns to flourish even while accepting the limits of her freedom in love and in life.

When we look at Natasha and Princess Marya, and all of the characters, in fact—women *and* men—who end up surviving and finding happiness in *War and Peace*, we detect a pattern: they find deep fulfillment in opening themselves up to the joys, pain, vulnerabilities, and yes, responsibilities, not of individual fulfillment, but family life.

Take a look at Princess Marya's family. Back in 1805, when things seemed more or less stable in Russia, a familiar gloominess reigned in the Bolkonsky household: the venerated old Prince Bolkonsky (father of both Princess Marya and Prince Andrei), a small-figured man with a brusque manner to go with his beetling brows, busies himself with his memoirs, his mathematical calculations, his energetic hobby of turning snuff boxes on a lathe, and of course supervising the ceaseless construction work on his estate. Nicknamed "the king of Prussia," this scion of the old order is respected and feared by nearly everybody, not least his own daughter, whom he force-feeds daily lessons in geometry and algebra. Feeling out of place in her father's enchanted castle of order and discipline, the physically frail and emotionally sensitive Princess Marya would rather lose herself in studying the Gospels, or writing long, heartfelt letters to her friend Julie in Moscow. And, of course, she is drawn to the notion of building a family of her own.

No wonder the arrival of the dashing Anatole Kuragin and his father Prince Vassily at Bald Hills in December 1805 is a welcome departure from her daily drudgery. Prince Bolkonsky may be less than enamored of this young cad and his fortune-hunting father, who have come to ask for the hand of the unattractive but very rich princess, but Marya is at once elated and terrified: "'Can it be—a husband?'" (227).

Try as he might to give his daughter the space in which to make her own sound decision, the old prince cannot bear the thought of her leaving him, least of all for someone like Anatole. And so when he notices Anatole's attraction to the provocative Mlle Bourienne, a family companion living with them, the old prince is as relieved as he is insulted. Nevertheless, he calls his daughter into his office for a consultation and explains that "'a proposal has been made to me concerning you, Miss.'" She is free to decide on her own, he tells her before proceeding to dispense what must be one of the stranger pieces of parental counsel in literature:

> "I desire only one thing—to do your will," she said, "but if my desire must needs be expressed . . ."
>
> She did not have time to finish. The prince interrupted her.
>
> "Splendid!" he cried. "He'll get you and your dowry and incidentally take along Mlle Bourienne. She'll be his wife, and you . . ."
>
> The prince stopped. He noticed the impression these words made on his daughter. She hung her head and was about to cry.
>
> "Well, well, I'm joking," he said. "Remember one thing, Princess. I hold to the rule that a girl has the full right to choose. And I give you freedom. Remember one thing: the happiness of your life depends on your decision. There's no point in talking about me." (230)

But freedom is exactly what this excessively controlling father hasn't a clue how to give his daughter. In his own rather awkward way, he is, of course, trying to protect her, for he sees perfectly clearly that her marriage to Anatole would be a disaster. Indeed, within minutes of this conversation, Princess Marya, strolling into their winter garden, notices her prospective fiancé whispering sweet nothings in Mlle Bourienne's ear while fondling her shapely waist. That this tête-à-tête occurs within a day of Anatole's arrival certainly does not augur well for Princess Marya's future with him. And so, rather than bemoaning her own fate, she suggests that Mlle Bourienne marry Anatole instead. After all, Marya concludes, Bourienne must be desperately in love with Anatole; otherwise, why would she have flirted with him so audaciously right under Princess Marya's nose? It doesn't occur to her that Bourienne is as much of a self-centered egoist as Anatole.

Things go from discouraging to downright depressing for Marya after the death of her brother Andrei's wife Liza and his subsequent proposal to Natasha Rostova. Andrei's father is opposed to this union, and as usual, Princess Marya receives the brunt of his angry outbursts, which have become more and more frequent. One day she receives a letter from her brother in which he requests that their father shorten the postponement of his marriage to Natasha by three months. When Marya communicates this request, the old man falls into a perfect rage, adding to an already steady barrage of attacks against his daughter fresh personal insults, including threats to marry Mlle Bourienne himself and hints that maybe Marya should move in with Andrei and Natasha, since the sight of her has become positively unbearable to him.

Utterly confused by her father's senseless cruelty, the princess mutes her sadness through prayer, writing long letters to Julie, and raising her nephew Nikolenka (Prince Andrei and Liza's son), and visiting with the holy wanderers who come to Bald Hills. Reflecting at one point on the sadness that fills her home, she realizes that spinsterhood is looking more and more like not only her best option, but her only one. And so she resolves to leave Bald Hills altogether and spend the rest of her days traveling the Russian countryside in rags, like one of her beloved holy wanderers, collecting a caftan, a black kerchief, and bast shoes for the journey. But in the end, she just can't go through with it: "[S]eeing her father and especially little [Nikolenka], her intention would weaken, she would weep in quiet and feel she was a sinful woman: she loved her father and her nephew more than God" (487). How shall we understand Marya's decision?

"No backbone," winces one of my students recently. "Stockholm syndrome!" exclaims another reader to whom I've posed the same question, referring, of course, to the psychological phenomenon in which a hostage who is in captivity for long enough begins to mistake her captor for a protector.

As the chorus of judgment and well-meaning criticism gains strength during such discussions, so does my discomfort. "Yikes!" I think to myself. "Am I myself such a product of a rigid upbringing, my entire being stamped indelibly by the notion that Thou Shalt Respect Thy Mother and Father, no matter what?" Maybe so, for to this day I remain unconvinced by readings of Princess Marya either as a chauvinist Tolstoyan fantasy of the ideal docile woman, or as somebody who really needs to get a life and begin standing up for herself.

The fact is, this character, who was inspired by Tolstoy's own late mother, *does* stand up for what she believes with every bit as much courage as we may find in a whole host of independent-minded nineteenth-century literary heroines, from Lizzy Bennet to Jane Eyre. It just so happens that what she believes, far from any notions of universal freedom or entitlement, is that the bonds of blood are thicker than even the sturdiest pair of bast shoes, and that sticking out a fundamentally imperfect family situation is, well, preferable to bolting.

But if this is a kind of wisdom Tolstoy seems quite clearly intent on privileging over various others in his novel, then why is it that he himself could not heed it in the course of his own life? Scholars, psychologists, and writers—even directors—have been debating this question for more than a century now, and still haven't come up with a satisfactory answer. That, in turn, prompts another question: Is it possible that the troubled relationship between Princess Marya and her father anticipated—perhaps even drew upon—the one slowly deteriorating between Tolstoy and his wife? Might Tolstoy not have sensed more than a little bit of himself in Prince Bolkonsky? And might that not in turn have prompted him to endow the princess with the qualities of stolid tolerance so abundantly demonstrated by his wife? Surely he understood that it required gargantuan patience to live with someone like himself. And therefore, it is also hard to imagine that, deep down, he wasn't grateful to have found someone equal to the task.

The fact is, without his family, Tolstoy would have been a very different kind of artist, if indeed an artist at *all*. His family was, quite simply, the wellspring of his imagination, and Sonya nursemaid to his abundant talents. He knew it, too: "I am a husband and a father, who is fully satisfied with his situation," Tolstoy wrote to his relative Alexandrine ("Granny") in 1863, around the time he started working on *War and Peace*. "I only *feel* my family circumstances, and don't think about them. This condition gives me an awful lot of intellectual scope. I've never felt my intellectual powers, and even all my moral powers, so free and so capable of work." Later, in a letter written shortly after his marriage, he compares himself to an apple tree that had once sprouted in all directions: but "now that it's trimmed, tied, and supported, its trunk and roots can grow without hindrance. And that's how I grow."

Yet nearly five decades after writing *War and Peace*, this avowedly well-nourished and well-supported man would find himself feeling stifled, and, like his character, would outfit himself in a caftan, kerchief, and bast shoes. Tolstoy, however, made good on those preparations, and left home. He wasn't sure, in his final hours, that he'd made the right decision: "I do not understand what it is I am supposed to do," he kept repeating—among the truest of utterances he made during those very conflicted last twenty years of his life.

Does any of us really know what we are supposed to do in a thorny family situation of the sort Tolstoy contended with? We struggle, we search, we hit impasses. But the minute we seize the solution we feel sure we've finally figured out—as Tolstoy did on that fall night of 1910—we lose our capacity to embrace alternative possibilities. Fortunately, he'd already left us *War and Peace*, a novel all *about* the possibilities lying right smack between such extreme measures. And if in the end Tolstoy was unable to embrace this wisdom in his own life, he at least created in Princess Marya a character who can be seen as its embodiment.

Marya's brother Andrei, by contrast, after his father's destructive interference in his relationship with Natasha, descends into a downward spiral of bitterness and depression. Upon returning to Moscow and discovering that his fiancée has been unfaithful, Andrei launches into a tirade against his father, against Natasha's seducer Anatole, even against Mlle Bourienne, who now openly flirts with the old prince right under Princess Marya's nose. Marya implores her brother to rise above it all, but try as he might, he cannot follow her path of all-forgiving love. His heart having grown cold, he sees only ugliness and deceit wherever he looks, not least in his own childhood home: Princess Marya is "'a pathetic, innocent being'" who "'stays to be devoured by a senile old man'" unable to change vicious habits. And as for Andrei's own son, well, he's growing up in a dog-eat-dog world, "'in which he will be the same as everybody else, the deceived or the deceiver'" (632).

But is that the lesson we are meant to learn from this situation? Princess Marya feels her brother's pain, all right; she just doesn't share his interpretation. Nor would she have agreed with the assessment of her father by one of Tolstoy's most outspoken contemporaries. "[I]n the course of the whole of his life," wrote the publicist V. V. Bervi-Flerovsky in a scathing 1868 character assassination of the male side of the Bolkonsky family, "he never, even unintentionally, expressed a human feeling towards his own daughter." But what could be more human, Princess Marya knows, than a proud old man painfully aware that his glory has passed? Or a widower at once desperate for his daughter's affection and constitutionally incapable of receiving, let alone returning, it? Or a frail father who fumbles around for his spectacles lying right next to him, who makes a false step with his weakening legs while looking up quickly to make sure nobody has noticed, who suddenly drops his napkin, dozes off, and hangs his tired, gray head over his plate at the dinner table? "'He's old and weak, and I dare to judge him!' she would think in such moments" (541). In which position Tolstoy would say there is not weakness, but rather wisdom.

Even that seemingly cold, old prince, in one of the novel's poignant moments, acknowledges his daughter's unique gifts: "'Thank you . . . daughter, dear friend . . . for everything, everything,'" mumbles the dying Prince Bolkonsky clumsily with his stroke-injured tongue, even as the invading French troops approach Bald Hills. "'Forgive me . . . thank you . . . forgive me . . . thank you!'" (716).

Now, I'm uncomfortably aware that my endorsement of Princess Marya has something to do with the fact that her situation hits rather close to home for me. You see, like Princess Marya, I grew up in a house filled more with the aura of intellectual sophistication than, say, the aroma of fresh-baked pies. The many paintings and sculptures I was not to touch sometimes gave me the impression that I was a visitor in a precious art gallery, much as Princess Marya feels like an uncertain guest in her old father's less-than-welcoming mansion.

Envious of friends who came from more ebullient, Rostov-like homes, I looked forward to Saturday playdates with Teddy, who had the latest toys and coolest gadgets; craved the afternoons with Chris, who would invite me home after school, treating me to forbidden delicacies like Doritos and Twinkies. One day, at the ripe age of eleven, I got up the courage to run away, making it as far as the Four Corners, about a mile away from home, only to realize that my feet hurt and I didn't even have enough money for a Slurpee. And so I borrowed the neighborhood pharmacist's phone, and minutes later the escape attempt ended with my dad dutifully showing up in the car to whisk me back to my four-thousand-square-foot prison overlooking Bear Lake, as I slunk down in the front seat, utterly defeated.

At least I came to discover a sense of purpose in my discontent, my listless, melancholy ambles through the house inevitably leading to my dad's large leather library chair, where I'd install myself, flipping carefully through the hundreds of leather-bound classics from his well-kept bookshelves. At sixteen, I even started penning verse about "my private passions and silent sufferings"; indeed, had I been as religiously inclined as Princess Marya, I might well have taken up the study of Talmud, rather than Tolstoy.

"All happy families are alike," he writes in the famous opening sentence of *Anna Karenina*. "Each unhappy family is unhappy in its own way." So which kind was mine? I've often wondered, secretly hoping I belonged to the latter, more distinctive category.

Scouring my memory bank, I mentally tallied my grievances against my parents, siblings, even relatives. Hundreds of hours and tens of thousands of dollars of therapy later, I can say that the hurts were certainly there; nor do I mean to minimize their impact. But do they earn me membership in Tolstoy's unhappy-family category? I'm afraid not. Having recently become a father myself, I've gained firsthand exposure to the challenges of child-rearing, and, as a result, a deeper appreciation of the many subtle manifestations of my parents' love for me that once went unnoticed. In the years since I first ventured forth from my cocoonlike existence on Bear Lake, I have met folks from broken families in which terribly destructive things actually do occur—things that make my weeklong grounding for scratching a painting, or even those dreadful pummelings from my older brother, appear rather insignificant by comparison.

The Kaufmans, then, like the Bolkonskys, while far from perfect, were by Tolstoy's standards a fairly happy lot. As are nearly all the families in *War and Peace*, for that matter. Even as their world is imploding under the weight of external pressures, most of them stay together. The Bolkonskys have their share of problems, true, but given all the horrible things that can and do happen in the world—watching your capital burn to the ground, for instance, or having the one you love die at your side—putting up with an insufferable old father would surely seem a small price to pay for the deeper consolations that one's family alone may provide.

After her father's death, the newly liberated princess has a whole set of practical decisions to make. Does she stay or leave in advance of the invading French army? Should she free the peasants now rebelling? Things are chaotic, and she is terrified to step into a leadership role for which she is unprepared. Yet step into that position she must, and she finds guidance in the knowledge that she is acting not for herself, but on behalf of her father and brother. "Whatever they would have said, whatever they would have done now, she felt it necessary to do the same" (725).

Tolstoy's male chauvinism, many would suggest, is evident in this passage; and such an assessment would not be entirely baseless. Then again, very much in evidence, too, is his insight into the facts of life: with Russia in the throes of war, her peasants rebelling and human relationships hanging in the balance, the one thing the princess has to fall back on is her connection to her family roots. Surely this is something that those of us living through our own troubled times might relate to. National hardship at any time, really, allows fresh insight into the meaning of family. The general mood in this country after September 11, 2001, for example, may not have been unlike that in Russia following Napoleon's invasion; I know it affected me personally. For years I had prided myself on being my own man. Then the attacks happened. Coming home alone to my apartment in Los Angeles, or sitting on airplanes, wondering whether I'd even make it to my destination in one piece, I suddenly realized that being "my own man" wasn't so important to me anymore; I wanted to be somebody *else's* man: a husband, a father, a son, a brother. No longer did all those family traditions—all the Shabbat dinners, the handcrafted birthday cards—seem quite such . . . an imposition. In fact, I found a strange sense of comfort knowing that I was a member of what I'd always supposed must be the world's most annoying family.

The old world may be disintegrating in *War and Peace*, but a fresh one is emerging, in much the same way as a dying-out beehive, which, appearing lifeless and inert, has already begun to gestate new life forms: the essential work of pairing, pollination, and reproduction having been completed, the queen bee is already off reproducing her eggs elsewhere. The novel is full, in fact, of such biological metaphors, with a particular emphasis on bee propagation and bird behavior. Playing, no doubt, off the fact that the word for "family" in Russian (*sem'ia*) is nearly identical to the word for "seed" (*semia*), Tolstoy emphasizes that family is the indestructible seed that, no matter what else is happening in the world, continually renews itself by adhering to a set of laws as universal as the processes of nature itself.

We see this process of transformation at work in the Rostov home right around the time Princess Marya buries her father. Life by this point is dangerous and chaotic. Natasha wants to give up the carts to the wounded soldiers; her mother's refusal results in a family argument ultimately resolved by the demands of the moment. In the final hours before they leave their home, the sense of imminent danger ever more palpable, Natasha becomes a managerial force in the house, overseeing the packing and issuing a number of instructions that even other members of her family begin to heed. The role of mother hen protecting her own before the storm, comes naturally to her, but of course it has taken a situation of extreme duress to propel her all the way into it. "'The eggs . . . the eggs are teaching the hen . . .' [Count Rostov] said through happy tears, and he embraced his wife, [who, embarrassed by her earlier refusal to give up the carts,] was glad to hide her ashamed face on his chest" (862).

By the time she turns twenty, life has dealt Natasha enough blows to temper her erstwhile joie de vivre with a hardy realism. Given all she's been through, it is hardly surprising that she fails to exude her once-infectious charm; indeed, after getting married, she even starts letting herself go, to the disappointment of some of her former society acquaintances and, indeed, many readers. But while somebody like the beautiful seductress Hélène Kuragin may continue to prance about the continent in search of multiple husbands who might inject her cheerless life with shots of instant adoration, all Natasha really needs now is one good man, a point Tolstoy makes by means of a rather unusual metaphor:

> If the purpose of dinner is nourishment, and the purpose of marriage is the family, then the whole question is solved simply by not eating more than the stomach can digest and not having more wives and husbands than are needed for a family, that is, one of each. Natasha needed a husband. A husband was given her. And the husband

gave her a family. And not only did she see no need for another, better husband, but as all her inner forces were directed at serving this husband and family, she could not even imagine and saw no interest in imagining how it would be if it were different. (1156)

While it may be tempting, then, to order any number of the entrees on the menu so as not to miss out on anything, that indulgence in the short term will surely lead to nausea, and over time, to obesity, an epidemic as prevalent today as venereal disease was in Tolstoy's day. So, too, with family life, the writer says. There might be a hundred mouth-watering reasons to put an end to that whole messy business, and either go it alone or to try it out with some more enticing combination of individuals. But there is one very good reason to stick it out, or, at least, to resist the all-too-familiar urge to escape from the messiness of marriage in the vague hopes of finding "something better out there": because only by doing so—by placing real limitations on our rampant desires—may we feed the soul what it needs to survive and flourish.

Tolstoy with his granddaughter Tanyechka in 1909.

9

COURAGE

"What would you call brave?"

"Brave? Brave?" the captain repeated with the air of someone considering a question for the first time. "*A brave man*," he said after some thought, "*is one who behaves as he ought to do.*"

—"The Raid: A Volunteer's Story," 1852

I t wasn't exactly what you'd call the Summer of Love:

On the twelfth of June, [1812,] the forces of western Europe crossed the borders of Russia, and war began—that is, an event took place contrary to human reason and to the whole of human nature. Millions of people committed against each other such a countless number of villainies, deceptions, betrayals, thefts, forgeries and distributions of false banknotes, robberies, arson, and murder as the annals of all the law courts in the world could not assemble in whole centuries, and which, at that period of time, the people who committed them did not look upon as crimes. (603)

Yet amid descriptions of carnage, widespread burning and looting, and mass exodus from cities and villages, Tolstoy keeps readers' attention equally focused on the private lives of individual characters, some of whom find themselves committing the most unexpected and irrational acts of goodness. There's longtime Rostov family servant Mavra Kuzminishna, for instance, who gives a twenty-five-ruble note of her own to a stranger who shows up at the doorstep, saying he's a relative of the count's. Then there's that unnamed Russian soldier on the corner of Ilyanka Street who, in the mayhem of the Moscow evacuation, steps outside his assigned duties to help an unknown pimple-faced shopkeeper protect his store from looters. And let's not forget about that dark-eyed French soldier who helps rescue a three-year-old Russian girl separated from her parents amid the confusion. These are the random, uncelebrated acts of goodness that Tolstoy considered to be the real stories of heroism of that time—a lesson that Nikolai Rostov, whom we haven't seen since his return to the regiment a year ago, following his extended leave in Otradnoe, is about to learn for himself.

A beloved squadron commander, confident and secure in his position in the regiment, the twenty-seven-year-old Nikolai has been enjoying the pleasures of inactive duty for some time now. He has no intention of submitting to his parents' request that he come home once again to assist with family troubles, the most recent of which is Natasha's mysterious and protracted illness, following the elopement fiasco. Nikolai isn't about to leave the regiment at such a critical moment, only to get involved in that mess, not least because he never approved of the match between his sister and Prince Andrei in the first place.

Nevertheless, Nikolai can't help thinking more and more of autumn in Otradnoe, with its mushroom-picking and hunting expeditions; winter, with its Christmastime celebrations; and, of course, the heartening promise of Sonya's unwavering love. All of this "had opened up before him the prospect of quiet gentlemanly joys and a tranquility that he had not known before and which beckoned to him" (645). But "'I would consider myself dishonorable not only before all my comrades, but also before my own self,'" he writes to Sonya, "'if I were to prefer happiness to my duty and love for the fatherland. . . . Believe me, right after the war, if I am alive and you still love me, I will abandon everything and come flying to you, to press you forever to my ardent breast'" (645).

Doth the man not profess his love a bit too . . . forcefully? And might that not call attention to the possibility that Nikolai isn't perhaps quite as clear about his feelings for his cousin Sonya as he believes himself to be? His mother has been imploring him for some time to forget about his adolescent promise to the poor, dowerless Sonya, and fall in love instead with a rich woman, someone who might even help dig the Rostovs out of their mounting financial troubles. Despite her best intentions, Nikolai's mother certainly doesn't help to clarify matters for him.

Even regimental life isn't quite as simple as it once seemed. The young man who seven years ago bragged about his heroic exploits in the battle of Schöngrabern now listens with bemusement to the pompous tale of the double-mustached officer Zdrzhinsky about the recent exploits of General Raevsky, who, in a showy feat of supposed courage, has just led his two sons onto a dam under intense gunfire. This juicy story of valor is precisely the kind that Nikolai himself used to eat up as generously as he served it, but now hearing it only fills him with . . . shame.

Nikolai has seen enough of war to know that all such stories are distortions, if not outright fabrications of what really happens under fire. For one thing, he thinks to himself, battles are so chaotic that nobody but a few dozen men would have noticed Raevsky's sons, not to mention the fact that the fate of the fatherland hardly depended on taking that particular dam anyway. So what was the point of Raevsky offering up such a grossly disproportionate sacrifice? "'I wouldn't lead my brother Petya into it, or even Ilyin [a young officer Nikolai has been mentoring], a nice boy but a stranger to me; I'd try to find some safe place to put him'" (647).

Nikolai is starting to think less like a cocky young fighter than like his own father, who back in 1805 had similar concerns about his eldest son's departure for the front. And, like Count Rostov, who listened to Nikolai's silly patriotic outbursts with a clenched lip, Nikolai knows as well that Zdrzhinsky's story, drivel though it almost certainly is, "contributed to the glory of our arms, and therefore one had to make it seem that one did not doubt it" (647).

After a long July night of card playing and flirting with the plump German wife of the regiment doctor, Nikolai and his men receive news of a skirmish to take place the next morning in the nearby village of Ostrovna. The sun is just rising when they arrive at the battle site, where columns of French and Russian troops are already lined up, and the crackling of lazily exchanged gunfire can be heard. Later, as the battle begins to heat up, with bullets whizzing and whining past him, Nikolai can barely contain his joy. "[W]ith his keen hunter's eye," he spots French dragoons pursuing the Russian hussars, and watches "what was happening before him as if it was a hunting scene" (652). And with his hunter's intuition, he knows that the moment to strike the unsuspecting French dragoons is now or never:

> "Andrei Sevastyanych," said Nikolai, "you know, we could crush them…"
> "It would be a daring thing," said the captain, "and in fact . . ." (653)

But Nikolai cuts the conversation short, spurs his horse, and charges. As the bullets whistle stirringly past him, that old, familiar thrill of the kill takes over. "He did it all as he did at the hunt, not thinking, not reflecting" (653). Nikolai gives free rein to his horse, and as soon as the disordered clump of French troops suddenly shifts directions and gallops away, he picks one out for himself and bears down on his target. As his own mount slams into the rump of the gray horse carrying his intended prey, Nikolai, "not knowing why himself, raised his saber and struck the Frenchman with it" (653). The Frenchman falls to the ground, not so much from the saber blow as from the equine collision and the horrors of the moment. Eagerly looking "to see whom he had vanquished" (653), Nikolai does something he's never done before in battle. He stops. He looks. And this is what he sees:

Narrowing his eyes fearfully, as if expecting a new blow any second, [the French officer] winced, glancing up at Nikolai from below with an expression of terror. His face, pale and mud-spattered, fair-haired, young, with a dimple on the chin and light blue eyes, was not at all for the battlefield, not an enemy's face, but a most simple, homelike face. (653)

What Nikolai sees, in other words, is a human being: a boy in his teens—the very same age as his own brother Petya, in fact, the same age as his protégé Ilyin.

On any other occasion, Nikolai would have been overjoyed by what happens next: Summoned by his commander, he is instructed that, rather than being punished for having attacked without being given orders to do so, he is to be recommended to the tsar for the St. George Cross. But something keeps troubling him. "'Ilyin? No, he's safe. Did I disgrace myself somehow? No, it's not that!' Something else tormented him, something like remorse. 'Yes, yes, that French officer with the dimple. And I remember how my arm stopped as I raised it'" (654).

This nervy hussar who once blurted out at the dinner table that "'the Russians must either die or conquer'" (64) has suddenly discovered yet another possibility he never considered before: that Russians can also feel compassion toward their enemies—a sense of charity that may well up every bit as powerfully and as suddenly as the instinct, in the heat of battle, to kill. Had Nikolai almost anticipated this sense of compassionate regret? He only grazed the young Frenchman, after all, where, had he plunged the saber in him with full force, he certainly would have killed him. For two days Nikolai is silent and pensive,

> thinking about that brilliant feat of his, which, to his surprise, had gained him the St. George Cross and even given him the reputation of a brave man—and there was something in that he was unable to understand. "So they're even more afraid than we are!" he thought. "So that's all there is to so-called heroism? And did I really do it for the fatherland? And what harm had he done, with his dimple and

his light blue eyes? But how frightened he was! He thought I'd kill him. Why should I kill him? My hand faltered. And they gave me the St. George Cross. I understand nothing, nothing!" (654)

But *we* understand perfectly well: his cherished ideas about what it means to be a hero, to defend the fatherland, to kill another person in battle, have just received a fatal blow. Nikolai has gone through similar moments of disillusionment before, of course—after being chided for calling out the purse thief Telyanin in front of other officers, for instance, or while nursing his wounds around the campfire after the battle of Schöngrabern, or while witnessing the disheartening treaty signing between Alexander and Napoleon in Tilsit. But if at Tilsit Nikolai buried his disappointment beneath drunken fist pounding on the canteen table, roaring at his comrades, "'Our business is to do our duty, to cut and slash, not to think, that's all'" (417), now, some five years later, he understands that there are also times when soldiers should refrain from cutting and slashing, take a moment to consider their actions—perhaps even make a split-second decision not to act at all. And that, for Nikolai, is a new paradigm altogether.

In the essay "Why Do Men Stupefy Themselves?," published in 1890 as a preface to a book, *Drunkenness*, Tolstoy wrote:

[T]rue life begins where the tiny bit begins—where what seem to us minute and infinitely small alterations take place. True life is not lived where great external changes take place—where people move about, clash, fight, and slay one another—it is lived only where these tiny, tiny, infinitesimally small changes occur.

The fact that Tolstoy offers this wisdom in an essay about addiction is significant. For the strength one needs to overcome addiction is most clearly exhibited at the first moment of desire for the cigarette or the bottle. If you don't resist in that second, you've had it. If Nikolai is something of a battle junkie, he overcomes his addiction to battlefield highs in the very second that he hesitates before plunging his saber into the chest of the young, dimple-chinned Frenchman. *That*, Tolstoy says, not the martial action it follows, is where courage resides. It is a pivotal step on the character's journey of transformation from young heroism addict to authentically heroic human being. The man who used to think that to be courageous meant slaying Frenchmen in battle as unthinkingly as one might slay wolves on a hunt now realizes that compassion and self-restraint may be braver still.

So is Nikolai transforming into some kind of Christian moralist, a pacifist of the sort Tolstoy himself became in his later years? Not at all. Far from losing his responsiveness to life's vital energies, Nikolai is actually gaining the capacity to channel them in richer and more nuanced ways than before. The difference between the battle at Ostrovna and the exhilaration he feels on the wolf hunt, for instance, or the ecstasy he experiences while listening to Natasha sing, is that Nikolai is now able to *choose* his response to those vital forces washing over him. In the singing scene, this happens only after the fact, when he settles back into reality and must decide how he's going to tell his father about what's happened. While in the hunting scene it occurs after the hunt is over and he is able to reflect calmly on the events of the day. In this scene, however, Nikolai chooses within the heat of battle, at the very moment when the thrill of the kill would seem to have him in its grip. He both feels the wild energy to which he's so well attuned and harnesses it toward constructive, life-affirming ends.

Theologian Paul Tillich, writing in the mid-twentieth century, identifies this sort of integration of vitality with morality as one of the hallmarks of genuine courage. "Pure vitality in man," writes Tillich in his celebrated *The Courage to Be* (1952), "is never pure but always distorted, because man's power of life is his freedom and the spirituality in which vitality and intentionality are united." But this sort of courage is rare—and never more so than during troubled times—as Tillich well knew. Living in Nazi Germany until he was extradited for his opposition to the regime in 1933, Tillich was intimately familiar with the ways in which pure vitality "can, if used by demagogues, produce the barbaric ideal of courage." No stranger to demagoguery himself, Tolstoy gives us plenty of examples of this phenomenon in *War and Peace*.

We might compare Nikolai's reaction to the blue-eyed French youth, for example, to Moscow governor Rostopchin's treatment of the adolescent Russian political prisoner Vereshchagin a few weeks later. Vereshchagin is accused of disseminating pro-French pamphlets. Afraid that he might be losing control of his city and enraged that the decision to abandon the Russian capital was made without his consent, Rostopchin vents his frustration by inciting the crowd to beat Vereshchagin to death: "'Beat him! . . . Let the traitor perish and not disgrace the Russian name!' Rostopchin began shouting. 'Cut him down! I order it!'" (889) The crowd, only too ready to oblige, roars wildly, kills the youth, and closes in over the bloody corpse. Rostopchin, chilled by the realization of what he's just done, escapes by carriage, and makes a point of comforting himself with the thought that he did it for *le bien public*, "the public good" (893). This is, of course, nonsense, for he acted out of desperation, his will not just blocked but seemingly threatened. Yet in his frenzied attempt to maintain his grip on his rapidly dwindling power, Rostopchin gives up the one power he actually does have: to choose good on the spur of the moment rather than evil. And that is a power Nikolai Rostov, even in the heat of battle, does not relinquish.

A month after Ostrovna, just before the battle of Borodino, Nikolai is out for a ride not far from enemy lines, along with his orderly Lavrushka and Ilyin. Being a thoughtful squadron commander, Nikolai wants to take advantage of this brief window of opportunity before the French close in; he hopes to find provisions and maybe even some pretty girls for his ragged troops. But the outing unexpectedly becomes a mission of a very different sort when the swashbuckling military men happen upon the country estate of a wealthy aristocratic family in the town of Bogucharovo. There they find a terrified princess whose father has just died, and whose agitated peasants, wrongly believing that their mistress intends to abandon them to the French, have unharnessed her horses and refused to let her leave the estate. Little does Nikolai know that this estate belongs to the late Prince Bolkonsky, and that the woman being held against her will is none other than Princess Marya Bolkonskaya, sister of Natasha's former fiancé, Prince Andrei.

"Yeah, right!" exclaims one student, skeptical of this unlikely encounter.

"Give me a break," chimes another.

"Ah, ye of little faith!" I respond. "I mean, synchronicities like this *do* happen now and then, don't they? You're going about your life, and you run into a friend of a friend of a friend you haven't seen for a long time, or you have a wildly unexpected encounter that has the potential to change the very course of your life. You may not know this at the time, of course, so the real question then becomes: How are you responding to each of these moments *as* they arise?"

Well, here's how Nikolai responds. As soon as he registers the seriousness of the situation, he dismounts and bolts down the road to the manor house in order to check up on the princess, who, upon seeing his familiar Russian face and recognizing in him a man of her own circle, looks at her savior "with her deep, luminous gaze" that touches Nikolai (733). He immediately imagines something romantic in this strange encounter: "'A defenseless, grief-stricken girl, alone, left to the mercy of coarse, mutinous muzhiks [peasants]! And what a strange fate has pushed me to come here!' thought Nikolai, listening to her and looking at her. 'And what meekness, what nobility in her features and expressions!' he thought, listening to her timid account" (733).

His reaction is sure to evoke a smile in the reader. But should that smile cross over into an ironic, cynical smirk, as I have seen often enough, then the reader, well, has missed Tolstoy's point entirely. "[D]o heroes see themselves acting as heroes?" wonders one slightly skeptical Slavic scholar about this scene. "[Nikolai's] very self-consciousness carries with it something of the parodic." Maybe so, yet whatever romantic explanation Nikolai might attempt to superimpose on his strange encounter with Princess Marya is less important to Tolstoy than his (and *our*) ability to recognize the power of the moment itself. The fact is, there is indeed something providential going on here, as we shall soon discover, and the sympathy each of these people feels for the other isn't just romantic fluff. It's quite real—as real, in fact, as the deep, luminous gaze that makes Nikolai forget the plainness of Marya's face, or the tears that well up in his own eyes as soon as he learns that all of this has befallen the princess the day after her father's death:

> "I cannot express to you, Princess, how happy I am that I have come here accidentally and will be in a position to show you my readiness," Nikolai said, getting up. "Go, please, and I will answer to you on my honor that not a single person will dare cause you any trouble, if only you will allow me to escort you," and bowing respectfully, as one bows to a lady of royal blood, he went to the door. (733)

A bit over the top? Okay, sure. But the most interesting thing about this courtly encounter is how genuine the refinement in behavior actually *is*. In contrast to the aristocratic niceties, those less-than-sincere expressions of noblesse oblige thrown about by other high-society characters in so many of the novel's drawing-room scenes, Nikolai's fine sentiments here are *fine* indeed, and entirely genuine. By his respectful tone he communicates to Marya that, fortunate as he may consider himself to have made her acquaintance, he has no intention of exploiting her misfortune to become closer to her. Yet closeness, much to his own surprise, is exactly what he feels.

Leaving Marya, he heads back to the village, where he spends all of a millisecond debating his course of action. His first order of business is to find out who the headman of Princess Marya's estate is. When the peasant Karp brazenly questions why Nikolai needs to know this, Nikolai responds with a right hook to Karp's jaw, sending the peasant's head flying sideways. His rage now at full throttle, Nikolai has the bruised and humbled peasant bound, an order that two other peasants are only too ready to oblige, removing their own belts in order to assist. Only then does the headman Dron finally step forward out of the crowd, his face pale and frowning. Suddenly, seeing the error of their ways, the peasants return to their homes; the rebellion is over. An hour later, they're back at work, cheerfully loading their masters' belongings onto carts. So what just happened?

It's possible of course that the peasants were just bluffing. But it is equally likely that they recognize in Nikolai someone not unlike their deceased master, the old Prince Bolkonsky, who, for all his faults, possessed both firm resolve and moral clarity, two qualities badly needed in this chaotic time. Whatever their motivations, Nikolai manages to convince the peasants that with the enemy approaching, maybe now isn't the best time to hold hostage their irreproachable and well-meaning mistress, who has just lost her father and is about to lose everything else if they all don't get the hell out of there, and fast. Even before Nikolai's fists start rolling, the head steward Alpatych and the other peasants sense that, whatever he's about to do, it's going to work:

> Without considering what he was going to do, unconsciously, at a quick, resolute pace, he moved towards the crowd. And the closer he came to it, the more Alpatych felt that his unreasonable action might produce good results. The muzhiks [peasants] in the crowd had the same feeling, looking at his quick and firm stride and resolute, frowning face. (734)

Nikolai isn't thinking about being a hero or savior, or even about what might come of his actions. He simply sees a young woman who needs help and a situation that needs to be rectified, and, putting his self-interest and fears aside, responds appropriately. These actions prove effective in a way that Tolstoy believed only uncalculated and spontaneous activity *can* be: "Only unconscious activity bears fruit," Tolstoy writes a little bit later in the novel, "and a man who plays a role in an historical event never understands its significance. If he attempts to understand it, he is struck with fruitlessness" (944).

If Nikolai's split-second decision not to act on the battlefield of Ostrovna, then, like his decision *to* act in Bogucharovo, is more effective and courageous than nearly anything else he's done up to that point in the novel, it is precisely because he's no longer trying to behave like the Hero. Which is precisely how any of us may be one. A hero in Tolstoy's estimation is, more often than not, just an ordinary person who finds himself doing the extraordinary things demanded by the circumstances he happens to *be* in.

For a number of veterans of the war of 1812, this notion of heroism wasn't, well, heroic enough. Prince Pyotr Vyazemsky, an influential cultural figure in the 1860s and a soldier in 1812, accused the author of *War and Peace* of being a nihilist, one of those "killers of history." He and other veterans found the novel downright blasphemous in the way it lampoons the leaders of the Russian military operation, includes trivial and unnecessary details about officers' daily lives, and depicts the war of 1812 as one giant conglomeration of circumstances beyond human planning or comprehension. Avraam Norov, a philologist and church historian in the 1860s who lost a leg as a young officer at Borodino, was particularly offended by Tolstoy's portrait of Commander in Chief Kutuzov, who, on the eve of the battle of Borodino, immerses himself in a cheap French novel:

> Before and after Borodino, all of us, from Kutuzov down to the last artillery lieutenant, like myself, burned with the same lofty and sacred fire of patriotism. We regarded our calling as some kind of a religious rite. I do not know how comrades-in-arms would treat someone who would have among his belongings a book for light-reading, especially a French one, such as a novel by Madame de Genlis.

Contemporary critic Nikolai Strakhov begged to differ, arguing that Tolstoy's depiction of Russian heroism is, in fact, *more* inspiring than that of any number of soon-to-be forgotten "patriotic" writers of the time, because Tolstoy manages to create real characters, with real flaws, whom every reader can recognize, yet who nonetheless exhibit the "spark of heroism" in the most unlikely circumstances. Far from denigrating the strength and nobility of the Russian spirit, then, Tolstoy's unflinching realism actually permits those qualities to "appear before us all the more powerfully and all the more truthfully."

Needless to say, I'm with Strakhov, and would suggest that Nikolai's actions at Bogucharovo are a good illustration of the point he is making. Clearly, Nikolai has some serious anger management issues, with a leadership style that isn't apt to win him many friends. And yet he *does* manage to influence people, at a time in history when many of the most famous and celebrated Russian leaders, according to Tolstoy, have revealed themselves to be as arrogant as they are ineffective. Maybe, then, in order to be a Russian patriot, it isn't really necessary to burn with the sacred fire of patriotism, to regard one's soldierly duty as a kind of religious rite, or even to forgo the pleasures of light French novels on the eve of an important battle; perhaps it's enough to be fully present to what is happening around you, and to respond with quiet strength and commitment to doing what's *right*. Nikolai used to talk a lot about things like honor and duty and the fatherland, and always came off sounding pretty immature and self-righteous. Whereas at Bogucharovo he doesn't do a lot of talking. He simply acts—bad temper, loose fists, and all—and winds up saving the life of the woman who will become his wife: an instance of unconscious activity that will quite literally bear fruit.

About a week after the episode at Bogucharovo, Nikolai is sent to Voronezh in order to remount the division. There he enjoys his status as mini-celebrity among the locals, and isn't above a little inappropriate flirting with the sweet-looking, blue-eyed wife of a provincial official. Nikolai, in other words, is just being Nikolai. But guess who happens to be in Voronezh staying with her aunt at that very moment? Bingo.

When the governor's wife offers to arrange a meeting between the dashing squadron commander and the princess he recently saved, Nikolai for some reason feels compelled to pour his heart out to this complete stranger. Confiding in her as he might in his own mother, he lets the self-designated matchmaker know that he has indeed taken a fancy to the princess, but could never marry her because of his long-standing promise to Sonya. Later on, he'll berate himself for that "stupid whimsy" of a confession, and yet, as he will eventually come to understand, "this impulse of unprovoked candor, along with other small events, had enormous consequences for him and for the whole family" (949). To begin with, it provokes a strong reaction from the governor's wife:

> "*Mon cher, mon cher*, how can you reason that way? Sophie [Sonya] has nothing, and you said yourself that your father's affairs are in disorder. And your *maman*? It will kill her, for one thing. Then Sophie, if she's a girl with a heart, what sort of life will it be for her? The mother in despair, affairs in disorder . . . No, *mon cher*, you and Sophie ought to understand that."
>
> Nikolai was silent. It was pleasant for him to hear these conclusions. (950)

An odd reaction from a guy who's had more than a few screaming matches with his mother on this very subject. But that was before the events of 1812, before Bogucharovo. The world is rapidly changing, and so is Nikolai. The remonstrations of the governor's wife serve only to reinforce his growing intuition that there is something as faulty about his plans to marry Sonya as there is something inexplicably right about the closeness he feels toward Marya.

These realizations, dawning upon him during the several-weeks stay of his in Voronezh, become strikingly clear when he sees the princess praying during a church service in honor of the Russian troops. "[W]ithout asking himself whether or not it would be good or proper for him to address her there in church," Nikolai strides up to Marya and expresses his sincere sympathy for her grief over her brother Andrei, about whose shrapnel wounds she only recently learned from the newspapers (954). And as Nikolai studies "[t]hat pale, fine, sorrowful face, that luminous gaze, those quiet, graceful movements, and above all that deep and tender sorrow which showed

in all her features," he is moved by the presence of a spiritual life
utterly foreign to him, yet weirdly irresistible (955). Marya illuminates impulses within him he never knew he had, and shines a fresh
light onto old truths he thought were settled:

> With Sonya he had already made up a future picture, and it was
> all simple and clear, precisely because it was all invented, and he
> knew everything there was in Sonya; but with Princess Marya it
> was impossible for him to picture a future life, because he did not
> understand her, but only loved her.
>
> Dreams about Sonya had something gay and toylike about
> them. But to think about Princess Marya was always difficult and a
> little frightening. (955)

Moved by his encounter with Marya at church, Nikolai returns to
his quarters in Voronezh and does something we've seen him do on
just one other occasion in the novel: he prays, only this time not for
a wolf to come his way, but for a resolution to the agonizing predicament in which he currently finds himself. "'What do I want? Freedom,
release from Sonya. . . . No, I don't love her as I should. My God! Lead
me out of this terrible, hopeless situation!'" (955) At this moment his
orderly Lavrushka comes barging in and hands him some mail, among
which happens to be a letter from Sonya granting Nikolai the very
freedom for which he was just praying! So astonished by the speediness
with which God has answered his prayer, the flabbergasted Nikolai
suspects that it must not have been the hand of God at all, but a matter of mere chance.

Well, which is it?

In the very next chapter Tolstoy reveals the circumstances under
which Sonya wrote that letter: Traveling with the Rostovs during their
evacuation, she has been receiving ever more pressure from the countess to show her respect for the family that brought her up by releasing
poor Nikolai from his obligation. Utterly crushed, Sonya nevertheless
finds some solace in the fact that Prince Andrei's health appears to be

his relations with Natasha rekindling. For if the two ~~~ their engagement and getting married, Sonya calcu- ~vent Marya from marrying Nikolai, about whose ... Sonya has just learned from Nikolai's most recent letter. (At that time marriage between a brother-in-law and sister-in-law was forbidden by the Russian Orthodox Church.) And so, "with tears in her eyes and a joyful awareness of performing a magnanimous act, she wrote, interrupted several times by the tears that clouded her velvety black eyes, that touching letter, the reception of which so struck Niko-lai" (960). It's moments like this that make it, well, difficult to like Sonya. But the fact is, in spite of herself, she has unintentionally done a good thing. Her calculations about Andrei's health will turn out to be wrong, just as by writing that less than entirely ingenuous letter, she manages to bring Nikolai and Marya even closer together. "[O]wing to this letter," Tolstoy writes, "Nikolai and the princess were suddenly brought together in almost familial relations" (956).

A chance here, a chance there, and pretty soon things are starting to look a lot like destiny, aren't they? What's important, though, is how Nikolai has been responding to all those chances every step of the way. Had he not done what he did in Bogucharovo, not blurted out his feelings about Marya to the governor's wife, not gone up to Marya in church, not been honest with himself during prayer about how he really feels about Sonya, it's quite likely the concatenation of random occurrences might have remained just that: entirely random. Fate, Tolstoy has it, is what happens to us; destiny is what we do with it. By remaining open to life, then, by responding authentically and fully in every instance, Nikolai has been slowly transforming all of those instances of raw chance into, yes, destiny.

Tolstoy develops this idea more abstractly in the second epilogue, where he distinguishes the concept of freedom (*svoboda*) from that of will (*volya*). Freedom, he argues, is an illusion; our lives are inevitably dependent on a multitude of forces beyond our control or comprehension. We can, however, choose how we assert our will in each moment, and in so doing, unconsciously bring into being the larger, hidden design of which our lives are part. "Man lives consciously for him self," Tolstoy writes, "but serves as an unconscious instrument for the achievement of historical, universally human goals" (605).

For Tolstoy's nineteenth-century audience, taken by hero worship of all stripes, this was a rather unusual reframing of the concept of courage. But, then, there wasn't anything typical about the way Russians defeated the French in 1812. Just as Nikolai, harnessing the swirling forces of change all around him, manifests his personal destiny moment by moment, so, too, Russia, absorbing blow after blow of an invading army, redirects that invasive energy to its own advantage. This rather backward sort of strength, so unlike the inflexible aggressiveness of their European foe, is precisely what allows Russia not only to defeat the French, but to transform the turmoil of 1812 into a moment of national self-awakening. Something rather similar happens with Nikolai, who comes to exhibit a unique sort of courage he never could have envisioned at the beginning of the book.

Nikolai meets Marya once again, more than a year later, in Moscow. Affairs in the Rostov family, in the winter of 1813, are now dire, and Nikolai is revolted by the thought of marrying a rich heiress, as his family has been pressuring him to do. So, when Marya calls on him at the small apartment the Rostovs have now been forced to rent, Nikolai is understandably embarrassed, distant, even cold. Marya leaves, convinced that she never really liked Nikolai in the first place. But another wiser, more intuitive voice deep within her suggests Nikolai is hiding something. A month and a half later, in the middle of winter, Nikolai calls on her again, initially carrying himself with what seems that same cold demeanor. But then something happens. Try as he might to hide behind whatever self-protective postures, the truth about his feelings suddenly breaks through in a moment of poignant, quintessentially Tolstoyan dialogue worth quoting in full. It is Princess Marya who speaks first here:

> "I had become so close to you . . . and to your family, and I thought you would not consider my sympathy misplaced; but I

" she said. Her voice suddenly quavered. "I don't
went on, having composed herself, "you were dif-
..."

are a thousand reasons *why*" (he placed special emphasis
on the word *why*). "Thank you, Princess," he said softly. "It's sometimes hard."

"So that's why! That's why!" an inner voice was saying in Princess Marya's soul. "No, it wasn't only that cheerful, kind, and open
gaze, not only that handsome appearance that I loved in him; I
guessed at his noble, firm, self-sacrificing soul," she said to herself.
"Yes, he's poor now, and I'm rich . . . Yes, it's only because of that . . .
Yes, if it weren't for that . . ." And, recalling his former tenderness
and looking now at his kind and sad face, she suddenly understood
the reason for his coldness.

"But why, Count, why?" she suddenly almost cried out involuntarily, moving towards him. "Why, tell me? You must tell me." He
was silent. "I don't know your *why*, Count," she went on. "But it's
hard for me, it's . . . I'll confess it to you. You want for some reason
to deprive me of your former friendship. And that pains me." There
were tears in her eyes and in her voice. "There has been so little happiness in my life that every loss is hard for me . . . Forgive me, good-
bye." She suddenly began to weep and started out of the room.

"Princess, wait, for God's sake!" he cried, trying to stop her.
"Princess!"

She glanced back. For a few seconds they looked silently into
each other's eyes, and the distant and impossible suddenly became
near, possible, and inevitable. . . . (1143–44)

What if Nikolai had held on to his pride? What if Marya hadn't
taken the risk of making herself vulnerable? By transcending their
fears, both characters manage to reverse the outcome of a moment
rapidly fading away. And their courage goes even deeper than this. In
order for this moment to turn out the way it does, both Nikolai and
Marya have to be ready to move beyond their former preconceptions

to embrace new possibilities for their lives. Marya now realizes that she has the opportunity to lead precisely the spiritually rich sort of life she's always cherished, without forgoing the more mundane pleasures of marriage and family life. Nikolai, for his part, discovers that he can do his duty to his financially strapped family *and* marry the woman he truly loves, that he can be both a man of honor *and* a man who remains true to his own wants and needs. Imagine that! Before the events of 1812, he himself most surely would not have been able to.

Even after his marriage to Marya and the death of his father, Nikolai will make yet another of his seemingly impetuous decisions when he disregards the counsel of some of his friends and relations who urge him to renounce his deceased father's estate, as it will saddle him with unbearable debt. Yet bear that debt is exactly what he does, raising the necessary funds by taking a post in the civil service and borrowing money where he can. For the fiercely proud and independent Nikolai, these actions would have seemed as likely as begging for alms in the street. But by swallowing his aristocratic pride—by being one of the very sort of sellout "diplomats" he has always professed to abhor—Nikolai paradoxically shows himself to be the very aristocrat he has always wanted to be. He soon grows into an effective estate manager, and within three years amasses enough money not only to pay back all of his father's debts, but to acquire another small estate, as well. It is precisely Nikolai's newfound mix of pragmatism, then, *combined* with what remains of his youthful impulsiveness, that allows him to achieve the dream he has cherished since childhood—to be a *man*:

> And—it must have been because Nikolai did not allow himself the thought that he was doing anything for others out of virtuousness—all that he did was fruitful: his fortune quickly increased; neighboring muzhiks came asking him to buy them; and long after his death, the pious memory of his management was preserved among the people. "He was a master . . . The muzhiks' affairs first, and then his own. But he never went easy on us. In short—a master!" (1146)

"The ancients," Tolstoy writes, "left us examples of heroic poems in which heroes constitute the entire interest of history, and we still cannot get used to the fact that, for our human time, history of this sort has no meaning" (754). What kind of history does have meaning, then? The sort Tolstoy models for us in *War and Peace*, in which courage isn't a gift from the gods to a chosen few, but can manifest itself in any person, anytime, anywhere. This view actually places more of a burden of responsibility on each one of us, rather than less, for it says: No matter what army has invaded our country, what sorts of brutality surround us, what fears and doubts may beset us, we nevertheless retain the choice either to hide our heads, ostrichlike, in the wild, shifting sands of change, or else strive to build small sandcastles of goodness and meaning on whatever tiny plot of land we happen to find ourselves.

10

DEATH

The closer we come to death, or rather, the more vividly we remember it . . . the more important becomes this single indispensable thing called life.

—Tolstoy's letter to Vladimir Chertkov, August 1910

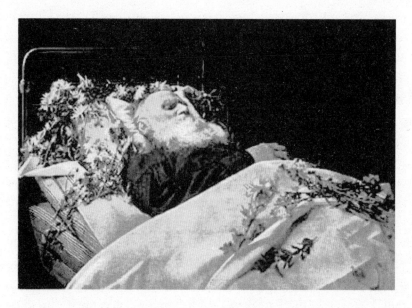

Tolstoy on his deathbed, Astapovo train station, 1910.

F   ew subjects are more integral to Tolstoy's writing than death. It
     flows from the writer's pen like an uncorked bottle of Russian
vodka—depicted in every imaginable flavor, texture, and color.
Whether a slow death in the bedroom or a sudden one on the battlefield,
an ignominious death by suicide or state-sponsored death through
public execution, dying is a topic on which he dwells attentively and
with no small fascination. But then, Tolstoy had considerable personal
experience with mortality. He'd lost both parents by the age of nine. He
witnessed wartime slaughter while serving as a soldier in the Caucasus
and in the Crimea. In 1856 his brother Dmitry died of consumption,
and in 1860 another brother, Nikolai, died of the same disease. For
weeks after his soul-wrenching panic attack during that land-buying
trip in 1869, Tolstoy was himself on the verge of suicide. He lost five
of his young children either to disease or complications in childbirth.
In fact, after the death of one of them, Petya, in 1873, he fled his estate
for Moscow out of fear that he, too, might catch death as one would a
cold. Given all his familiarity with the topic, can it be any wonder that
Tolstoy penned what is surely the most bloodcurdling death journey
in world literature? There is a reason Tolstoy's *The Death of Ivan Ilyich*
(1886) is still read in medical schools today, where it teaches doctors
in training exactly what dying looks, smells, and feels like, in all its
grim detail.

Yet this writer who affirmed in *What I Believe* (1884) that "death,
death, death, attends us every second" found it extremely difficult to
deal with the reality of death in his own life. "Yesterday a soldier was
found hanged in the Zaseka wood," he wrote years earlier in his diary
in 1856, at twenty-seven, "and I rode round to have a look at him."
Not before taking time to muse about the prettiness of the forester's

wife, however, or seriously considering whether to order a soldier to bring him an attractive young woman. A few weeks later, awakening to the news that a peasant had drowned in his pond, the count was in no rush to respond: "Two hours have gone by and I've done nothing about it."

Stranger still is his response to the news in 1856 that his brother Dmitry was dying. "I was particularly loathsome at the time," Tolstoy would later write in his *Recollections*. "I had come from Petersburg, where I was very active in society, and I was bursting with conceit! I felt sorry for [Dmitry], but not very. I simply put in an appearance at Orel and left immediately." He even admits to being rather annoyed that the whole affair made him miss a performance at Court to which he'd been invited. Three weeks later he received the news that Dmitry had died. He didn't go to the funeral, however, because of a prior social commitment.

Four years later Tolstoy had another chance to get it right when he learned that another brother, Nikolai, lay dying in Soden, Germany. On this occasion he did manage to pull himself away from his travels through Europe long enough to accompany his brother and their sister Marya and her three children to the south of France, where Nikolai died a month later. "Terrible though it is," Tolstoy wrote to his surviving brother Sergei, "I am glad it all happened before my eyes and affected me as it should have done. It is not like the death of [Dmitry], which I learned of at a time when my mind was completely taken up with other things." Still, as Tolstoy would admit in a long, heartfelt letter to his friend Afanasy Fet, Nikolai's death shook him to the core:

> Nothing in life has made such an impression on me. [Nikolai] was telling the truth when he said there is nothing worse than death. And if you really think that death is after all the end of everything, then there's nothing worse than life either. What's the point of struggling and trying, if nothing remains of what used to be [Nikolai] Tolstoy? . . . What's the point of everything, when tomorrow the torments of death will begin, with all the abomina-

tion of meanness, lies, and self-deceit, and end in nothingness, in the annihilation of the self. An amusing trick! Be useful, be virtuous, be happy while you're alive, people have said to each other for centuries—we as well—and happiness and virtue and usefulness are truth; but the truth that I've taken away from my 32 years is that the situation in which someone has placed us is the most terrible fraud and crime for which words have failed us. . . . So that when you see it clearly and truly, you come to, and say with horror like my brother: "What does it all mean?"

Tolstoy with his brothers in 1854. From left: Sergei, Nikolai, Dmitry, Tolstoy on far right.

What does it all mean? Now, *there's* a question Tolstoy would certainly return to over and over again throughout his lifetime. "Why should I live?" the writer would ask, some two decades later, in his *Confession.* "Why should I wish for anything or do anything? Or to put it still differently: Is there any meaning in my life that will not be destroyed by my inevitably approaching death?" One of his most earnest attempts to answer these questions came in the tract "On Life," the essay that would have such a profound effect on the young Ernest Crosby. Written in 1887, when Tolstoy was nearly sixty, the work argues that death as we know and fear it doesn't actually exist; we only *think* it does, because we have the wrong view of reality. Most of us take as real those things we can see and touch, including our own physical selves. But true life, he argues, begins when we acknowledge our connection to an eternal spiritual whole, which existed long before we arrived in this world and will exist long after we're gone. If we don't voluntarily accept this more accurate view of reality, then it will be forced upon us surely enough at the time of our physical death, at which too-late point it is certain to cause us unnecessary suffering. Only "by renouncing what is perishing and must perish—that is to say, our animal personality—can we obtain our true life which does not and cannot perish."

Yet surely this exceptionally vital man who fathered thirteen children—who on multiple occasions in his sixties and seventies trekked 125 miles by foot from Moscow to Yasnaya Polyana, who rode horseback in his eighties, who tossed his grandchildren up in the air and then caught them with one hand—surely this man didn't really believe that the body was an illusion, did he? Surely this writer who with his own eyes saw corpses lying in blood-drenched battlefields, watched a brother die in his arms, and described death as vividly as anyone ever managed to—surely he did not believe that death is a mere figment of an unenlightened imagination?

The writer Maxim Gorky, for one, wasn't buying these arguments, and went so far as to accuse the bearded sage of not a little hypocrisy. "Although I admire him," the young Gorky wrote, "I do not like him. He is exaggeratedly preoccupied, he sees nothing and knows nothing outside himself. . . . He lowers himself in my eyes by his fear of death and his pitiful flirtation with it; as a rabid individualist, it gives him a sort of illusion of immortality." Gorky's characteristically incisive remarks expose an aspect of Tolstoy's personality that has long troubled even his most ardent admirers, myself included: the nearly pathological obsession with death that seems as out of step with his exceedingly vital nature as it does with the selflessly life-affirming message of his greatest novel.

But then, maybe there's not such a contradiction, after all. For pretty much his whole life, Tolstoy had searched for a justification of life in the face of death—for a way of living, in other words, "so that death cannot destroy our life," as he puts it in *What I Believe*. Yet if the later sage achieves this goal simply by rendering death irrelevant, then the author of *War and Peace*, struggling with the same issues decades earlier, takes a different approach: he urges us to fully embrace our finitude, precisely in order to enhance our engagement with the things of this world, and to deepen our appreciation of the short time we've been allotted in it. In *War and Peace*, nothing lights a fire in a person's belly more than an awareness that one day in the not-too-distant future that belly will be filled not with caviar and cream puffs, but maggots and dirt. Not only do things of this world inevitably start looking and smelling and tasting better, but some characters learn to start living as *if* they were dying, which, as Tolstoy reminds us, we all are, however slowly, every minute of every day.

Early in the novel, when young Nikolai Rostov believes he is about to be popped off by attacking French soldiers, his first thought is about what a nice thing it is to be alive. He looks upon the glistening blue waters of the Danube, the glorious sky, the pine forests bathed in mist, and is suddenly struck by

> [h]ow good the sky seemed, how blue, calm, and deep! How bright and solemn the setting sun! How tenderly and lustrously glistened the waters of the distant Danube! [. . .] And his fear of death and the stretcher, and his love of the sun and life—all merged into one painfully disturbing impression. (148)

Hundreds of pages later, at the battle of Borodino, the usually aloof Prince Andrei discovers that even reeking wormwood smells pretty good when your head is about to be lopped off by an exploding grenade:

"Can this be death?" thought Prince Andrei, gazing with completely new, envious eyes at the grass, at the wormwood, and at the little stream of smoke curling up from the spinning black ball. "I can't, I don't want to die, I love life, I love this grass, the earth, the air..." (810–11)

Are you noticing a pattern? Were the author of *War and Peace* alive today, he might be grateful enough for advanced methods of dampening the physical pain of dying, but we can safely guess that he wouldn't be jumping on the cryonics bandwagon. Because when you take away a human being's consciousness of dying, you also take away his capacity for *living*. The problem, Tolstoy would say, is that most of us don't do either one particularly well.

In my classes and workshops about *The Death of Ivan Ilyich* I ask participants to imagine that they have six months to live: How would they spend their time? Most participants find it all but impossible to respond honestly. Many just nervously giggle or tune out entirely, while not a few say what they think someone with six months to live would or *should* say. For the most part, this remains a purely hypothetical exercise, leading one to conclude that most of us have plenty of ideas and stereotypes about death, but find it extremely difficult to make it real to ourselves.

Now, there might be some good reasons for this. It could well be the case that we human beings are hardwired not to dwell too much on the fact of our own extinction. Doing so, after all, can put us in the position of soldiers who die in battle not from gunshot wounds but from the fear of being killed that causes them to seize up, to make fatal mistakes, to give up. Tolstoy's own fear of death several times led him to the brink of suicide. Yet, as the residents at Beaumont Juvenile Correctional Center in Virginia (where my students and I discuss *Ivan* as part of my class "Books Behind Bars: Life, Literature, and Leadership") insist, *not* thinking about death can be no less frightening or debilitating: Pushing death out of their minds, they explain with astonishing candor and insight, is one technique they employ for protecting themselves emotionally amid the violence that is a regular part of their lives. And yet what such screens have done in the end, they confess, is to make it a bit too convenient for them to avoid asking the hard questions about their behavior and their lives that need to be asked.

It is gratifying to an extreme to see how Tolstoy's tale about a man who comes alive only when he realizes he's dying inspires these young men of seventeen to twenty to open up to my students and me about people they've watched die, mistakes they've made, opportunities they've squandered, or perhaps never had in the first place. Inevitably, it makes all of us feel a little more connected as human beings, reinforcing my conviction that Tolstoy is perhaps the most universal of all the great Russian writers, and death his most accessible theme.

Now, *War and Peace* isn't nearly so compact a parable as this later work. Still, it too is wise about death in the same sort of direct, jolting way. Most of us don't like to think about death, Tolstoy shows us on this much larger canvas, and with all of the delights life has to offer, maybe there's no need to overdo it. Still, at some visceral level we get it, and Tolstoy *gets* that we get it: death, like sex and war, is here to stay, and we, alas, are anything but. So if we want to make our short life on this earth count, we'd best come to terms with that fact. Or, as Tolstoy would put it in *What I Believe*: "Life is life, and we must use it as best we can."

Indeed, the sad truth about the most tragic character in *War and Peace*, Prince Andrei Bolkonsky, is that he ultimately fails to embrace this wisdom. Like his sudden transformation while lying wounded at Austerlitz, chatting with Pierre on the ferry raft, or encountering that dark-haired, slender girl at Otradnoe, Andrei's passionate love of life on the battlefield of Borodino lasts only briefly—for all of about two seconds. No sooner does he think about how much he loves the grass, the earth, and the air, than he "remembered that he was being looked at" (811). And so, rather than hitting the dirt like the other officers, he just stands there, undecided, watching the spinning shell about to explode in his face. And he says to the adjutant: "'Shame on you, officer!'" (811). For what? For trying to save his own life? This man who

is so concerned about what the world will think of him, thinks himself right out of making a spontaneous, potentially lifesaving decision.
But then, this isn't terribly surprising in someone who, on the evening
before battle, has already concluded that his entire life has been one
long, cruel illusion:

> The whole of life presented itself to him as a magic lantern, into
> which he had long been looking through a glass and in artificial
> light. Now he suddenly saw these badly daubed pictures without a
> glass, in bright daylight. "Yes, yes, there they are, those false images
> that excited and delighted and tormented me," he said to himself,
> turning over in his imagination the main pictures of his magic lan-
> tern of life, looking at them now in that cold, white daylight—the
> clear notion of death. "There they are, those crudely daubed fig-
> ures, which had presented themselves as something beautiful and
> mysterious. Glory, the general good, the love of a woman, the
> fatherland itself—how grand those pictures seemed to me, how
> filled with deep meaning! And it's all so simple, pale, and crude in
> the cold, white light of the morning that I feel is dawning for me."
> (769)

Anybody who has gone through the dark night of the soul knows
exactly what Andrei is feeling here, but if you've come through to the
other side, you know something *else*, too—something conspicuously
absent from Andrei's analysis of the way things are: yes, life is full of
deception and pain and disappointment, but it has beauty and magic
and meaning, as well. These Prince Andrei can no longer see, precisely because he has seen—or rather, *thinks* he has seen—too much.
"'Ah, dear heart, lately it's become hard for me to live,'" he confesses
that same evening to Pierre, who has come to the front to witness the
upcoming battle. "'I see that I've begun to understand too much. And
it's not good for a man to taste of the tree of the knowledge of good
and evil . . . Well, it won't be for long!' he added" (776). Indeed, his
premonition proves right.

After the stopover in Mytyshchi, Andrei travels with the Rostovs some 125 miles east to Yaroslavl, away from advancing French troops, and is offered refuge in the house of a town merchant. By this point, he

> not only knew that he would die, but felt that he was dying, that he was already half dead. He experienced an awareness of estrangement from everything earthly and a joyful and strange lightness of being. Without haste or worry, he waited for what lay ahead of him. The dread, the eternal, the unknown and far off, of which he had never ceased to feel the presence throughout his life, was now close to him and—by that strange lightness of being he experienced—almost comprehensible and palpable. (982)

As he lies there, mentally reviewing the past few weeks of his life, Andrei remembers Anatole in the operating tent, and is tormented by the question of whether the young cad is even still alive. (Tolstoy doesn't answer this question for the reader: after his leg is amputated, we never hear of Anatole again.) And then Andrei recalls his recent, inexplicable surge of love for Natasha in Mytyshchi; but that too has been transformed into something like bitter regret. Can it be, he now wonders, that fate has once again brought them together, only so that he should now die? That "'the truth of life has been revealed to me so that I should live in a lie? I love her more than anything in the world. But what am I to do if I love her?' he said and suddenly moaned involuntarily, by a habit acquired during his sufferings" (983). Even if he really wanted to do something about his love for Natasha (and it's no clearer here than elsewhere in the novel that he does), there's not much he *can* do, and it is precisely this sense of powerlessness in the face of the radical unknown that pains him most.

Princess Marya, meanwhile, gets the news of her brother's grave condition and whereabouts. Taking Andrei's seven-year-old son, Nikolenka, with her, she braves the treacherous roads to be with him. The first person she meets upon her arrival in Yaroslavl is Natasha, who has been at Andrei's side for weeks, and whom the princess hasn't seen since their chilly meeting in Moscow long ago, when Natasha and Andrei were first engaged. But it takes Marya just one glance into the eyes of that flighty young girl who repelled her two years ago to see "a sincere companion in grief, and therefore her friend" (977). For her part, Natasha, looking into Marya's luminous eyes, which seem to penetrate into her very soul, feels an immediate closeness to this woman who once appeared so strange and distant. Natasha's lips begin to tremble, ugly wrinkles begin to form around her mouth, and, without saying a word, she bursts into sobs and covers her face. "Princess Marya understood everything" (978).

Well, almost. In her imagination, Marya sees the gentle face of her dear brother Andryusha, which she remembers so well from childhood, and, preparing herself to be moved by the tender words he will certainly speak to her, she enters the room. What she finds is a man she hardly recognizes:

> In his words, in his tone, especially in that gaze—a cold, almost hostile gaze—there could be felt an alienation from everything of this world that was frightening in a living man. He clearly had difficulty now in understanding anything living; but at the same time it could be felt that he did not understand the living, not because he lacked the power of understanding, but because he understood something else, such as the living could not understand, and which absorbed him entirely. (979)

Clearly, Andrei is going through what psychologists sometimes refer to as decathexis, or a letting go, a withdrawal from earthly attachments that accompanies the acceptance of death. But withdrawal isn't necessarily the same thing as wisdom, and just what exactly that "something else" Andrei now understands *is*, Tolstoy never tells us. Still, that hasn't stopped scholars and readers alike from assuming that Tolstoy intends to show here how Andrei has indeed attained a wisdom to live by, often citing as evidence Andrei's poignant musings about love in these delirious final hours:

"Love? What is love?" he thought. "Love hinders death. Love is life. Everything, everything I understand, I understand only because I love. Everything is, everything exists, only because I love. Everything is connected only by that. Love is God, and to die—means that I, a part of love, return to the common and eternal source." (984)

Yet as touching as Andrei's reflections are—painfully close as they are to the very heart of the matter—they are for Andrei just thoughts. True, these words echo Tolstoy's own argument in "On Life," and the principle the dying man articulates is fundamental to many spiritual traditions, including Buddhism and Hinduism, both of which deeply influenced the author. Yet, when placed on Andrei's cold, parched lips, half animated by that hostile gaze, his reflections about love and the eternal life seem . . . only detached, distant. Even he senses it: "These thoughts seemed comforting to him. But . . . [s]omething was lacking in them, there was something one-sidedly personal, cerebral" (984). Quite right: How could it be otherwise, really? What the dying prince says about love is beautiful; how he has actually expressed that love, though, whether here or elsewhere in the novel, is anything but.

Critic George Steiner has argued that there are a number of scenes in *War and Peace*, such as this one, in which Tolstoy "conveyed a psychological truth through a rhetorical, external statement, or by putting in the minds of his characters a train of thought which impresses one as prematurely didactic." Steiner's observation is accurate enough, but his attribution, less so: the philosophical abstraction in this moment belongs not to Tolstoy, but Andrei. For the author knows what we know: Andrei's failure to connect on a visceral, emotional level with the world around him while dying is more than a matter of decathexis; it is also a natural reflection of how he's lived his entire life.

"'Yes, this must seem pitiful to them!'" Andrei thinks. "'Yet it's so simple!'" (981). And, gathering up his strength, he tries to recall a line from the Gospels, only to conclude that Princess Marya and Natasha will understand it in their own way. So he remains silent, thinking:

"'This they cannot understand, that all these feelings they value, all these thoughts of ours, which seem so important to us—that they're *unnecessary*'" (981).

At one level, of course, he's right. So many of the things we do and value in this world, when illuminated by that cold, white light of death, *are* unnecessary. But it isn't just our worldly ambitions and strivings Andrei has in mind, as on the evening before the battle of Borodino. No, he is also referring to those "silly" little things Princess Marya does in this moment to comfort him, as well as herself—like suggesting, for instance, that she bring in his son Nikolenka; to which Andrei responds, with a "smile not of joy, not of tenderness for his son, but of quiet, mild mockery of Princess Marya, who, in his opinion, was using her last means to bring him to his senses" (980). Marya is horrified, and can we blame her? What she wants is for her brother to affirm his kinship by seeing his very own, only son—by connecting with him, recognizing him, and giving him his fatherly blessing before his death. That Andrei cannot comprehend this, and is even mildly contemptuous of his sister's efforts, is proof, as Marya rightly surmises, of "how terribly far he now was from everything living" (980). Andrei is still denying his primal connection to the living, and worse, he is mocking the need for a comforting ritual by those who watch him die.

As I write this, I catch myself glancing out into the yard. There is the oak tree beneath which my kitten Monkey lies buried. I recall those many hours my wife Corinne and I spent choosing that very spot, with just the right balance of sunlight and shade; those countless vet visits and thousands of dollars paid to specialists to see if there was something, anything, we could do to cure his congenital illness; that assortment of wooden caskets I considered, wanting to make sure my little guy was buried in just the right one. I've even kept letters I wrote to him after his death, asking forgiveness for our failure to be at his side when he died—quite unexpectedly, of a different disease we never even knew he had (on our honeymoon, no less). I can only imagine how pathetic all this would have appeared to someone like Prince

Andrei, not least when such mawkish attention was being lavished on a mere pet. But to *me* these "ridiculous" actions were absolutely necessary, just as everything Princess Marya and Natasha do in the days leading up to Andrei's death are necessary for them.

"What a jerk!" blurts out one of my students during a discussion of this scene. "Look at how he treats his own sister on his deathbed!"

"Yes, *do* look, but don't . . . *judge*," I respond with uncharacteristic forcefulness, as if I need to defend the guy. "How, after all, are we *supposed* to treat others when we're dying?" I ask. "Where are the guidebooks informing us about such things?"

The fact is, Tolstoy takes us completely out of the realm of right and wrong in this scene—beyond the reach of pat answers—and puts us instead face-to-face with life's deepest mysteries. Tolstoy's contemporaries, raised on romantic literary fare, would have been used to deathbed scenes filled with fulsome professions of love, tender tours down memory lane, maybe even a bit of hysterical wailing. But Tolstoy gives us none of that. No, he is here to tell all of us that death is never what we think it is, neither for the person dying nor the people witnessing it. Death, like life itself, is infinitely more surprising and mysterious than our rational mind may ever fathom. Look at it, Tolstoy says, get curious about it. Be with it, and then be quiet, like Princess Marya and Natasha, who, in Andrei's final hours, "did not weep, did not shudder, . . . [and] also never spoke of him between themselves. They felt that they could not express what they understood in words" (985).

In 1865, a few years into the writing of *War and Peace*, Tolstoy "needed a brilliant young man to die at Austerlitz," but then changed his mind, deciding that this son of old Prince Bolkonsky was only to be wounded, since he was needed for later on. For what purpose Tolstoy never did say, but having followed the character to the end of his journey, perhaps we now know. You see, Tolstoy needed Andrei Bolkonsky to illustrate the fate of a man who never quite learns how to integrate his high ideals with ordinary reality, who never learns how to allow his genuine insight into that greater something out there to deepen his appreciation of this messy world down here.

There is a telling moment much earlier in the novel in which Andrei, who has just begun to court Natasha, is so moved by her singing he finds himself on the verge of tears over "a sudden, vivid awareness of the terrible opposition between something infinitely great that was in him, and something narrow and fleshly that he himself, and even she, was. This opposition tormented him and gladdened him while she sang" (467). This same opposition continues to torment and, in an odd way, gladden him throughout the novel, right up until his end, as he slips quietly into eternity, something he appears to have been prepared to do for quite some time. What Tolstoy gives us in Prince Andrei is the portrait of a man, not yet thirty-five years old, who has made his peace with death, rather than life.

And yet, with the possible exception of Hadji-Murat, I know of no other character in all of Tolstoy's fiction or elsewhere in Russian litera- ture whose death is described with such tragic beauty. Anna Karenina's famous death is just plain gruesome, and even Ivan Ilyich's end, for all its trenchant physical and psychological detail, doesn't reach the poetic heights to which Tolstoy takes us in these pages. And this is the case, I would argue, not just because Tolstoy was capable of the same as a writer, but because Andrei's complexity and depth as a human being called for such treatment in this book.

For all his massive failings—perhaps even because of them—Prince Andrei is nevertheless attuned to some higher dimension of experience that eludes most other characters. In early drafts of the novel, before there was any Andrei, there was Boris Drubetskoi, who was endowed with many of the features of the character who would become Andrei. Early on these two characters were conflated in Tolstoy's imagination, but all that later changed in an important and telling way. Although Andrei would continue to share with Boris the traits of egoism and ambition in the final version of the novel, Andrei's fatal flaw—an inability to come to terms with the world as it is—stems from a far deeper engagement with life than Boris ever musters; the latter is unable even to recognize, let alone grapple with, the sorts of existential questions that haunt Andrei throughout. From the shell of one of the novel's major careerists, then, emerged one of Russian literature's great and tragic seekers.

Nowhere is his tragic depth more poignantly captured perhaps than in the description of Andrei's dream, our last encounter with him in the novel. In the prince's dream he is lying in the very same room he happens to be in. There are all sorts of people there, and he argues with them about "something unnecessary." They are preparing to go somewhere, but Andrei "recalls that it is all insignificant and that he has other, more important concerns." Not that this stops him from engaging the group, to everybody's surprise, "speaking some sort of empty, witty words" (984). Sound familiar? This is the Andrei we met at the beginning of the novel, bored to death by everyone and everything at Anna Pavlovna's soiree, balking at the fakeness all around him, and yet carrying on as sure-footedly as anyone there. This brilliant young aristocrat was about to embark on an exceptional career—one he hoped would win him the admiration of the very high society he so despised.

But then Austerlitz happened; so, too, something happens in the dream:

Gradually, imperceptibly, all these people begin to disappear, and everything is replaced by the question of the closed door. He gets up and goes to the door to slide the bolt and lock it. *Everything* depends on whether he does or does not manage to lock the door, but still, he painfully strains all his force. And a tormenting fear seizes him. And this fear is the fear of death: *it* is standing behind the door. But as he is crawling strengthlessly and awkwardly towards the door, this terrible something is already pushing against it from the other side, forcing it. Something inhuman—death— is forcing the door, and he has to hold it shut. He lays hold of the door, strains in a last effort—to lock it is already impossible—just to hold it shut; but his attempts are weak, clumsy, and pushed by the terrible thing, the door keeps opening and shutting again.

Once more it pushes from the other side. His last supernatural efforts are in vain, and the two halves open noiselessly. *It* comes in, and *it* is death. And Prince Andrei died.

But in the same instant that he died, Prince Andrei remembered that he was asleep, and . . . he made an effort within himself and woke up. (984–85)

If you've been reading *War and Peace* carefully, you may recall that Tolstoy uses an identical image several hundred pages earlier, when Andrei comes home on that snowy March night and finds his wife Liza going into labor. After being instructed to wait in an adjacent room, he covers his face while listening in bewilderment to the shrieking, animal moans coming from the other side of the door. "Prince Andrei got up, went to the door, and wanted to open it. Someone was holding the door" (327). Now, it's impossible to say with any certainty whether Tolstoy had recently reread this scene, written some three years earlier, while composing Andrei's deathbed scene, but this much is clear: whether consciously or subliminally, the two moments are in the writer's mind connected—so much so that the later sentence "He gets up and goes to the door to slide the bolt and lock it" is not just a nearly exact echo of the earlier one, but a rather neat reversal—"Prince Andrei got up, went to the door, and wanted to open it." What are we to make of this?

Taken together, these two moments may be seen to embody the core of Andrei's character, and the essence of his spiritual journey: he has always sensed there must be something on the other side of that proverbial door—something as attractive to him as it is repellent. He wanted to be in the room, after all, from which those animal-like moans were coming, where Liza was busy creating new life. Little did he know at the time that death, too, was lurking behind the closed door in that very moment; Liza, recall, died during childbirth. Now, hundreds of pages later, Tolstoy craftily realizes the metaphor, when that "[s]omething inhuman—death" finally breaks through, the door swings open and closed, and all separation between what's on this side of it and what's on that one is eradicated. *It* is there. *It* is here. *It* is everywhere. At once radically strange yet completely ordinary, death, like life itself, is happening all around him. Only now, for perhaps the very first time, Andrei truly *sees* and *understands*:

> "Yes, that was death. I died—I woke up. Yes, death is an awaken-ing." Clarity suddenly came to his soul, and the curtain that until then had concealed the unknown was raised before his inner gaze. He felt the release of a force that previously had been as if bound in him and that strange lightness which from then on did not leave him. (985)

At the funeral a few days later, the onlookers go up to the clothed, washed body lying in the coffin and bid it farewell, each one weeping for different reasons: young Nikolenka, Andrei's son, from the confusion in his heart; Countess Rostova and Sonya, out of pity for Natasha; and the old Count Rostov, because he knows that "soon he, too, would have to take that dreadful step" (986). Tolstoy's own perspective in this moment is perhaps closest to that of Natasha and Princess Marya, who now allow themselves to weep, as well, though "they did not weep from their own personal grief; they wept from a reverent emotion that came over their souls before the awareness of the simple and solemn mystery of death that had been accomplished before them" (986).

11

PERSEVERANCE

"The hardest and most blissful thing is to love this life in one's suffering."

—*War and Peace*, Volume 4, Part 3, Chapter 15

Even as Prince Andrei enters into the final mystery, his great friend Pierre finds himself embroiled in the continued horrors and absurdities of war. It is August 1812. Two months ago, in June, Napoleon crossed the western Russian border. Now Pierre is dropping in on the battle of Borodino, a nonmilitary onlooker, roaming around in his white hat and green tailcoat, watching wide-eyed as his world is suddenly transformed into a collage of whining cannonballs, glistening bayonets, bleeding bodies, and rays of sun piercing the morning mist to illuminate the purple-gray cannon smoke.

His gaze falls upon a young officer lying in a pool of blood, on disfigured soldiers walking, crawling, and being carried off the battlefield on stretchers. At one point he has a skirmish with a French soldier, which ends with neither man knowing just who has captured whom; both end up running away in fright, Pierre stumbling over dead bodies as he bolts frantically down a hill. The exoticism of war for Pierre by now utterly exhausted, he wishes only to return to the ordinary conditions of his home life back in Moscow, to fall soundly asleep in the blessed safety of his large, eiderdown bed.

By the time he arrives, however, Moscow has been almost completely abandoned. Nothing is left of the city he knew but a few familiar sites rising up from among the charred ruins. In this state of total confusion an idea pops into his head: he'll assassinate Napoleon and thereby liberate his country. But on his way to saving the world, Pierre instead accidentally saves a French captain, Ramballe, who has just been attacked by a drunken, half-crazy man. Pierre and the Frenchman then proceed to spend the evening drinking wine and waxing poetic about the mysteries of love.

Waking the next day with a hangover, Pierre grabs the pistol, dagger, and peasant coat disguise he had acquired earlier in preparation for his heroic assassination, and makes one final attempt to revive his original intention. Alas, on his way to the center of Moscow, where he believes Napoleon to be, his grand plan is interrupted yet again, first by a mother who begs him to save her child from a burning building, and then by a shrieking Armenian woman being harassed by a French soldier. Pierre pummels the soldier, gets beaten himself, and then is arrested on suspicion of arson. Seven years earlier, this bearlike, bespectacled twenty-year-old Russian count inherited the largest fortune in Russia. Now he is a prisoner of war.

For six weeks he marches with a caravan of prisoners. In captivity Pierre's attention shrinks from grandiose plans all the way down to the miserable reality of his swollen feet in their shredded moccasins, the sharp ache of his empty stomach. No wonder he develops an affinity for the little blue-gray stray dog who tags along with the marching prisoners. Homeless and feeding on horseflesh to stay alive, both of them are leading a dog's life.

Then, just when he thinks things can't possibly get worse, Pierre is brought before a firing squad. Prepared to die, he discovers, miraculously, that he has been escorted there only as a witness. Still, the sight of the blindfolded factory worker being shot in the head (which Pierre well realizes might just as easily have been him) is enough to shatter his every intellectual conceit about life—every illusion he's ever had about his own power, every ounce of his faith in "the world's good order, in humanity's and his own soul, and in God" (968). His world utterly crumbled, he feels that "to return to faith in life was not in his power" (969).

In a sense, he's right. It *is* beyond his power. He stops fighting, planning, and searching, and simply . . . submits. French soldiers toss him into a small, dark shed, where he sits silently in a corner on a heap of straw, waiting to die.

But then something interesting happens. In that shed Pierre is struck by the strong smell of sweat emanating from a small man sitting beside him. He studies the steady, flowing movements of the man's arms as he removes his foot wrappings, and then the smooth, even undulation of his hands cutting something Pierre doesn't at first quite recognize:

> Pierre felt something pleasant, soothing, and rounded in these deft movements, in this well-arranged domain of his in the corner, even in the smell of this man, and he looked at him without taking his eyes away.
>
> "So you've seen a lot of misery, master? Eh?" the little man suddenly said. And in the man's melodious voice there was such an expression of tenderness and simplicity that Pierre wanted to reply, but his jaw trembled, and he felt tears rising. (969)

The man sitting next to Pierre is Platon Karataev, an old peasant who has ended up in French captivity while serving a mandatory twenty-five-year service in the Russian imperial army as punishment for having once trespassed on a neighbor's property. No stranger to suffering himself, Platon knows what Pierre is going through; and so he consoles the young fellow, not only with his soothing words, but by doing something seemingly quite unremarkable: he gives Pierre some potatoes.

Now, these are not the first potatoes Pierre has ever eaten. If you've ever glanced at a menu in a Russian restaurant, you know that Russians have as many ways of preparing this ubiquitous national vegetable as Eskimos have of naming snow. But these might be the first potatoes he has ever really . . . *tasted*. More than physical nourishment, these modest little hunks of carbohydrate, handed to him in an act of simple kindness, are spiritual sustenance, as well. Reconnecting him to the human family, to the earth, to himself, they bring Pierre back to life.

His spiritual rebirth, then, begins not under the intoxicating influence of any of those grand plans, or indeed from the realm of heroic fantasy, but in the fulfillment of his most basic bodily needs. Seldom have the ordinary rhythms of everyday life or the details of his immediate surroundings so enraptured Pierre. Rarely has he immersed himself so fully and yet so unpretentiously in the greatest pleasure of all—the joy of simply being alive.

There in that dark shed, on the darkest day of his life, Pierre touches something solid and transcendent in his now-pulverized world. He glimpses that elusive "it," the "real thing." We've all had that moment when our ordinary, perhaps even crummy, life suddenly strikes us as something pretty extraordinary *after* all. Just when you're ready to throw in the towel over a job, a relationship, an addiction, an illness— over life itself—grace may magically intervene, illuminating a fresh possibility you hadn't imagined, offering an entirely new way of seeing an all-too-familiar problem. "Ah, *now* it makes sense!" you are tempted to shout. You don't, of course—for you've discovered a secret gift that need not be advertised to the world. And that private little heaven is what we have earned by marching through hell.

Had Pierre merely been told that he might have achieved that illumination by following the prepackaged advice offered by the Freemason Bazdeyev all those chapters back, his discovery surely would have seemed less striking, dull and cheap even. His realization in captivity is so compelling to him—and thus to the reader—in direct proportion to how long he has had to fight in order to achieve it. For seven years we've followed this young man through the ups and downs of his tumultuous journey as he careers from one grand failure to another. To find any nuggets of wisdom, he has first had to dig deep in the dirt, sift well through the dross. He has had to go through War, in short, before he could find his Peace:

> And precisely in that time he received the peace and contentment with himself which he had previously striven for in vain. In his life he had long sought in various directions for that peace, that harmony with himself, which had struck him so much in the soldiers during the battle of Borodino—he had sought it in philanthropy, in Freemasonry, in the distractions of social life, in wine, in a heroic deed of self-sacrifice, in romantic love for Natasha; he had sought it by way of thought, and all this seeking and trying had disappointed him. And, without thinking, he had received that peace and harmony with himself only through the horror of death, through privation, and through what he had understood in Karataev. (1012)

What Pierre sees in Platon is how, in a troubled world, to maintain one's inner strength, one's true north. In contrast to one of Pierre's earlier "teachers," the fast-talking spirituality peddler, Bazdeyev, who tries to wheel and deal his way into Pierre's heart (and pocketbook) with so much Freemasonry mumbo jumbo, Platon doesn't say much at all, and yet. . . and yet he communicates volumes.

Here is a man to whom life has been anything but kind; yet, rather than bemoaning his hard fate, all he can say of his grossly unjust sentence is that "'we thought it was grief, but it was joy!'" (971). His explanation? It saved his brother, who had four children, from being conscripted. This sort of moral courage is part and parcel of Platon's entire attitude toward life. Instead of focusing on what he lacks in every moment, he is grateful for what he *does* have. Some of us might dismiss this man as little more than a Pollyanna, perhaps even a rather pathetic one. This would be a mistake. Platon's approach to life is in fact quite pragmatic. Indeed, it's what allows him to survive nearly unbearable hardship:

Karataev had no attachments, friendships, or loves, as Pierre understood them; but he loved and lived lovingly with everything that life brought his way, especially other people—not any specific people, but those who were there before his eyes. He loved his mutt, his comrades, the French, he loved Pierre, who was his neighbor; but Pierre sensed that, despite all his gentle tenderness towards him (by which he involuntarily gave Pierre's spiritual life its due), Karataev would not have been upset for a moment to be parted from him. And Pierre was beginning to experience the same feeling towards Karataev. (973–74)

The famous Soviet literary scholar Viktor Shklovksy criticized Tolstoy for making Platon Karataev almost too good to be true. Nor is his position hard to understand: Shklovksy was writing about *War and Peace* in the 1920s, an era in which his country was still being torn apart in the long aftermath of the Russian Revolution, a particularly brutal time in which soulful Karataev types would have been few and far between.

Yet Tolstoy, who also happened to live in tumultuous times, *did* find Platon Karataevs among the Cossacks who dwelled in the Caucasus Mountains of the Russian south, not to mention among the Bashkirs, a nomadic tribe in the Samara region, which Tolstoy often visited for spiritual regeneration. Moved by the Bashkir way of life, Tolstoy even began to adopt some of their customs—studying the Koran, for instance, smoking hashish, and getting drunk on *kumis*, an alcoholic drink made from mare's milk. "As is proper when taking a *kumis* cure," he wrote to the poet Afanasy Fet during one of his trips to the Bashkirs, "I'm drunk and sweat from morning til night, and I find pleasure in it." It's probably no coincidence that one of the first things Tolstoy has Pierre notice about Platon is "the strong smell of sweat that came from him" (969).

Just as Platon consoles Pierre and shows him what in the worst of times is humanly possible, so Pierre, in turn, gives moral support to his fellow prisoners, who need him every bit as much as he needed

Platon. These men look up to Pierre for his education, his strength, his authenticity, his simplicity, and his ability, "which they found incomprehensible, to sit motionless and think, doing nothing" (1014). The very qualities that always made Pierre an oddball in the eyes of high society, then, are what among his suffering compatriots give him moral authority.

They are also what permit him to overcome his wartime trials. Not only does the Russian count attain his own Karataev-like peace while in captivity, he manages to experience . . . *happiness*. Awakening one day, Pierre walks outside the shed and is moved by the glorious morning sun lighting up the Russian capital:

> Pierre felt a new, never yet experienced feeling of the joy and strength of life.
>
> And that feeling not only did not abandon him through all the time of his captivity, but, on the contrary, kept growing in him as the hardships of his situation increased. (1014)

Unless we suppose that Tolstoy intended his hero to be some kind of Russian masochist of the sort we're more likely to encounter in Dostoevsky, we must find another explanation for the fact that Pierre's joy increases even as his hardships mount. The ever-intuitive Natasha Rostova, upon meeting Pierre after he returns from captivity, has the answer to this apparent paradox: "'He's become somehow clean, smooth, fresh,'" she remarks to Princess Marya, "as if from the bathhouse, you understand? Morally from the bathhouse. Hasn't he?'" (1118).

This reference to the bathhouse (in Russian, *banya*) has an even deeper layer of significance than may at first meet the eye, for in the Russian *banya* physical pain and cleanliness absolutely go together, as I myself (achingly) experience whenever I go to Russia. There is this odd *banya* whipping ritual, in which you lie naked, totally exposed on the hot wooden bench, while a large naked comrade—how to put this?—lashes your backside, already burning from the unbearably hot steam, with sharp dried birch leaves, in order to stir up still more sensation. By the end of that little torture session, you really *do* feel cleansed, spiritually as well as physically. Something rather similar has, indeed, happened to Pierre in captivity.

Before his wartime trials, Pierre makes the mistake, familiar to many of us, of equating happiness with the pursuit of, first, personal gratification and, second, the attainment of certain very elusive goals. Only in captivity does this frustrating pattern of high expectation and bitter disappointment finally come to an end. Suddenly there is no better place to be—no world to save, no utopia to create, no alcohol or beautiful woman or poker game in which to seek intoxication. Circumstances force Pierre to get off that loopy roller-coaster ride—to plant his feet firmly on the ground, and live, like Platon, in the here and *now*:

> He experienced the feeling of a man who has found what he was seeking under his own feet, while he had been straining his eyes looking far away from himself. All his life he had looked off somewhere, over the heads of people around him, yet there was no need to strain his eyes, but only to look right in front of him. (1104)

And what he discovers right in front of him is perfect and beautiful just as it is:

> Now he had learned to see the great, the eternal, and the infinite in everything, and therefore, in order to see it, to enjoy contemplating it, he had naturally abandoned the mental telescope he had been looking through until then over people's heads, and joyfully contemplated the ever-changing, ever-great, unfathomable, and infinite life around him. And the closer he looked, the calmer and happier he became. (1104)

You've heard the old saw about the man who complained that he didn't have any shoes until he met the man who didn't have any feet.

Tolstoy is using Pierre to say something similar: the man who thought only a short time before that a bullet was about to blow his brains out, no longer bemoans the fact that he isn't as brilliant or successful as his best friend, Prince Andrei, or that things haven't exactly turned out as he had hoped. Pierre is simply grateful his skull is in one piece. And this fresh way of seeing gives him renewed strength.

Now, with everything stripped from him—his status, his money, his possessions, his comforts, even his name—when he is about as *un*free as a person can possibly be, Pierre feels, paradoxically, as free as he ever has:

> [F]or the whole of his life Pierre thought and spoke with rapture of that month in captivity, of those irrevocable, strong, and joyful sensations, and above all of that full peace of mind, that perfect inner freedom, which he experienced only in that time. (1013)

These sentences might strike some of us as odd, if not unsettling. How can Pierre experience "perfect inner freedom" in *captivity*? Because, Tolstoy says, he joyfully recognizes, for perhaps the first time, that one freedom nobody can ever take away from him: the freedom to choose how he will respond to his conditions. And *that*, in the end, is the only choice he—or any of us—really has. For the harsh truth of the matter is that our individual fates are largely determined by external forces over which we have little if any control.

Just think, for instance, of all the circumstances, great and small, leading Pierre to his current situation. What if, for instance, he hadn't come to the rescue of that Armenian woman being harassed by the French soldier, hadn't in that very moment been found to be carrying a pistol and a dagger, and hadn't, in "that ecstasy of fury in which he was oblivious to everything," appeared so terrifying to the Frenchmen? (930). Might his captors in that case simply have assumed him to be the harmless innocent that he in fact is, and just let him go? Or what if Pierre—a bastard to begin with and in the wake of his mother's death, an orphan—had grown up, say, in a more nurturing family? Might he have been more internally secure and perhaps less inclined to search for fulfillment in all what you might call the wrong places?

Panning the lens out even further, what if Pierre hadn't been born in an era when some French megalomaniac decided to invade his country? Had he come of age only a decade later, for instance, at a time with no national war tearing his homeland apart, how easily might he have become a plump country squire?—a man whose interest in national affairs could have been satisfied by the quarterly delivery of the *Library for Reading* to his rural mansion. We might chuckle at such hypotheticals, but Tolstoy's point is that it is precisely these sorts of totally unpredictable circumstances that define our lives, affecting us in profound, unforeseeable ways. Indeed, it is a truth Pierre apprehends just before he is about, he thinks, to be executed:

> Who was it, finally, who was executing, killing, depriving him of life, him—Pierre—with all his memories, longings, hopes, thoughts? Who was doing it? And Pierre felt that it was no one.
>
> It was the order of things, the turn of circumstances.
>
> Some order of things was killing him—Pierre—depriving him of life, of everything, annihilating him. (965)

That "order of things" is, of course, the well-oiled French killing machine, but it is also, on a deeper level, the concatenation of forces and circumstances that have led Pierre to this moment.

How, then, are we supposed to live in a world of such brutal whim? Well, we trudge along as we must, and make the best choices we can. We visit the shrink and pop our pills in the hopes that things might acquire a rosier hue in our eyes. Sometimes they do; at least as often, they don't. And *then* what are we to do? Curl up in a ball of fear, hide behind a rosy façade, or just give up? None of the above, says Tolstoy.

Once we accept that we are not masters of our own respective destinies, that hardship and suffering are a necessary part of our lives, we must then focus on those things we *can* change: how we respond to what is happening in the moment, how we treat others around us, whether we bear our cross with grace or with cowardice . . . "There is only one thing that I dread," Dostoevsky purportedly once admitted: "not to be worthy of my sufferings." In Pierre, Tolstoy has created the unforgettable portrait of a man who, against all odds, proves absolutely worthy of his.

This Tolstoyan wisdom doesn't require us to live up to some superhuman standard. Nor does it recommend that we try to convince ourselves that the deadly rapids we find ourselves navigating are nothing more than a series of tranquil streams. Tragedy is out there, Tolstoy insists, suffering is unavoidable, and the limits of our power are real enough—and *not*, as Rhonda Byrne, author of *The Secret*, might suggest, merely the result of an insufficiently positive attitude. Byrne's can-do mentality is oh-so-inspiring, so twenty-first century and "user-friendly," and, um . . . so utterly naïve. For how far is it going to take you, really, when your world has fallen to pieces?

Imagine, for instance, Pierre's response, had Platon Karataev attempted to console him not through the quiet, simple act of handing him potatoes, but by the inspirational sort of boosterism we hear so much today: "Just *do* it, Pierre!" Well, the fact is, *it* wouldn't have taken him far. Frankly, there's nothing for Pierre to do, really. He doesn't even have shoes to put on his bleeding, bruised feet, let alone any fancy performance-enhancing arch support. No, the real secret to survival, Tolstoy helps us to see, is learning to live courageously in a world filled with real uncertainty, real hardship, and real suffering.

Were external freedom and good fortune prerequisites to human fulfillment, Platon Karataev and Pierre Bezukhov would be utterly out of luck. And not only them: pretty much everyone in this novel—and, indeed, *most* Russians who have ever lived—would be a rather sad lot. Yet Pierre is *happy* in captivity. Just as many Russians I know demonstrate the same almost preternatural capacity for joy belying their often tragic history. When you grow up in a nation that has witnessed about twenty-five years of something resembling democracy set against the larger inevitability of a thousand years of authoritarianism, I suppose you learn not to hang all your hopes for fulfillment on ideals of freedom, fairness, or the gratification of one's personal desires.

Most Russians, by the time they reach adulthood, harbor few illusions about life's inequities. Stalin, they know well, murdered some twenty million of his own people. Russian poets were routinely imprisoned and even executed in the Soviet era for what they wrote. What kind of a country, a Russian friend of mine recently wondered, still incarcerates its own citizens for political reasons, or for simply failing to provide a valid passport when stopped for any reason whatsoever on the streets of the nation's capital? Yet, in spite of such pervasive, even relentless injustice, the best Russians I know display a remarkable inner strength and a commitment to living with as much dignity as they can. Pierre Bezukhov and Platon Karataev are the embodiment of this.

Not all Russians are so admirable, of course. A Moscow cabbie in the late 1980s once tried to rip me off, only to discover that I wasn't quite as clueless about Russian cab fare customs as my Ralph Lauren polo shirt and JanSport backpack might have led him to believe. When I called him on his deception in fluent Russian, he knew he had some 'splainin' to do, which he proceeded to do by describing to me how hard it was to feed one's family and clothe one's children in those economically chaotic Gorbachev years. Who was I—a bookish, clean-shaven, twenty-year-old Russian major from Amherst College— to lecture this man on morality? Not that I didn't try—unsuccessfully, of course—and though I'm now a bit embarrassed by that exhibition of naïveté laced with arrogance, I still believe I might have been onto something. There are, after all, many different responses to hardship: I've ridden with hundreds of hard-up Russian cabbies over the years who made no move to take advantage of me.

We human beings are badly blemished, and seldom is this fact more evident than in our response to tough times. Then again, equally likely to come out at such times is our capacity to rise above the very worst aspects of our nature. Yet even Pierre falters in his newfound wisdom.

My undergraduate students are particularly bothered by the moment when Pierre, realizing that Platon, weak and sick, will soon be executed, "pretended that he had not seen [Platon's] look and hurriedly walked away" (1064).

"How could he do that?" they ask, with disappointment.

"Well, have you ever *been* in such a situation?" I ask. Whereupon a prolonged silence generally ensues. "Right, and neither have *I*," I continue. "So, you know, I can't say for sure that I wouldn't have acted similarly if I were in his shoes—if I were scared for my life."

Pierre is only a man, after all—no more, no less. He stumbles, as we all do. Yet despite his many mistakes, he marches on, feeling the world's pain, imbibing its pleasures, and embracing its possibilities as few of us ever have occasion to. Perhaps, rather than judging him for his faults, we would do better to appreciate his unique strengths, not least of which is his commitment to living as fully and humanely as he possibly can in the very darkest of times.

The contentment he experiences in captivity doesn't last, of course. Life flows on. Eventually, Pierre and his fellow prisoners are freed by a detachment of Russian soldiers. And as soon as he returns to Moscow after the war and reenters the world of ordinary, everyday living, new battles await him: the fight to reform a corrupt government, at one end of the spectrum—and, at the other, the struggle to keep his baby's bottom clean (at which, according to his proud wife Natasha, he happens to be rather good, actually). But Pierre's memory of those transformative weeks in captivity continues to influence him in important if subtle ways, remaining for him an ever-present symbol of what life is all about.

"He who has a *why* to live for can bear almost any *how*," Nietzsche once said. And though Tolstoy was hardly a fan of the German existentialist, he agreed with him on this point: if to live is to suffer, then to persevere is to find meaning in one's suffering. Does hardship make us beasts, Tolstoy asks, or better human beings? Do we continually focus on getting what we think we want, or on making something meaningful out of what we have, no matter how minuscule or shabby it might seem?

Nelson Mandela, whose favorite book happens to have been *War and Peace*, did the latter. As did Mahatma Gandhi, who, at twenty-four, was changed after reading Tolstoy's *The Kingdom of God Is Within You*. Rather than being dragged down by their surroundings, they rose above them, transforming their own personal pain into spiritual possibility for the benefit of humanity at large. Not that one must be famous or touched by some grand destiny in order to exhibit that kind of inner strength. If an unprepossessing nineteenth-century Russian count or an obscure Russian peasant can do it, Tolstoy shows us, then surely any one of us can, if we choose to.

Given the value of what he finds in the end, would Pierre do it all over again? Here he is after the war, in his own words, speaking to Natasha and Princess Marya:

> "They say: misfortunes, sufferings . . . Well, if somebody said to me right now, this minute: do you want to remain the way you were before captivity, or live through it all over again? For God's sake, captivity again and horsemeat! Once we're thrown off our habitual paths, we think all is lost; but it's only here that the new and the good begins." (1118)

Not such a bad message for our own times.

12

TRUTH

The hero of my tale—whom I love with all the power of
my soul, whom I have tried to portray in all its beauty,
who has been, is, and always will be beautiful—is Truth.

—"Sevastopol in May," 1855

Pick an ism, *any* ism: Materialism, Atheism, Liberalism, Positivism,
Pietism, Spiritualism, Communism, Slavophilism, Pan-Slavism,
or—if you'd just like to do away with the whole rotten mess and start
from scratch—Anarchism. Such was the veritable smorgasbord of
warring ideological agendas gracing the Russian intellectual scene in
the 1860s. All this ideological mudslinging rather saddened Tolstoy,
not only because he believed it to be responsible for a fair amount
of the pain we humans persistently inflict on one another, but also
because he believed that smug claims about knowing the truth almost
certainly never succeed in leading us there. Amid this maelstrom of
competing agendas, he ruefully noted in an 1858 letter to the literary
critic Vassily Botkin, "there are no people who would simply bring
others together and reconcile them through the power of goodness."
Or, he might have added, through the power of art.

War and Peace challenges intellectual arrogance of *all* stripes, shows
life to be infinitely more complex than acknowledged by any of our

beliefs and theories—so often motivated by blind self-interest. Indeed, a character's certainty about something is a pretty good indication of his or her being wrong about it, or at the very least, insufficiently *right* . . . Perhaps a healthy serving of good ol' Russian self-doubt isn't such a bad thing, after all—by which Tolstoy means the sort of searching honesty and self-awareness exhibited by Pierre in the end. "'I don't say we should oppose this or that. We may be mistaken,'" he tells his wife Natasha just after returning from Petersburg, where Pierre has been trying to unite conservatives and liberals, who are at each other's throats over the future direction of the country. "'What I say is: let's join hands with those who love the good, and let there be one banner—active virtue'" (1176). Exactly what form that virtue will take is not yet clear to Pierre, for he is not so arrogant as to assume *he* knows the precise destination to be reached, let alone quite how to get there. Experience has taught him the wisdom of Turgenev's observation in an 1857 letter to Tolstoy that "the truth is like a lizard; it leaves the tail in your hand and escapes, knowing that it will soon grow another."

It's this sort of humility and honest self-reflection, Tolstoy believed, that was lacking among most of the people working in the "truth business," that is, pundits, scientists, historians, academics, and fanatics of all persuasions—of which there were quite a few in Russia in those days. The explosion of knowledge and advances in science in the second half of the nineteenth century created many new academic specialties and subspecialties. Yet even if Russia's last great Renaissance man was widely read, and counted among his friends some of the era's leading scientists and academics, Tolstoy remained as skeptical of scientific knowledge as he was of social and political agendas to address life's deepest challenges. Social scientists, who claim to have come up with the solution to perennial human questions by means of their experimental techniques and analytical arguments, are, he says in *War and Peace,*

> like plasterers assigned to plaster one side of a church wall, who, taking advantage of the foreman's absence, in a fit of zeal smear

their plaster all over the windows, the icons, the scaffolding, and the as yet unreinforced walls, and rejoice at how, from their plastering point of view, everything comes out flat and smooth. (1203)

Then there were the historians, whose books Tolstoy read by the hundreds in preparation for writing *War and Peace*. Not surprisingly, he found many of them lacking, especially the ones arguing that Napoleon was perhaps the greatest military genius the world had ever known. Why, then, Tolstoy asks, did he make decisions that led directly to the destruction of his 422,000-man army, followed a few years later by confinement on the South Atlantic island of St. Helena, where he died of stomach cancer? His rapid string of military successes must have lulled him into the false belief that he had the world all figured out . . . He didn't. None of us does; least of all anyone who insists on it. Yet too many of these authors saw the world through the lens of Great Man theory, which assumes that it is powerful men and women who shape historical events. Not true, Tolstoy says:

[W]e need only inquire into the essence of any historical event, that is, into the activity of the entire mass of people who took part in the event, to become convinced that the will of the historical hero not only does not guide the actions of the masses, but is itself constantly guided. (987)

Far better, if you want the truth about how history really happens, to study works of fiction:

A historian and an artist, describing an historical epoch, have two completely different objects. . . . For a historian, considering the contribution rendered by some person towards a certain goal, there are heroes; for the artist, considering the correspondence of this person to all sides of life, there cannot and should not be any heroes, but there should be people.

And indeed, we eventually come to realize that there are no great people in *War and Peace*, just multifaceted, full-blooded human beings who in their essence are strikingly similar to those who came before them and will continue to come after. Some things, Tolstoy tells us, don't much change over time. And human nature is one of them.

The nature of the world is another. Nowhere does Tolstoy make this more wrenchingly clear than in the fate of young Petya Rostov. At the very moment that Pierre is suffering in captivity, Tolstoy reintroduces us to Petya, the youngest of the Rostov children, and a character we have met briefly at various points throughout the novel—first as a young boy, later as a budding adolescent. Now, in the very last section of the novel, this relatively minor character is suddenly thrust into the foreground for eight unforgettable chapters.

It is 1813, and Napoleon's army is on its way out of Russia, yet the partisan efforts continue, and battles are still being fought, to the delight of fifteen-year-old Petya, who has just been promoted to officer. He volunteers and is chosen to be sent to a detachment of Russian partisans, which, by some gigantic coincidence, happens to be commanded by one Vassily Denisov, the man who had once mentored Petya's brother Nikolai when *he* was just starting out eight years earlier, eventually becoming one of Nikolai's dearest friends. No wonder Denisov feels both a special bond with, as well as a sense of responsibility toward, this boy, who is like family to him.

And he certainly has his hands full. The general who sent Petya over to Denisov's detachment expressly forbade Petya to take part in any more military action, because of the way the young man galloped right into a line under French fire during a recent battle and shot off his pistol like some wild Cossack. But Petya just hasn't been able to help himself: ever since being promoted to officer and taking part in active duty, he has "constantly been in a state of happily excited joy that he was grown up, and in constantly rapturous haste not to miss any occasion for real heroism" (1045). He therefore decides not to tell anyone about the general's order, especially after learning that Denisov and his men are planning an attack on the evening of his arrival. *They are real heroes*, after all, whom Petya wouldn't dream of abandoning in this difficult moment.

That familiar Rostovian impetuousness, then, is alive and well in Petya, as is his family's largeness of spirit, evident in the way Petya wants to take care of a recently captured drummer boy, and showers the men in his detachment with one gift after another: his pocketknife, coffeepot, flint, and anything else he might happen to have on him. "'Good heavens! I completely forgot,'" he suddenly cries at one point. "'I've got wonderful raisins, you know, the seedless kind. . . . I bought ten pounds. I'm used to something sweet. Would you like some?'" (1046). Indeed, Petya is used to something sweet—he's a happy, coddled Rostov, after all—and his overflowing youth and kindness cannot but infect the men and the reader alike.

Later that night, as Petya dozes off, dreamily anticipating the upcoming battle, his first real action in weeks, he imagines that he

was in a magic kingdom, in which there was nothing resembling reality. Maybe the big black spot was indeed the guardhouse, but maybe it was a cave that led into the very depths of the earth. Maybe he is indeed sitting on a wagon now, but it very well may be that he is sitting, not on a wagon, but on a terribly tall tower, from which, if you fell, it would take you a whole day, a whole month, to reach the earth—you would keep falling and never get there. Maybe it is simply the Cossack Likhachev sitting under the wagon [sharpening Petya's saber], but it very well may be that he is the kindest, bravest, most wonderful, most excellent man in the world, whom nobody knows. Maybe it was indeed a hussar who came for water and went back into the hollow, but maybe he just vanished from sight, vanished completely, and never was.

Whatever Petya might have seen now, nothing would have astonished him. He was in a magic kingdom in which everything was possible. (1054–55)

Then, as he quietly rocks himself to sleep, he enjoys an extraordinary concert unlike any he's ever heard before. Listen in:

Drops dripped. Quiet talk went on. Horses neighed and scuffled. Someone snored.

"Ozhik, zhik, ozhik, zhik . . ." whistled the saber being sharpened. And suddenly Petya heard a harmonious chorus of music, playing some unknown, solemnly sweet hymn. Petya was musical, like Natasha, and more so than Nikolai, but he had never studied music or thought about music, and therefore the melodies that unexpectedly came to his head were especially new and attractive to him. The music played more and more audibly. The melody grew, passing from one instrument to another. What is known as a fugue was going on, though Petya had not the slightest idea of what a fugue was. Each instrument, now resembling a violin, now trumpets—but better and clearer than violins and trumpets— each instrument played its own part and, before finishing its motif, merged with another, starting out almost the same, and with a third, and with a fourth, and they all merged into one and scattered again, and merged again, now solemn and churchly, now brightly brilliant and victorious.

"Ah, yes, it's me dreaming," Petya said to himself, rocking forward. "It's in my ears. And maybe it's my music. Well, again . . . Go on, my music! Now! . . ."

He closed his eyes. And on all sides, as if from far away, sounds trembled, began to harmonize, scattered, merged, and again all joined in the same sweet and solemn hymn. "Ah, how lovely that is! As much as I like and however I like," Petya said to himself. He attempted to conduct this huge chorus of instruments.

"Softer, softer now, fade away." And the sounds obeyed him. "Fuller now, merrier. More, more joyful." And swelling, solemn sounds rose from an unknown depth. "Now, voices, join in!" Petya ordered. And voices, first men's, then women's, came from far away. The voices grew, grew in a measured, solemn effort. Petya felt frightened and joyful hearkening to their uncommon beauty.

The song merged with the solemn, victorious march, and drops dripped, and bzhik, zhik, zhik . . . whistled the saber, and again the horse scuffled and neighed, not disrupting the chorus, but entering into it. (1055)

This is one of those scenes in *War and Peace*, like the hunt, in which all of the teeming diversity of life is concentrated into one shining moment. It's all here: the human and natural worlds, the sounds of impending battle and the incredible calm, the laserlike specificity of the senses, and, encompassing all of it, the sense of life's mysterious, musical grandeur.

When the battle commences at the crack of dawn, a very stimulated (and very tired) Petya is hardly able to contain his excitement. Hearing the sound of whistling bullets, seeing the dense, undulating smoke, he gallops down a village road ahead of the other troops toward the place the shots seem to be coming from. Approaching a courtyard where, unbeknownst to him, French soldiers are ensconced behind a wattle fence, Petya lets out a giant "Hurra-a-h!" and breathlessly charges straight into a thick cloud of magical powder smoke.

Somewhere deep in that cloud a bullet pierces his skull and kills him.

"I can't believe it!" exclaims one upset reader.

"No *way!*" rues another. "Aren't we supposed to be, like, inspired by Petya's spirit? Isn't this the very sort of . . . vitality Tolstoy's been celebrating the whole way through?"

The sadness and shock readers feel at Petya's sudden death is perfectly understandable. It breaks my heart, too, every time I read it.

How, after all, can we blame this happy, gung ho fifteen-year-old for being the coddled kid that he is, reveling in the seemingly limitless possibilities of his young life? Reading these pages in the novel, you feel Tolstoy's almost paternal tenderness toward this character, this boy so full of sweetness and pluck. But no amount of wishful thinking can get around the hard facts of reality: a fortified French encampment being ambushed at dawn by a Russian infantry in the middle of war is not, and never will be, a magic kingdom. No, this is a venue where inexperienced adolescent boys charging happily into gun smoke are going to get killed. Tolstoy was too honest a writer to pretend otherwise. Perhaps if he had eventually become a Hollywood screenwriter, like his son Ilya, Tolstoy might have ended the Petya story line with his young hero, say, skillfully slicing up the Frenchmen ensconced behind the wattle fence to become one of the youngest Russian soldiers ever to win the St. George Cross. Fortunately for our sake, Tolstoy stayed put in Yasnaya Polyana, and decided to tell the truth. And the truth, like life itself . . . hurts.

It can also heal us, though, in a way that our rational concepts, or abstract ideas—to say nothing of our fantasies about the world—rarely can. The bittersweet reality is that each one of our lives is but a note—even a melody—in the gorgeous concert of life. Those notes and melodies may be fully appreciated on their own, but far more important is how they're heard in conjunction with all the others. That Petya is attuned to this higher reality makes perfect sense, for he possesses the same vitality and sensitivity to the musicality of life that all of the Rostovs seem to share. Alas, in his final, fatal moment of youthful rapture, he seeks to conduct the fugue, to control all those instruments and notes and melodies, when in reality, he is merely one of them.

But does his song ever truly vanish, in the same way that the hussar in his magic kingdom "just vanished from sight, vanished completely, and never was"? (1054). Not exactly. Tolstoy, who studied musical theory in his youth, had considered a career as a composer. Often reduced to tears while listening to Bach, he knew well the power of music to affect listeners—even long after a performance has ended. Not surprisingly, he is equally attuned to the ways in which every human life, even as it eventually fades back into the whole, leaves its indelible trace on the world, in often unpredictable ways. At some deep, intuitive level, the Rostovs, too, know this. They know that Petya's death, crushing as it is, in a strange, terrible way, remains part of the music of life—serves, indeed, as Natasha will herself discover, as a clarion call *to* life.

Distraught over the death of Prince Andrei, she has been wandering around the house ghostlike for days, annoyed by the humdrum concerns of all those people around her whose "words and feelings seemed to her an insult to that world in which she had been living recently, and she was not only indifferent, but looked at them with hostility" (1078).

And then the Rostovs get the news about Petya. Natasha, not yet aware of what has happened, notices her father stumbling over to a chair into which he collapses, and covering his eyes, he begins to weep. In an instant she is transformed from self-absorbed child back to keenly aware adult; Tolstoy describes this sudden shift of perspective as an experience almost of physical violence: "She felt a terrible pain; it seemed to her that something had torn inside her and she was dying. . . . Seeing her father and hearing her mother's terrible, coarse cry from behind the door, she instantly forgot herself and her grief" (1079)—in fact, Tolstoy goes on, "[t]his was the way Natasha's wound healed. She thought her life was over. But suddenly her love for her mother showed her that the essence of life—love—was still alive in her. Love awoke, and life awoke" (1080).

Love awoke, and life awoke. These five words strike to the very core of *War and Peace*: To love, Tolstoy says, is to see. To see is to know the truth. And to know the truth is to truly live. No wonder, then, that this novel chock full of clear, honest reflection about the pain of living is also one of the most life-affirming works of fiction one will encounter.

It is not just Natasha whose experience is upended by Petya's death. As we discover, Pierre is saved by the very detachment with which Petya was fighting when he died. Nor is this the only coincidence at play here. A certain Dolokhov, who happens to be one of the commanders of those Russian troops, marches with the Cossacks as they escort Petya's body to a pit dug in the garden. Dolokhov, the very man who once nearly destroyed Petya's brother Nikolai at the poker table, and almost killed Pierre in a duel! This rather dreadful fellow, it seems, has found an outlet for his native cruelty on the killing fields, an embodiment of Tolstoy's belief that evil, too, plays a necessary role in the larger scheme of things. "'Finished,'" he says with characteristic iciness upon seeing Petya's lifeless body, "as if uttering this word gave him pleasure" (1058). Denisov, present as well at that moment, says nothing after learning what has happened. Instead, with trembling hands, he turns the pale, blood- and mud-stained face of young Petya toward him, and, wailing hysterically while grabbing hold of a nearby wattle fence, suddenly recalls Petya's words from the night before: "'I'm used to something sweet. Excellent raisins, take them all'" (1058). That sweetness will continue to live on through Pierre's and Natasha's third child, a son, whom they name Petya. All of this, taken together, creates the impression that the world is indeed a mysterious place, with a unique sort of poetic justice, and with its own special kind of "harmony," which, as Tolstoy wrote in an 1863 diary entry, "only art feels."

We tap into this harmony when we loosen our attachment to our own ideas, to our egos, when we overcome our insistence that the world be the way we *think* it should be: when, in other words, we learn to see as Tolstoy sees. Sure, it might be comforting if Tolstoy were to offer some clear rational or religious justification for why young Petya Rostov has to die while his namesake Pierre Bezukhov survives. His goal as an artist is not to offer a superficial prescription for what ails us, however, but merely an accurate description of the way things are. And the way things are, he suggests, is neither as lovely as we might wish, nor as bleakly senseless as we often fear. Joy and tragedy, sweetness and sadness, are the yin and yang of life, forever giving meaning to each other, even as they balance each other out. Not that this sort of awareness does much to lessen the very real grief felt by the Rostovs; nor should it. But it may at least create a wider context for understanding the meaning of that grief: a context that allows the Rostovs to discover

possibilities within their pain, just as it helps all of us to recognize sorrow as an essential, and in its own way, beautiful, refrain in the whole
concert of life.

Four short chapters and six or so pages after we learn of Petya's death,
Pierre, still in captivity and worn-out from hunger and exhaustion,
falls into a half-delirious sleep and recalls a long-forgotten old geography teacher of his back in Switzerland. In the dream the teacher shows
him a globe:

> This globe was a living, wavering ball of no dimensions. The entire
> surface of the ball consisted of drops tightly packed together. And
> these drops all moved and shifted, and now merged from several
> into one, now divided from one into many. Each drop strove to
> spread and take up the most space, but the others, striving to do
> the same, pressed it, sometimes destroying, sometimes merging
> with it.
>   "This is life," said the old teacher.
>   "How simple and clear it is," thought Pierre. "How could I have
> not known this before?" (1064–65)

Because, Tolstoy would say, it often requires years of struggle and
searching before the simplest, most obvious truths become evident to
us. Much of our lives is but a drop on that wavering globe, isn't it? As
each of us journeys through life, striving to realize ourselves according
to our ideas, our ideals, while at the same time continually buffeted
by outside circumstances, we come into contact with others on their
own trajectories. Our paths cross and collide, sometimes with sudden
intensity, as with Nikolai and Marya, amid the turmoil of 1812; at
other times, as with Pierre and Natasha, slowly, over long periods of
time. Now and again entire populations clash, as do the French and
Russians here, resulting in a reordering of the political and cultural

landscape. Yet through it all, life flows endlessly on, forever changing, forever renewing itself.

Why, we may well wonder, on top of that lengthy description of the nighttime fugue Petya hears, would Tolstoy employ yet another elaborate metaphor to convey life's beautiful fluidity? For the same reason that he has marshaled nearly six hundred characters over the span of more than a thousand pages in order to describe the countless variations on the novel's central theme of man's search for meaning in a relentlessly unstable world: just as no individual experience encapsulates the meaning of human existence, so no single metaphor is going to capture the whole truth about life. And so Tolstoy just kept on writing, creating new characters and scenes, revisiting familiar characters in fresh contexts, exploring metaphor after metaphor in his quest to contain in words that which is not readily contained. In the same way that every human journey in the novel is at once unique and integrally connected with those of the other characters, so the fugue and the globe offer two slightly different versions of one and the same idea of what Tolstoy once referred to as "life in all its countless, inexhaustible manifestations." If the fugue is an embodiment of some higher musical harmony in the world, then the globe suggests life's inevitable conflict and instability. *War and Peace* embodies both of these dimensions of experience as powerfully as any novel ever has. And in the epilogue, they are brought together and held in perfect, creative tension.

So there they are after the war: three generations of Rostovs living under one roof along with the Bezukhovs, as aristocratic families often did in those days, at Bald Hills, the Bolkonskys' country seat. The world has changed. Gone is the Russia before the Napoleonic Wars, when the Rostovs threw parties at their home on Povarskaya Street, the count's corpulent body heavily twisting and twirling on the dance floor, while young Natasha clapped and demanded that all her guests "look at papa!" Nikolai, now a father himself, is so worn-out from the hard work of digging the Rostov family out of debt and securing a future for his children that he spends much of his time on the couch in his study; only occasionally will he allow himself to give *his* daughter Natasha "a little gallop around the room" before putting her down, out of breath (1153). Gone, too, are the wonderfully eccentric old Prince Bolkonskys, those scions of an old aristocratic order who presided, tsarlike, over their vast estates, suspicious of anybody or anything that might threaten their traditional way of life. Russia at the end of *War and Peace* is a country no longer quite so certain about its collective national identity; indeed, it seems headed for yet another upheaval:

> Seven years had passed since 1812. The churned-up historical sea of Europe settled back within its shores. It seemed to have grown still; but the mysterious forces that move mankind (mysterious because the laws that determine their movement are unknown to us) continued their action.
>
> Though the surface of the historical sea seemed immobile, mankind moved as ceaselessly as the movement of time. Various groups and human connections were made and unmade; causes were prepared for the formation and decomposition of states, for the displacement of peoples.
>
> The historical sea did not, as formerly, direct its surges from one shore to another: it seethed in its depths. (1129)

The defeat of Napoleon in 1812 unleashed a surge of patriotism resulting in calls for reform, which were themselves snuffed out by a conservative crackdown in the capital. Pierre, now in his thirties, is at the center of a movement to form a secret society of aristocrats and government figures who will work to reform Russian society, ridding it of corruption. Listening to him speak, one can't help hearing strong echoes of the idealist he once was, under the influence of Freemasonry, who'd always wanted to bring about a more just world: "'My whole thought,'" he now tells Natasha, "'is that, since vicious people band together and constitute a force, honest people need only do the same'" (1177). At last, then, his reformist intentions of so many years ago are beginning to bear actual fruit, although in a form Pierre could never have predicted. We have this sneaky suspicion, moreover, that the older, wiser Pierre might even succeed this time around—albeit, again, in a way that neither he nor we can quite envision.

Pierre's brother-in-law Nikolai Rostov, on the other hand, insists during one of their many fiery debates that the government for which he and millions of other Russians sacrificed so much back in 1812 is not nearly as corrupt as Pierre thinks. As for Pierre's secret society, well, it is as dangerous as it is unnecessary. In fact, were Nikolai ordered this instant by the infamous, iron-fisted chief counselor to the tsar, Arakcheev, to go against Pierre with a squadron and cut him down, then by God, he'd do it! Really? We know enough about Nikolai's character to be certain that, for all his bluster, he is a good and kind man who, were he ever forced to make such a choice, would choose his family ties over his political loyalties. Indeed, this particular argument with Pierre ends, as the debates at Bald Hills always do, with the disputing sides parting "on the most friendly terms" (1171): "As in every real family, several totally different worlds lived together in the house at Bald Hills, each maintaining its own particularity and yielding to the others, but merging into one harmonious whole" (1160).

What, then, are we to make of Nikolenka Bolkonsky, Prince Andrei's son born on that wintry March night fifteen years earlier, who now often sits alone in corners, breaks pens and sticks of sealing wax, and dreams of conquering the world like the Roman generals he reads about in Plutarch? With no memory of his biological father, Nikolenka is being raised by Uncle Nikolai and Aunt Marya, who admittedly have trouble connecting to this odd, curly-headed, sickly-looking boy. "'I'm afraid I forget about him because of my own,'" Marya confesses to Nikolai. "'We all have children, we all have relations; but he has nobody. He's eternally alone with his thoughts'" (1173). Of which Nikolenka has quite a few, stirred up in no small measure by the sorts of heated political arguments he often overhears at Bald Hills.

As a matter of fact, Nikolenka happens to be sitting in the shadows at a writing table by the window in Uncle Nikolai's study during the argument in which Nikolai tells Pierre that he'd cut him down if

Arakcheev ordered him to. That night Nikolenka has a dream. He dreams that he and Uncle Pierre are marching at the head of a huge army consisting of slanting white lines like the spiderwebs that hang in the air in the fall. Just ahead of them is their destination, "glory," a slightly denser version of those very webs. As Nikolenka and Uncle Pierre close in on their goal, the threads supporting them and their army weaken and tangle, and suddenly Uncle Nikolai stands menacingly before them. Pointing to the broken-up wax and pencils, he tells Nikolenka that Arakcheev has given him orders to kill the boy. Nikolenka turns immediately to look at Uncle Pierre, but instead of Pierre he sees his father, who has no image or form, but who nevertheless caresses his son and fills him with tender love. Still, that love isn't quite strong enough to stop Uncle Nikolai from moving closer and closer, at which point the boy awakens in a cold sweat, a flurry of thoughts rushing through his head:

> "Father," he thought. "Father" (though there were two portraits of a good likeness in the house, Nikolenka never pictured Prince Andrei in his human image), "father was with me and caressed me. He approved of me, he approved of Uncle Pierre. Whatever he says—I'll do . . . I know they want me to study. And I will study. But some day I'll stop. And then I'll do it. I ask God for only one thing: that it's the same with me as with the men in Plutarch, and I'll do the same. I'll do better. Everybody will know me, love me, admire me." (1178)

Sound familiar? Many years earlier, on the eve of the battle of Austerlitz, Prince Andrei had similar thoughts: "'[I]f I want this, want glory, want to be known by people, loved by them,'" he thinks, "'it's not my fault that I want it, that it's the only thing I want, the only thing I live for'" (265). Fortunately, Nikolenka is still young, and will have many more opportunities to define, and redefine, his personal definition of "glory" before actually throwing himself in front of enemy fire on the battlefield. He also has his tutor Dessales to comfort and guide him:

"Are you unwell?" Dessales asks in French.

"*Non*," replied Nikolenka, and he lay back on the pillow. "He's kind and good, I love him," he thought of Dessales. "But Uncle Pierre! Oh, what a wonderful man! And father? Father! Yes, I'll do something that even *he* would be pleased with...." (1178)

With his idealistic and ambitious nature, Nikolenka might well go on to do good and important things in the world. But then again, if the tragic circumstances of his birth as well as this terrifying nightmare on the last page of the book are any indication, he might not. Nikolenka will come of age, after all, at a time when his compatriots will march on Senate Square in Petersburg in 1825, demanding political reforms, only to wind up in Siberian exile—or hanged. Might Nikolenka, who will be twenty-one at that time, himself become one of those very Decembrists?

We cannot know—Tolstoy never tells us. What *is* clear is that the cocoonlike environment in which his parents grew up has dissipated, becoming tangled up like those airy spiderwebs in his dream. For now, Dessales is at his side, but at some point Nikolenka will be on his own in the world, the mounting tensions of Russian political life battling it out within his soul. Soon enough it will be his turn to seek answers to the very questions his forebears grappled with so intensely: What does he value? What kind of a person does he wish to be? What sort of society does he want to help build for his children?

Having recently become a father, I find myself thinking more and more about these questions from a perspective rather different than the one I had when I began this book some years ago. As I watched that tiny being emerge, with his wobbling limbs, his swollen eyes, his shrieking little mouth, love awoke and life awoke within me as never before. Suddenly, the ending of *War and Peace* took on fresh personal significance, compelling me to consider questions I'd never thought to ask before: Given all he'd experienced, what advice would Prince Andrei, were he alive, offer his son? After all my years of studying Tolstoy, what advice will I offer my own son?

What would please Prince Andrei most, I'd venture to guess, would be for Nikolenka to carve out a path though life inspired by the traditions and memories of those who came before him, yet illuminated by a light uniquely his own. Surely, though, he would wish Nikolenka to know something that he himself discovered only in the end: that one is much more than his successes and failures, his plans and frustrations, or the circumstances in which he may happen to find himself at any given point in time.

Andrei would probably encourage Nikolenka to spend more time listening to the stories of wonderful, old Uncle Pierre—for instance, the tale about that one evening, while in captivity, when Pierre tries to cross to the other side of a road, in order to chat with another group of captive soldiers, only to be stopped by a French sentry who tells him to go back. Pierre does go back—only not to the campfire or to his comrades, but rather to an unhitched cart, beside which he sits alone on the cold ground. After an hour of sitting there with crossed legs and a lowered head, he suddenly bursts into a hearty, good-natured laugh:

> "Ha, ha, ha," laughed Pierre. And he said aloud to himself: "The soldiers wouldn't let me go. They caught me, they locked me up. They're holding me prisoner. Who, me? Me? Me—my immortal soul! Ha, ha, ha! . . . Ha, ha, ha!" he laughed, with tears brimming his eyes. (1020)

Whereupon he looks up at the full moon standing high in the bright sky, sees the forest and fields spreading into the wavering, endless distance, peers into the depths of the retreating, twinkling stars, and thinks joyously to himself: "'And all this is mine, and all this is in me, and all this is me!'" (1020)

There, Nikolenka—dear reader—is the truth, in all its stark, liberating beauty, the truth Tolstoy managed to give us before he was done.

*The Artist as an Old Man: Tolstoy taking a walk
along a snowy avenue at Yasnaya Polyana in 1909.*

Acknowledgments

In "A Few Words Apropos of the Book *War and Peace*," Tolstoy admitted that he wrote the novel "under the best conditions of life." Thanks to the support and kindness I've received from many people, I can say the same for this book.

From the day I met my agent Rob McQuilkin—perhaps the most fortunate day of my writing career—I have understood why a handful of writers speak so passionately about their agents. With consummate professional and intellectual integrity, creativity, and tenacity he has given me spot-on guidance throughout the writing and publishing process.

Sharon Leiter, one of my dearest friends and most trusted readers, brought her poetic ear and scholarly precision to every page of this book, holding my writing to her own highest literary and intellectual standards.

My friend and fellow writer Marietta McCarty has been an invaluable literary companion, bringing wisdom, kindness, and dry logs to our regular fireside chats.

John Gray helped me to tune out the noise and tune into Tolstoy's—and my own—deepest truths, and James Yates helped to deepen my thinking about *War and Peace* through his penetrating philosophical insights.

With deepest respect and admiration I thank Dana Gioia, Jay Parini, Richard Gustafson, James Billington, Irwin Weil, the late Joseph Frank, Lazar Fleishman, Hugh McLean, Donna Orwin, and Carol Apollonio for their scholarly generosity as well as their feedback on my Tolstoy scholarship over the years.

I owe a special thank you to Pyotr Palievsky of the Gorky Institute of World Literature, one of my most sensitive and encouraging readers, and to my longtime mentor Aida Abuashvili-Lominadze, who played a pivotal role in my decision to dedicate my life to the study of Russian literature. I also thank Galina Alekseeva and the staff at the Leo Tolstoy Museum and Estate at Yasnaya Polyana for their scholarly assistance, and Vladimir Tolstoy for encouraging my efforts to bring his great-great-grandfather's ideas to a wider audience.

Many of the ideas in this book were deepened by conversations with my University of Virginia students, the residents at Beaumont Juvenile Correctional Center, and the members of two Charlottesville, Virginia reading groups I've been a part of. Other friends and colleagues have given me professional and personal support during the writing of this book. Mike Signer inspired me with rich conversation about literature and life during our regular breakfast chats. Aaron Fein and Dahlia Lithwick gave me valuable feedback on my writing. Jonathan Coleman mentored me through the thicket of the publishing world. Julie Gronlund and Annette Owens helped with the proofreading. Dorothy Kolomeisky made suggestions that improved parts of the manuscript. Jane Barnes and I shared tales from the literary trenches. Lilia Travisano assisted with translations. Dorothe Bach, Marva Barnett, Rob Wolman, Karen Inkelas, and David Herman at the University of Virginia have been generous colleagues, supporting my efforts to develop new methods of teaching Tolstoy and Russian literature.

I have had the good fortune to be able to work with a wonderful team at Simon & Schuster. Millicent Bennett inherited this book from a previous editor, yet treated it like one of her own. I thank Millicent, her assistants Ed Winstead and Sarah Nalle, and Kathryn Higuchi and the entire Simon & Schuster production team for their steadfast enthusiasm for the project, and for helping to nurture my manuscript into the present book.

I owe an immeasurable debt of gratitude to my parents, two of my staunchest, longtime supporters, who encouraged me to pursue my creative dreams, and who wisely suggested many years ago that I start learning Russian—a piece of advice that would lead directly to my decades-long relationship with Tolstoy. My three older brothers, Greg, Bob, and Mike, were never too busy to offer support and guidance; and I especially thank Mike, a fellow academic and writer, who has continually challenged me to stay true to my best intellectual and emotional instincts.

My deepest gratitude goes to my wife Corinne, who has stood by my side with unwavering love and encouragement during every step of the long and difficult writing process. She has also given me the greatest gift of all: our son Ian, whose sparkling goodness fills me with daily joy and love. While I was writing about Tolstoyan wisdom, Corinne and Ian were showing me every day what it means to *live* it.

Appendix 1

Meet Leo Tolstoy: A Chronology of the Writer's Life

aking it to the age of eighty-two would be an accomplishment in any era. But at a time when the life expectancy for a man was roughly half that number of years, it was nothing short of heroic. Tolstoy packed a lot of living into those eight-plus decades, too: from his youthful (mis)adventures on the battlefield, at the gambling table, and in the bedroom, to his later years as a father of thirteen children, the founder of a religion, and the internationally famous social thinker who would inspire the likes of Mahatma Gandhi and Martin Luther King. No stranger to the upheavals of nineteenth- and early-twentieth-century life, Tolstoy was born a few years after the failed Decembrist uprising of 1825, came of age during the Crimean War of the 1850s, witnessed the Great Reforms of Alexander II in the 1860s, and then watched as his country barreled toward the failed, bloody Russian Revolution of 1905. And through it all this graphomaniac just kept on writing, producing ninety volumes of prose in all, among which there happen to be not one, but two of the world's greatest novels, as well as a handful of essays that would influence the course of modern civilization.

How do you choose details from such a life to be included in a brief chronological summary? Very, very selectively. Which is why the chronology of Tolstoy's life I offer below is meant simply as a useful reference point for readers wanting to keep track of what Tolstoy did, what he wrote, and when. The book you are holding in your hands will certainly fill in a number of the details relating to the writing and themes of *War and Peace*. For the complete story of Tolstoy's life and times, however, I recommend one of the excellent biographies mentioned in the Suggestions for Further Reading.

1828   Tolstoy is born in his inherited ancestral estate, Yasnaya Polyana, or "Clear Glade."

1830   Mother dies.

1836   Tolstoy moves to Moscow with his family.

1837   Tolstoy's father dies. Children raised by their distant relative, T. A. Yergolskaya, beloved "Aunty."

1844   Moves to Kazan, where he enters Kazan University to study Oriental languages, then transfers to the Faculty of Law.

1847   Withdraws from Kazan University and returns to Yasnaya Polyana. Begins his Benjamin Franklin–inspired journal, writing down daily rules of conduct.

1848   Moves to Moscow, where he frequents high society.

1849   Moves to Petersburg, plans to enroll in the university and enter civil service, but instead returns to Yasnaya Polyana. Opens a school for peasant children on his estate.

1851   Returns with his brother Nikolai to the Caucasus, Russia's southern frontier.

1852   Joins the military as a cadet stationed in the North Caucasus. Publishes "Childhood."

1854   Promoted to rank of ensign. Publishes "Boyhood."

1855   Forced to sell the house he was born in to pay off a gambling loss of six thousand rubles. Serves at Sevastopol on the notoriously bloody fourth bastion during the Crimean War. Goes to Petersburg, where he becomes acquainted with writer Ivan Turgenev.

1856   Publishes "Sevastopol in August 1855," "Two Hussars," and "A Landowner's Morning." Meets radical philosopher and critic Nikolai Chernyshevsky.

1857   Publishes "Youth." Travels through Europe.

1859   Publishes "Family Happiness." Reopens his school for peasant children at Yasnaya Polyana.

1860   Brother Nikolai dies.

1862   Marries Sofya [Sonya] Andreyevna Behrs. Secret police raid Tolstoy's Yasnaya Polyana school in search of seditious educational materials.

1863   Publishes *The Cossacks*. Son Sergei, first of thirteen children, is born.

1864   Begins work on the first draft of *War and Peace*, then called *1805*. First daughter, Tatyana, is born.

1865   *1805* (first two volumes of what will become *War and Peace*) is published in the *Russian Herald*.

1866   Second son, Ilya, is born.

1867   Works on the third and fourth volumes of *War and Peace*.

1868   Works on the fifth volume of *War and Peace*.

1869   Works on the sixth volume of *War and Peace*. Travels to Penza Province for a possible land purchase, stops overnight in a hotel in Arzamas, where he suffers a severe panic attack, the beginning of a long period of intense religious searching. Third son, Lev (Leo), is born.

1871   Suffers severe depression. Travels to the steppes of Samara, lives with the Bashkirs. Meets philosopher and critic Nikolai Strakhov. Second daughter, Marya, is born.

1872   Fourth son, Pyotr, is born.

1873   Begins work on *Anna Karenina*. Publishes his collected works in four volumes, included a revised edition of *War and Peace*. Baby Pyotr dies of croup.

1874   Fifth son, Nikolai, is born. Beloved "Aunty" T. A. Ergolskaya dies.

1875   Beginning of *Anna Karenina* published in the *Russian Messenger*. Baby Nikolai dies of meningitis. Third daughter, Varvara, is born prematurely, dies within two hours.

1877   Completes *Anna Karenina*, published the following year in a single edition. His religious quest intensifies. Sixth son, Andrei, is born.

1879   Seventh son, Mikhail, is born.

1880   Writes *Confession*. Begins work on *A Translation and Harmony of the Four Gospels*.

1881   Visits Optina-Pustyn Monastery, some seventy miles from Yasnaya Polyana. Writes a letter to Tsar Alexander III requesting that the tsar not execute the revolutionary terrorists who assassinated his father, Tsar Alexander II. The tsar responds that he doesn't have the right to forgive the criminals; the assassins are executed. Moves with his family to Moscow and hates city life. Eighth son, Alexei, is born.

1882   Buys a house in Moscow (today the site of the L. N. Tolstoy Museum).

1883   Finishes working on the religious treatise "What I Believe," published the following year. Reads the Bible in Hebrew. Meets Vladimir Chertkov, who will eventually become a prominent Tolstoyan.

1884   Threatens to leave home, but soon returns. Reads and admires the essay "Self-Reliance" by American transcendentalist Ralph Waldo Emerson. Fourth daughter, Alexandra, is born.

1886   Publishes *The Death of Ivan Ilyich*, "How Much Land Does a Man Need?," and the play *The Power of Darkness*. Four-year-old Alexei dies of croup.

1887   Works on *The Kreutzer Sonata* and the essay "On Life." Struggles to give up smoking and drinking.

1888   Walks from Moscow to Yasnaya Polyana. Quits smoking. Thirteenth and last child, Ivan (Vanya), is born. First grandchild, Anna (daughter of son Ilya), is born.

1889   Begins the novel *Resurrection* and writes the novella *The Devil*.

1890   Works on the tale "Father Sergius." Censor refuses to publish *The Kreutzer Sonata*. Writes article "Why Do Men Stupefy Themselves?"

1891   Renounces the copyright on all works published before 1881. Gives up meat and alcohol. Organizes a relief effort for the famine in Tula and Ryazan. Writes several articles about the famine, including "On Hunger," which sharply criticizes the government.

1892   Finishes work on *The Kingdom of God Is Within You* and sends it abroad for translation and publication.

1893   Writes an introduction to the essays of Guy de Maupassant. Meets theater director Konstantin Stanislavsky.

1894   Meets writer Ivan Bunin.

1895   Finishes "Master and Man." Youngest son, Vanya, dies suddenly from scarlet fever. Meets writer Anton Chekhov.

1896   Writes the first draft of the novella *Hadji-Murat*.

1897   Travels to Petersburg. Works on the tract *What Is Art?*

1898   Works on the novel *Resurrection* and the tale *Father Sergius* with the intention of donating the proceeds to help the Dukhobors, a persecuted religious sect in Russia, emigrate to Canada.

1899   Meets German poet Rainer Maria Rilke.

1900   Writes articles, "The Slavery of Our Times," "Patriotism and Government," and "Thou Shalt Not Kill." Works on drama *The Living*

Corpse (published posthumously). Meets writer and revolutionary activist Maxim Gorky. Having read Nietzsche, condemns the German philosopher for his moral "savagery."

1901   Excommunicated from the Russian Orthodox Church, and in response, publishes "A Reply to the Holy Synod's Edict." Comes down with malaria and travels to the Crimea to recuperate. Visited by Anton Chekhov and Maxim Gorky in the Crimea.

1902   Returns to Yasnaya Polyana. Finishes *What Is Religion and Wherein Lies Its Essence?* Sends a letter to Tsar Nikolai II criticizing the Russian government. Decides to commission his biography in order to share with people the "vileness of my life until my awakening."

1903   Protests Jewish pogroms in Kishinev. American politician William Jennings Bryan visits Yasnaya Polyana. Writes the story "After the Ball."

1904   Publishes the influential antiwar tract "Bethink Yourselves" in response to the Russo-Japanese War. Finishes *Hadji-Murat.* Beloved brother Sergei dies.

1905   Deplores the violence of the revolution. Writes articles such as "The End of an Age," applying principles of nonviolent resistance to the political turmoil in Russia. Writes the story "Alyosha the Pot."

1906   Publishes the story "For What?" Prepares stories for the instructional publication *Cycles of Reading.* Daughter Marya dies of pneumonia.

1907   Tells British playwright George Bernard Shaw in a letter that he is "not sufficiently serious." Brother-in-law Vyacheslav Behrs, a transportation engineer, is murdered during a strike in Petersburg. Russian painter Ilya Repin paints portrait of Tolstoy.

1908   Publishes "I Cannot Be Silent," condemning the death penalty. Receives Dictaphone from American inventor Thomas Edison.

1909   Writes his will leaving control of all of his works to daughter Alexandra after his death. Considers giving away all of his property.

1910   Leaves Yasnaya Polyana in secret. Dies in the stationmaster's house at the Astapovo train station with international media looking on. Buried, according to his wishes, in the forest where he and his brother Nikolai first discovered the "little green stick," on which they believed was inscribed the secret to universal happiness.

Appendix 2

Who's Who in *War and Peace*?:
A Guide to Characters' Names

If the prospect of keeping track of those nearly six hundred characters in *War and Peace* with their weird Russian, French, and German
names terrifies you, well, you're not alone. But the task isn't nearly as
difficult as you might think. All you need to do is understand a few basic
naming principles, recognize the five major families and the handful of
other characters that are most important in the novel, and avail yourself
of the character list below.

Russian names consist of a first name, a patronymic (based on the
father's first name, and usually ending in *-ovich* or *-ich* for males and
-ovna or *-ichna* for females), and a family name. In formal settings, it
is common to call a person by his or her first name and patronymic.
Among family and friends only the first name is used, or the more
endearing diminutive form (Natasha for Natalya, or Nikolenka for
Nikolai). In informal settings characters will also sometimes call one
another by their last name only (Rostov instead of Nikolai Rostov, or
Dolokhov instead of Fyodor Dolokhov), or even by their patronymic
alone (as in Alpatych). An *-a* or an *-aya* is often added to the end of a
family name to indicate feminine gender (as in Natasha Rostova and
Marya Bolkonskaya).

I have put the accented syllables of each Russian name in italics, and have included a pronunciation guide in brackets in cases where the pronunciation may not be obvious based on the spelling.

The Be*zu*khovs [beh-*zoo*-khuffs]

Count Kir*ill* Vla*dim*irovich Be*zu*khov

Count *Pyo*tr Kir*ill*ovich [kee-*ree*-luh-veech] (Pierre), his son

The Bol*kon*skys [bahl-*cone*-skeez]

Prince *N*ikolai An*dree*vich Bol*kon*sky

Prince And*rei* Niko*la*evich (Andr*yu*sha), his son

Princess *Ma*rya Niko*la*evna (*Ma*sha), his daughter

Princess Eliza*ve*ta *Kar*lovna (*Li*za), Prince Andrei's wife

Prince Nikolai An*dree*vich (Ni*ko*lenka), Andrei's son by Liza

The Ros*tov*s [rah-*stohffs*]

Count Il*ya* And*ree*vich Ros*tov*

Countess Na*ta*lya (no patronymic given) (Nata*lie*), his wife

Countess *Ve*ra Ily*in*ichna, their elder daughter

Count Niko*lai* Ily*ich*, their elder son

Countess Na*ta*lya Ily*in*ichna (Na*ta*sha), their younger daughter

Count *Pyo*tr Ily*ich* (*Pe*tya), their younger son

*So*fya Alex*an*drovna (no family name given) (*So*nya, So*phie*)— orphaned Rostov cousin brought up in the family

The Ku*ra*gins [koo-*rah*-geenz]

Prince Vas*si*ly [vah-*see*-lee] Ku*ra*gin

Prince Ana*tole* Vas*si*lievich, his eldest son

Prince Ippo*lit* Vas*si*lievich (Hippolyte), his younger son

Princess E*le*na Vas*si*lievna (Hélène), his daughter, later Pierre Bezukhov's wife

The Drubetskois [droo-buts-*koyz*]

Princess *An*na Mi*khai*lovna Drubetsk*a*ya

Prince Bor*is* [bah-*rees*] (no patronymic given) Drubetsk*oi*, her son

Other Important Characters

*Ma*rya *Dmi*trievna Akhros*i*mova, society matron and friend of the Rostovs

*Ya*kov Alp*a*tych (no family name given), steward of old Prince Bolkonsky

*O*sip Alex*e*evich Baz*de*yev, prominent Freemason who has a strong influence on Pierre Bezukhov

Al*phonse Karl*ovich Berg, a young Russian officer who marries Vera Rostova

Mademoiselle A*ma*lia Evg*e*nievna Bouri*enne*, a French companion living with the Bolkonskys

Vass*i*ly *Dmi*trich De*ni*sov (*Va*ska), hussar officer and close friend of Nikolai Rostov

*Fyo*dor I*van*ovich *Do*lokhov (*Fe*dya), Russian officer who befriends Nikolai Rostov

Dron, village headman at Bolkonsky family estate at Bogucharovo

I*la*gin (no first name or patronymic given), wealthy landowner and neighbor of Rostovs

Il*yin* (no first name or patronymic given), young officer being mentored by Nikolai Rostov

Julie Kar*a*gin (no Russian first name or patronymic given), a wealthy heiress and friend of Marya Bolkonskaya

Pla*ton* Kara*ta*ev, simple peasant soldier who influences Pierre Bezukhov

Karp, insubordinate serf at Bogucharovo, the Bolkonsky country estate

Mavra Kuz*min*ishna, Rostov family servant

Lav*rush*ka (no patronymic or family name given), Denisov's and Nikolai Rostov's orderly

*An*na *Pav*lovna *Sche*rer, a well-known Petersburg salon hostess

Captain *Tu*shin (no first name or patronymic given), Russian artillery captain at the battle of Schöngrabern

Major Historical Figures in *War and Peace*

Alexander I (1777–1825), tsar of Russia, often called "Emperor"

Napoleon I (1769–1821), French emperor

Prince *Pyo*tr I*van*ovich Bagratio*n* [buh-grah-tee-*own*] (1765–1812), Russian general

Prince Mikha*il* Illario*n*ovich Ku*tu*zov (1745–1813), Russian commander in chief at the battle of Borodino

Count *Fyo*dor Vas*si*lievich Rostopch*in* [ruh-stahp-*cheen*] (1763–1826), governor of Moscow

Mikha*il* Mi*khail*ovich Spe*ran*sky (1772–1839), government reformer under Tsar Alexander I

Notes

NOTE TO READERS: Page numbers in parentheses in the main body of my text refer to *War and Peace* by Leo Tolstoy, translated by Richard Pevear and Larissa Volokhonsky, translation copyright © 2007 by Richard Pevear and Larissa Volokhonsky. Used by permission of Alfred A. Knopf, an imprint of the Knopf Doubleday Publishing Goup, a division of Random House LLC. All rights reserved. Unless otherwise indicated, all other translations from Russian language sources are mine.

All dates from Tolstoy's life are given according to the old-style Julian calendar, in effect in Russian until 1918. The Julian calendar was twelve days behind the Western (Gregorian) calendar in the nineteenth century, and thirteen days behind it in the twentieth.

Book Epigraph

vii **"To be able to"**: Diary entry, December 19, 1900. Quoted in L. N. Tolstoi, *Polnoe sobranie sochinenii* [*The Complete Collected Works of L. N. Tolstoy*], 90 vols. (Moscow, 1928–58), vol. 54, p. 74.

An Invitation to the Reader

xiii **"It's the same"**: L. N. Tolstoi, *Sobranie sochinenii v dvadtsati dvukh tomakh* [*Collected Works in 22 Volumes*] (Moskva: Khudozhestvennaia literatura, 1978–85), vol. 14, p. 477.

xiv **"In clever art criticism"**: R. F. Christian, ed. and trans., *Tolstoy's Letters*, vol. 1, *1828–1879* (New York: Scribner, 1978), p. 295.

xiv **"we need people"**: A. A. Donskov, ed., *L. N. Tolstoy and N. N. Strakhov: Complete Correspondence*, 2 vols. (Slavic Research Group at the University of Ottawa and L. N. Tolstoy State Museum, 2003), p. 268. Also quoted in *Lev Tolstoi ob iskusstve i literature* (Moscow: Sovetskii pisatel', 1958), p. 517.

Introduction

3   **"The storm is approaching"**: Alexander Herzen, "The Russian People and Socialism. A Letter to Michelet" (1851), in *The Memoirs of Alexander Herzen*, vol. 4 (London: Chatto & Windus, 1968), p. 1649.

3   **"We are starting"**: Quoted in Boris Eikhenbaum, *Tolstoi in the Sixties*, trans. Duffield White (Ann Arbor, MI: Ardis, 1982), p. 29.

3   **"The day before"**: Letter of September 1869, in R. F. Christian, ed. and trans., *Tolstoy's Letters*, vol. 1, *1828–1879* (New York: Scribner, 1978), p. 222.

4   **"What, indeed, had I done"**: Leo Tolstoy, *Confession*, trans. David Patterson (New York: Norton, 1983), Part 11, p. 70.

5   **"a reflector as vast"**: Quoted in Leo Tolstoy, *War and Peace*, 2nd ed. (New York: Norton, 1996), p. 1114.

6   **"I must have"**: Entry from May 1853. Quoted in R. F. Christian, ed. and trans., *Tolstoy's Diaries*, vol. 1, *1847–1894* (London: Athlone Press, 1985), p. 67.

6   **"Sensuality torments me"**: Entry from August 1857. Ibid., p. 141.

6   **"I'm so disgusted"**: Entry from January 1855. Ibid., p. 100.

6   **"Played cards again"**: Ibid., p. 100.

6   **"It's absurd"**: Entry from June 1855. Ibid., p. 105.

7   **One John Levitt**: His letter can be found in N. Velikanova and R. Wittaker, eds., *L. N. Tolstoi i S.Sh.A.: Perepiska* [*L.N Tolstoy and the U.S.A: Correspondence*] (Moscow: Gorky Institute of World Literature of the Russian Academy of Sciences, 2004), p. 937.

7   **"I am sure"**: Quoted in ibid., p. 500.

9   **"That the novelist"**: *New York Times*, November 13, 1910.

9   **"No man is justified"**: Quoted in ibid.

9   **"There probably isn't"**: Diary of September 26, 1865. Quoted in Christian, ed., *Diaries,* vol. 1, p. 184.

10 **"No matter how old"**: Letter to V. G. Chertkov, February 1890; L. N. Tolstoi, *Polnoe sobranie sochinenii L. N. Tolstogo* [*The Complete Collected Works of L. N. Tolstoy*], 90 vols. (Moscow, 1928–58), vol. 87, p. 10.

10 **"Man is flowing"**: Tolstoy, *Polnoe sobranie sochinenii*, vol. 5, p. 262.

11 **"Take a broom"**: Quoted in Alexandra Popoff, *Sophia Tolstoy: A Biography* (New York: Free Press, 2010), p. 163.

11 **"Every activity"**: M. N. Bakhtin, *Literaturno-kriticheskie stat'i* (Moscow: Khudozhestvennaia literatura, 1986), p. 113.

13 **"The hero of my tale"**: From the short story "Sevastopol in May" (1855), in Michael R. Katz, ed., *Tolstoy's Short Fiction* (New York: Norton, 1991), p. 43.

14 **"The goal of the artist"**: Letter to P. D. Boborykin, published in Leo Tolstoy, *War and Peace*, ed. George Gibian (New York: Norton, 1996), p. 1084.

Chapter 1: Plans

15 **_Epigraph_**: "The mind's game": Diary entry from March 3, 1863, in R. F. Christian, ed. and trans., *Tolstoy's Diaries*, vol. 1., *1847–1894* (London: Athlone Press, 1985), p. 177.

15 **"(1) To study the whole"**: Ibid., p. 11.

16 **"RULES FOR DEVELOPING"**: Ibid., pp. 12–16.

16 **"The first rule"**: Ibid., p. 11.

17 **"It is easier to write"**: Ibid., p. 4.

17 **"The mind's game"**: Diary entry from March 3, 1863, in ibid., p. 177.

23 **"I cannot determine"**: Quoted in Leo Tolstoy, *War and Peace*, 2nd ed. (New York: Norton, 1996), p. 1089.

Chapter 2: Imagination

27 **_Epigraph:_** "What is *War and Peace?*": "A Few Words Apropos of the Book *War and Peace*," originally published in *Russkii Arckhiv* (*Russian Archive*) in 1868. Quoted in Appendix of Leo Tolstoy, *War and Peace*, trans. Richard Pevear and Larissa Volokhonsky (New York: Knopf, 2007), p. 1217.

27 **"loose baggy monster"**: Quoted in Leo Tolstoy, *War and Peace,* ed. George Gibian (New York: Norton, 1996), p. 1395.

28 **"[T]his *1805* presents"**: Quoted in Boris Eikhenbaum, *Tolstoi in the Sixties*, trans. Duffield White (Ann Arbor, MI: Ardis, 1982), p. 169.

28 **"everything is mixed"**: V. A. Zelinskii, ed., *Russkaia kriticheskaiia literatura o proizvedeniiakh L. N. Tolstogo: khronologicheskii sbornik kritiko-bibliograficheskikh statei*, 8 vols. (Ann Arbor, MI: University Microfilms, 1966), vol. 3, pp. 143–44.

29 **"a disordered heap"**: Eikhenbaum, *Tolstoi in the Sixties,* p. 236.

29 **"Evidently the author"**: Zelinskii, ed., *Russkaia kriticheskaiia literatura,* vol. 3, p. 3.

29 **"To my own"**: Eikhenbaum, *Tolstoi in the Sixties,* p. 164.

29 **"What is *War and Peace?*"**: "A Few Words Apropos of the Book *War and Peace,*" quoted in Appendix of Leo Tolstoy, *War and Peace,* trans. Richard Pevear and Larissa Volokhonsky (New York: Knopf, 2007), p. 1217.

31 **"Free entrance and exit"**: Eikhenbaum, *Tolstoi in the Sixties,* p. 30.

31 **"It seemed so strange"**: Ibid., p. 71.

32 **"I am now"**: R. F. Christian, ed. and trans., *Tolstoy's Letters,* vol. 1, *1828–1879* (New York: Scribner, 1978), p. 170.

33 **"—Eh bien, mon prince"**: L. N. Tolstoi, *Polnoe sobranie sochinenii* [*The Complete Works of L. N. Tolstoy*], 90 vols. (Moscow, 1928–58), vol. 9, p. 3.

34 **"The reproach that people"**: Tolstoy, *War and Peace,* trans. Pevear and Volokhonsky, p. 1218.

34 **"that French way"**: Ibid.

37 **"relate, portray, but do not judge"**: R. F. Christian, *Tolstoy's 'War and Peace': A Study* (Oxford: Clarendon Press, 1962), p. 178.

40 **"I was afraid"**: Leo Tolstoy, *War and Peace,* 2nd ed. (New York: Norton, 1996), p. 1087.

42 **"A complete picture"**: From Strakhov's 1870 essay about *War and Peace,* republished in Nikolai Strakhov, *Kriticheskie stat'i ob I. S. Turgeneve i L. N. Tolstom (1862–1885),* vol. 1, 4th ed. (Kiev: Izdanie I.P. Matchenko, 1901; reprint: The Hague: Mouton, 1968), p. 277.

43 **"realist in the higher sense"**: In his notebooks Dostoevsky writes: "I am called a psychologist: that is not true, I am only a realist in the higher sense, that is, I portray all the depths of the human soul." Cited in Donald Fanger, *Dostoevsky and Romantic Realism: A Study of Dostoevsky in Relation to Balzac, Dickens, and Gogol* (Evanston, IL: Northwestern University Press, 1998), p. 215.

Chapter 3: Rupture

45 *Epigraph*: "Once we're thrown": Leo Tolstoy, *War and Peace,* trans. Richard Pevear and Larissa Volokhonsky (New York: Knopf, 2007), vol. 4, part 4, chapter 17, p. 1118.

52   **"When shall I cease"**: R. F. Christian, ed. and trans., *Tolstoy's Diaries*, vol. 1, *1847–1894* (London: Athlone Press, 1985), p. 97.

52   **"really the soul"**: Quoted in Ernest J. Simmons, *Leo Tolstoy* (Boston: Little, Brown, 1946), p. 116.

53   **"the dirtiest creature"**: Christian, ed., *Diaries*, p. 100.

55   **"a great idea"**: Ibid., p. 101.

56   **"It's amazing how loathsome"**: Ibid., p. 105.

59   **"you are not sufficiently serious"**: This letter was written in response to Shaw's play *Man and Superman*, which the playwright had recently sent to Tolstoy. Quoted in R. F. Christian, ed., *Tolstoy's Diaries,* vol. 2, *1895–1910* (London: Athlone Press, 1985), p. 678.

Chapter 4: Success

61   *Epigraph*: "There is no greatness": Leo Tolstoy, *War and Peace*, trans. Richard Pevear and Larissa Volokhonsky (New York: Knopf, 2007), vol. 4, part 3, chapter 18, p. 1071.

63   **"[T]here are things"**: R. F. Christian, ed. and trans., *Tolstoy's Diaries*, vol. 1, *1847–1894* (London: Athlone Press, 1985), p. 90.

63   **"Lying, stealing, promiscuity"**: Leo Tolstoy, *Confession*, trans. David Patterson (New York: Norton, 1983), p. 18.

63   **"vanity, self-interest, and pride"**: Ibid., p. 18.

63   **"Very well, you will have"**: Ibid., p. 27.

63   **"was meaningless and evil"**: Ibid., p. 58.

69   **"Six feet from his head to his heels"**: Leo Tolstoy, *The Raid and Other Stories*, trans. Louise and Aylmer Maude (Oxford: Oxford University Press, 1982), p. 227.

71   **"The essential difference"**: A. V. Knowles, ed., *Tolstoy: The Critical Heritage* (London: Routledge & Kegan Paul, 1978), p. 115.

75   **"If the cause"**: Leo Tolstoy, *War and Peace*, ed. George Gibian (New York: Norton, 1996), p. 1088.

Chapter 5: Idealism

79   *Epigraph*: "To seek, always to seek": Quoted in Ernest J. Simmons, *Leo Tolstoy* (Boston: Little, Brown, 1946), p. 772

81   **"And just as I believed"**: Quoted in ibid., pp. 21–22.

82   **"Blessedness"**: Leo Tolstoy, *The Kingdom of God Is Within You,* trans. Constance Garnett (Lincoln: University of Nebraska Press, 1984), p. 52.

83 **"is just like telling"**: Ibid., p. 99

83 **"[O]verwhelmed"**: Mohandas Gandhi, *An Autobiography* (Boston: Beacon Press, 1957), pp. 137–38.

94 **"those Russian people"**: Fyodor Dostoevsky, *A Writer's Diary*, vol. 1, *1873–1876*, trans. Kenneth Lantz (Evanston, IL: Northwestern University Press, 1994), p. 876.

Chapter 6: Happiness

95 **"He who is happy"**: R. F. Christian, ed. *Tolstoy's Diaries*, vol. 1, *1847–1894* (London: Athlone Press, 1985), p. 177.

96 **"[T]he best way"**: Entry from May 12, 1856, quoted in ibid., p. 113.

96 **"I will never serve"**: Quoted in Chronology, Donna Tussing Orwin, ed., *The Cambridge Companion to Tolstoy* (Cambridge: Cambridge University Press, 2002), p. 6.

96 **"[i]n Russia things are"**: Letter of August 18, 1857, in R. F. Christian, ed. and trans., *Tolstoy's Letters*, vol. 1, *1828–1879* (New York: Scribner, 1978), p. 106.

96 **"life in Russia"**: Ibid., p. 106.

96 **"I experienced a feeling"**: Ibid., p. 108.

98 **"It's only honest anxiety"**: Ibid., p. 110.

98 **"that it's possible"**: Ibid.

100 **The original intention**: Martin E. P. Seligman and Mihaly Csikszentmihalyi, "Positive Psychology: An Introduction," *American Psychologist* 55, no. 1 (2000): 5–14.

101 **"the whole philosophy"**: Nikolai Ivanovich Kareev, *Istoricheskaia filosofiia gr. L. N. Tolstogo v 'Voine i mire'* (Petersburg, 1888), p. 43.

101 **"So-called self-sacrifice"**: Christian, ed., *Tolstoy's Diaries*, vol. 1., p. 177.

102 **"very good at saying"**: R. F. Christian, *Tolstoy's 'War and Peace': A Study* (Oxford: Clarendon Press, 1962), p. 168.

102 **"Since the world of thought"**: From Pisarev's essay "The Old Gentry," quoted in Leo Tolstoy, *War and Peace*, ed. George Gibian (New York: Norton, 1996), p. 1101.

108 **Here is life**: "Without false modesty," Tolstoy told the young writer Maxim Gorky, "*War and Peace* is like the *Iliad*." Quoted in Maxim Gorky, *Reminiscences of Tolstoy, Chekhov, and Andreyev* (London: Hogarth 1948), p. 57.

111 **"piece of life"**: From Arnold's essay "Count Leo Tolstoy," which was first published in the *Fortnighlty Review*, December 1887. Citation taken from Leo Tolstoy, *Anna Karenina*, 2nd ed. (New York: Norton, 1995), p. 766.

111 **"The hunt is described"**: L. N. Tolstoi, *Polnoe sobranie sochinenii* [*The Complete Works of L. N. Tolstoy*], 90 vols. (Moscow, 1928–58), vol. 15, p. 241. Also cited in Sergei Bocharov, *Roman L. N. Tolstogo "Voina i mir,"* 4th ed. (Moskva: Khudozhestvennaia literatura, 1987), p. 33.

Chapter 7: Love

113 *Epigraph*: "Everything I understand": Leo Tolstoy, *War and Peace*, trans. Richard Pevear and Larissa Volokhonsky (New York: Knopf, 2007), vol. 4, book 1, chapter 16, p. 984.

113 **"It could have been better"**: Alexandra Popoff, *Sophia Tolstoy: A Biography* (New York: Free Press, 2010), p. 167.

114 **"I've come to say"**: This whole scene is described in Sonya's letter to her sister, Tanya, quoted in ibid, pp. 150–51.

115 **"My departure will"**: R. F. Christian, *Tolstoy's Letters,* vol. 2, *1880–1910* (New York: Scribner, 1978), p. 710–711.

115 **"And really the main feeling"**: R. F. Christian, *Tolstoy's Letters,* vol. 1, *1828–1879* (New York: Scribner, 1978), p. 70.

117 **"[O]ur happiness is terrifying"**: Diary entry from March 1, 1863, quoted in R. F. Christian, ed. and trans., *Tolstoy's Diaries,* vol. 1, *1847–1894* (London: Athlone Press, 1985), p.176.

117 **"Every time he speaks"**: Henri Troyat, *Tolstoy*, trans. Nancy Amphoux (Garden City, NY: Doubleday, 1967), p. 259.

117 **"It's awful, terrible"**: Christian, ed., *Tolstoy's Diaries*, vol. 1, p. 178.

117 **"impossibly pure and good"**: Diary entry from March 3, 1863, quoted in ibid., p. 177.

128 **"One can't help loving"**: Diary entry from September 15, 1858, quoted in ibid., p.152.

129 **"Forgive me"**: Troyat, *Tolstoy,* p. 692.

132 **"Oh, constantly"**: *New York Times*, December 27, 1925.

Chapter 8: Family

133 *Epigraph*: "The family is flesh": Quoted in L. N. Tolstoi, *Polnoe sobranie sochinenii* [*The Complete Works of L. N. Tolstoy*], 90 vols. (Moscow, 1928–58), vol. 49, p. 32.

135 **"The novel of contemporary man"**: From Introduction to Fyodor Dostoevsky, *The Adolescent: A Novel*, trans. Richard Pevear and Larissa Volokhonsky (New York: Vintage Classics/Random House, 2003), p. vii.

136 **"[I]t really is"**: Quoted in Joseph Frank, *Dostoevsky: The Miraculous Years, 1865–1871* (Princeton: Princeton University Press, 1996), p. 434.

143 **"I am a husband"**: R. F. Christian, ed. and trans., *Tolstoy's Letters,* vol. 1, *1828–1879* (New York: Scribner, 1978), p. 182.

143 **"now that it's trimmed"**: Alexandra Popoff, *Sophia Tolstoy: A Biography* (New York: Free Press, 2010), p. 48.

143 **"I do not understand"**: Aylmer Maude, *The Life of Tolstoy: Later Years* (London: Constable, 1911), p. 669.

144 **"[I]n the course of"**: A. V. Knowles, ed., *Tolstoy: The Critical Heritage* (London: Routledge, 1978), p. 146.

149 **While it may be**: A. N. Wilson points out that ads for products claiming to cure venereal disease were a staple of Petersburg newspapers in the nineteenth century, and that sexual promiscuity and venereal disease were widespread throughout provincial Russia. A. N. Wilson, *Tolstoy* (New York: Norton, 1988), p. 374.

Chapter 9: Courage

151 *Epigraph*: "What would you call": L. Tolstoy, *Father Sergius and Other Stories* (Moscow: Raduga, 1988), p. 9.

156 **"[T]rue life begins"**: Leo Tolstoy, "Why Do Men Stupefy Themselves?" in *Recollections and Essays*, trans. Aylmer Maude, reprint ed. (London: Oxford University Press, 1961), p. 81.

157 **"Pure vitality in man"**: Paul Tillich, *The Courage to Be*, 2nd ed. (New Haven: Yale University Press, 2000), p. 84.

157 **"can, if used by demagogues"**: Ibid.

159 **"[D]o heroes see themselves"**: Patricia Carden, "Nicholas and Mary: An Inquiry into the Moral Structure of '*Vojna i Mir*,'" *Russian Literature* 51 (2002): 14. In fairness to Carden, it should be pointed out she qualifies her skepticism with the observation that both "humor and sympathy play out" (p. 14) during the course of this scene.

162 **"killers of history"**: Quoted in Dan Ungurianu, "Visions and Versions of History: Veterans of 1812 on Tolstoy's *War and Peace*," *Slavic and East European Journal* 44, no. 1 (Spring 2000): 48.

162 **"Before and after Borodino"**: Ibid., p. 49.

162 **"spark of heroism"**: From Strakhov's 1869 essay about *War and Peace*, republished in Nikolai Strakhov, *Kriticheskie stat'i ob I. S. Turgeneve i L. N. Tolstom (1862–1885)*, vol. 1, 4th ed. (Kiev: Izdanie I. P. Matchenko, 1901; Reprint: The Hague: Mouton, 1968), p. 196.

163 **"appear before us"**: Ibid., p. 208.

Chapter 10: Death

171 *Epigraph*: "The closer we come": Letter to Vladimir Chertkov, August 1910, quoted in Vladimir Chertkov, *The Last Days of Leo Tolstoy* (Moscow, 1911), trans. Benjamin Sher, http://www.linguadex.com/tolstoy/chapter 3.htm. Original source: V. F. Chertkov, *O poslednikh dniakh L'va Nikolaevicha Tolstogo* (Ranenburg, 1911), December 27, 1910, p. 30, http://feb-web.ru/feb/tolstoy/critics/pdt/pdt-001-.htm. According to Chertkov, Tolstoy wrote these words in a letter to him.

172 **"death, death, death"**: Leo Tolstoy, *What I Believe*, trans. Constantine Popoff (New York: Cosimo Classics, 2009), p. 131.

172 **"and I rode round"**: In R. F. Christian, ed. and trans., *Tolstoy's Diaries*, vol. 1, *1847–1894* (London: Athlone Press, 1985), p. 118.

173 **"Two hours have gone by"**: Ibid., p. 119.

173 **"I had come"**: Quoted in Henri Troyat, *Tolstoy*, trans. Nancy Amphoux (Garden City, NY: Doubleday, 1967), p. 135.

173 **"I am glad"**: Ibid., p. 199.

173 **"Nothing in life"**: Letter of October 1860, quoted in Christian, ed., *Tolstoy's Diaries*, vol. 1, pp. 141–42.

174 **"Why should I live?"**: Leo Tolstoy, *Confession*, trans. David Patterson (New York: Norton, 1983), Part 5, p. 35.

175 **"by renouncing what"**: Lev Tolstoi, *On Life and Essays on Religion*, trans. Aylmer Maude (London: Oxford University Press, 1934), p. 72.

175 **"Although I admire"**: Quoted in introduction to Leo Tolstoy, *The Death of Ivan Ilyich*, trans. Lynn Solotaroff (New York: Bantam, 1982), p. 25.

176 **"so that death"**: *What I Believe*, p. 131.

178 **"Life is life"**: *What I Believe*, quoted in George J. Gutsche, "Moral Fiction: Tolstoy's *The Death of Ivan Ilyich*," in Gary R. Jahn, ed., *Tolstoy's The Death of Ivan Il'ich: A Critical Companion* (Evanston, IL: Northwestern University Press, 1999), p. 90. Original text found in L. N. Tolstoi, *Polnoe sobranie sochinenii [The Complete Works of L. N. Tolstoy]*, 90 vols. (Moscow, 1928–58), vol. 23, p. 399.

182 **"conveyed a psychological truth"**: George Steiner, *Tolstoy or Dostoevsky: An Essay in the Old Criticism* (New York: Knopf, 1959), p. 274.

184 **"needed a brilliant young man"**: Letter to L. I. Volkonsaya, May 3, 1865, quoted in R. F. Christian, *Tolstoy's 'War and Peace': A Study* (Oxford: Clarendon Press, 1962), p. 17.

Chapter 11: Perseverance

189 ***Epigraph***: "The hardest and most blissful thing": Leo Tolstoy, *War and Peace*, trans. Richard Pevear and Larissa Volokhonsky (New York: Knopf, 2007), vol. 4, part 3, chapter 15, p. 1064.

194 **The famous Soviet**: In Viktor Shklovsky, *Lev Tolstoy* (Moscow: Progress, 1978), pp. 378–81.

194 **"As is proper"**: Quoted in Ernest J. Simmons, *Leo Tolstoy* (Boston: Little, Brown, 1946), p. 291.

199 **"There is only one thing"**: Quoted in Viktor Frankl, *Man's Search for Meaning* (New York: Simon & Schuster, 1984), p. 87.

201 **"He who has a *why*"**: Friedrich Nietzsche, "Maxims and Arrows," in *Twilight of the Idols*. Quoted in ibid, p. 109.

Chapter 12: Truth

203 ***Epigraph***: "The hero of my tale": From the short story "Sevastopol in May" (1855), In Michael R. Katz, ed., *Tolstoy's Short Fiction* (New York: Norton, 1991), p. 43.

203 **"there are no people"**: Quoted in Boris Eikhenbaum, *Tolstoi in the Sixties*, trans. Duffield White (Ann Arbor: Ardis, 1982), p. 8.

204 **"the truth is like"**: Quoted in V. Vinogradov, *O iazyke khudozhestvennoi literatury* (Moscow, 1959), p. 506.

205 **"A historian and an artist"**: "A Few Words Apropos of the Book *War and Peace*," quoted in Appendix of Leo Tolstoy *War and Peace*, trans. Richard Pevear and Larissa Volokhonsky (New York: Knopf, 2007), p. 1219 .

212 **"only art feels"**: March 3, 1863. Quoted in R. F. Christian, ed. and trans., *Tolstoy's Diaries*, vol. 1, *1847–1894* (London: Athlone Press, 1985), p. 177.

Suggestions for Further Reading

Having spent nearly twenty-five years reading and researching Tolstoy, I gratefully acknowledge the vast body of research about the writer that I have drawn on in the writing of this as well as my previous book, *Understanding Tolstoy*. For readers wanting to delve further into *War and Peace*, Tolstoy's life, and his art, below is a list of some of the books in English I have found particularly useful and hope you enjoy, too.

I am often asked about the best film adaptations of *War and Peace*. While there is much to recommend the BBC's 1972 production, starring Anthony Hopkins as Pierre, I would say that the single greatest adaptation to date is the 1967 Soviet film directed by Sergei Bondarchuk. Scrupulously faithful to the content and spirit of the original novel, this eight-hour epic is a masterpiece of filmmaking in its own right. It is available in Russian with English subtitles. And, because we can never have enough of a good thing, BBC One has announced that in 2015 it will be releasing a new adaptation of *War and Peace*, a six-part TV series written by Andrew Davies.

I also recommend *The Last Station*, an Academy Award–nominated movie starring Christopher Plummer and Helen Mirren about the last year of Tolstoy's life. Released in 2009, this movie is based on Jay Parini's excellent novel of the same name.

As for biographies of Tolstoy, the three best in English are:

Bartlett, Rosamund. *Tolstoy: A Russian Life*. Boston: Houghton Mifflin Harcourt, 2011.

Simmons, Ernest J. *Leo Tolstoy.* Boston: Little, Brown, 1946.

Wilson, A. N. *Tolstoy*. New York: Norton, 1988.

Other books I recommend:

Bayley, John. *Tolstoy and the Novel*. London: Chatto & Windus, 1966.

An informative, stylishly written work of Tolstoy criticism that situates the writer's novels in both their Russian and European literary context.

Berlin, Isaiah. *The Hedgehog and the Fox: An Essay on Tolstoy's View of History*. 2nd ed. Princeton, NJ: Princeton University Press, 2013. [Original editions: *The Hedgehog and the Fox: An Essay on Tolstoy's View of History*, London: Weidenfeld & Nicolson, 1953; New York: Simon & Schuster, 1953 and 1986.]

A classic of both Tolstoy scholarship and intellectual history, this erudite essay analyzing the writer's theory of history is both thought-provoking and a joy to read.

Christian, R. F. *Tolstoy: A Critical Introduction*. Cambridge: Cambridge University Press, 1970.

A solid, systematic, and useful introduction to Tolstoy's major fiction that focuses on sources and influences, as well as the literary techniques of Tolstoy's magisterial prose.

Eikhenbaum, Boris. *Tolstoi in the Sixties*. Trans. Duffield White. Ann Arbor, MI: Ardis, 1982.

A classic of Tolstoy scholarship that will tell you everything you ever wanted to know (and then some) about the social, cultural, and intellectual context of the 1860s, during which Tolstoy wrote *War and Peace*.

Feuer, Kathryn B. *Tolstoy and the Genesis of* War and Peace. Ed. Robin Feuer Miller and Donna Tussing Orwin. Ithaca, NY: Cornell University Press, 1996.

An engagingly written book by a respected Tolstoy scholar and novelist, tracing the process by which *War and Peace* grew from a sociopolitical novel with overt ideological intentions into an artistic masterpiece that transcends ideology altogether.

Gustafson, Richard. *Leo Tolstoy: Resident and Stranger: A Study in Fiction and Theology*. Princeton, NJ: Princeton University Press, 1986.

An important and serious book by a prominent Tolstoy scholar that illuminates the ways in which all of Tolstoy's works, both fictional and philosophical, are an expression of the writer's lifelong religious searchings.

Kaufman, Andrew. *Understanding Tolstoy*. Columbus: The Ohio State University Press, 2011.

A broad and accessible analysis of Tolstoy's major novels and novellas in the context of his life and times that speaks to the ways in which Tolstoy, despite living in a manner far removed from the experiences of most modern-day Americans, is still applicable and contemporary.

Lieven, Dominic. *Russia Against Napoleon: The True Story of the Campaigns of* War and Peace. New York: Viking, 2010.

The go-to resource for those readers wanting a fuller discussion of the power politics and military strategies behind the events described in *War and Peace*.

Nickell, William. *The Death of Tolstoy: Russia on the Eve, Astapovo Station, 1910*. Ithaca, NY: Cornell University Press, 2010.

A detailed account of Tolstoy's final flight from Yasnaya Polyana and his eventual death in the Astapovo train station, emphasizing how those events became a public spectacle and celebrity media event unlike any other the world had seen.

Orwin, Donna Tussing, ed. *Anniversary Essays on Tolstoy*. Cambridge: Cambridge University Press, 2010.

A collection of original essays by leading scholars containing some of the latest thinking about Tolstoy in areas ranging from the writer's attitudes toward music and death to the way in which he was presented during the revolutionary period in Russia.

Popoff, Alexandra. *Sophia Tolstoy: A Biography*. New York: Free Press, 2010.

The only biography of Tolstoy's wife available in English, Popoff's book provides fascinating insight into the troubled Tolstoy marriage, as well as a deeper appreciation of the heroism and humanity of the woman without whom *War and Peace* would never have been written.

Riasanovsky Nicholas V., and Mark D. Steinberg. *A History of Russia.* 8th ed. Oxford: Oxford University Press, 2010.

The best single-volume introduction in English to Russian history, spanning ancient Russia through the postcommunist present era.

Steiner, George. *Tolstoy or Dostoevsky: An Essay in the Old Criticism.* 2nd ed. New Haven, CT: Yale University Press,1996.

This wide-ranging comparative study of two giants of nineteenth-century Russian literature is erudite, accessible, and passionate, arising as it does out of Steiner's self-proclaimed "debt of love" for the writers he discusses.

Tolstoy, Sofia. *The Diaries of Sofia Tolstoy.* Trans. Cathy Porter. New York: Harper Perennial, 2009.

The best book available in English about the Tolstoy marriage, as seen from the point of view of Tolstoy's wife.

Tolstoy, Leo. *Correspondence.* 2 vols. Selected, edited, and translated by R. F. Christian. New York: Scribner, 1978.

———. *Diaries.* Edited and translated by R. F. Christian. New York: Scribner, 1985.

The best compilation in English of Tolstoy's letters and diaries, which make for fascinating reading in themselves.

Author's Note on
Translations of *War and Peace*

There are many fine translations of *War and Peace* available in English, and my recommendation is that you choose the one that you think you'll enjoy the most and that will make you want to read the novel from beginning to end. And you needn't fret too much about your choice: Tolstoy is one of those writers who loses surprisingly little in translation. His lucid prose, utterly recognizable characters, and universal truths seem to speak for themselves in any language, and through any translator.

Nevertheless, my personal favorite translation of *War and Peace* is the one by Richard Pevear and Larissa Volokhonsky, published by Alfred A. Knopf. It is scrupulously accurate, it beautifully captures the stylistic subtleties of the original novel, and it is wonderfully readable. That's the translation I recommend to my students, and the one I suggest you try first. In this book all the citations from *War and Peace* are from the Pevear and Volokhonsky translation.

Index

About the Author

An innovative, award-winning teacher of Russian language, literature, and culture, Dr. Andrew D. Kaufman holds a Ph.D. in Slavic languages and literatures from Stanford University and has spent the last twenty years bringing alive the Russian classics to Americans young and old. Dr. Kaufman, whose previous titles include *Understanding Tolstoy* and *Russian for Dummies* (coauthor), is a featured Tolstoy expert on Oprah.com, and he is frequently invited to discuss Russian literature and culture on national and international television and radio programs. An internationally recognized Tolstoy scholar, Dr. Kaufman has lectured at the National Endowment for the Arts, the Gorky Institute of World Literature of the Russian Academy of Sciences, and at the Leo Tolstoy Museum and Estate at Yasnaya Polyana. Currently he is a Lecturer and Faculty Fellow at the University of Virginia, where he founded and teaches a community-based literature course, "Books Behind Bars: Life, Literature, and Leadership," in which students lead discussions about Russian literature with incarcerated youth at juvenile correctional centers in Virginia. To learn more about Dr. Kaufman and his work, please visit his website:

www.andrewdkaufman.com